Fragile Evidence

A Critique of Reading Assessment

Sharon Murphy
York University

with

Patrick Shannon
Pennsylvania State University

Peter Johnston
State University of New York at Albany

Jane Hansen
University of New Hampshire

LEA LAWRENCE ERLBAUM ASSOCIATES, PUBLISHERS
1998   Mahwah, New Jersey   London

Lawrence Erlbaum Associates, Inc., Publishers
10 Industrial Avenue
Mahwah, New Jersey 07430

Cover design by Kathryn Houghtaling Lacey

Library of Congress Cataloging-in-Publication Data

    Fragile evidence : a critique of reading assessment / Sharon
Murphy . . . [et al.].
       p. cm.
    Includes bibliographical references and index.
    ISBN 0-8058-2529-0 (cloth : alk. paper). — ISBN 0-8058-
2530-4 (pbk. : alk. paper)
    1. Reading —Ability testing—Evaluation. 2. Educational tests
and measurements. I. Murphy, Sharon, 1955-
    LB1050.46.F72   1998
    428.4'076—dc21
                                   98-42352
                                        CIP

Books published by Lawrence Erlbaum Associates are printed on acid-
free paper, and their bindings are chosen for strength and durability.

Printed in the United States of America
10 9 8 7 6 5 4 3 2

Contents

Preface

> This study can be used to illustrate a number of more general themes. I have mentioned one ... the idea of making up people. I claim that enumeration requires categorization, and that defining new classes of people for the purposes of statistics has consequences for the ways in which we conceive of others and think of our own possibilities and potentialities.
>
> —I. Hacking (1990, p. 6)

Like Hacking's (1990) study of statistics, *Fragile Evidence: A Critique of Reading Assessment* is a study of the making up of people—but with a particular emphasis on the making up of readers as a result of reading assessment. Witness, for instance, recent events in the state of California. Millions of dollars went into the production and implementation of a new reading assessment—a new way to categorize someone as a reader. The results of the assessment were deemed, however, by popular press interpretations to be unsatisfactory. As an answer to the seeming plummeting of performance, a panel was commissioned, and a report was produced and circulated throughout the state. New monies were provided to reduce class size. More monies were expended to pay for academic "consultants" who jumped on the professional inservice bandwagon. Even more monies were spent by school districts on the materials produced to try to ensure that the students in their schools were named as readers in the next round of assessments.[1]

How did this state of affairs arise? What gives testing and assessment[2] such authority? Do they merit this authority? *Fragile Evidence: A Critique of Reading Assessment* is a critical exploration of these questions. Drawing on theorizing in two fields, psychometry and reading, we consider the evidence and values that undergird reading assessment as it is practiced. The approach taken in the book is unusual in that it applies questions of contemporary psychological theorizing about validity to the field of reading and brings together two areas that have often existed in separate spaces in educational writing. Because of this dual focus, the text cuts across educational psychology and reading and may be useful in graduate or senior undergraduate courses in educational assessment in general or in reading assessment in particular.

The chapters in Part I introduce a variety of conceptualizations of validity. From the building of evidence in the courtroom dramas of television to the everyday concepts of validity that underlie arguments in daily life, evidence and the values that bear on what counts as evidence are considered. The focus of validation in the field of psychometrics had for a time shifted from its conceptual underpinnings in efforts to create a technology of assessment, but recent theorizing about validity in the fields of both psychology and reading has returned to the seemingly commonsense views of validity.

The discussions in Parts II and III are critical of the results of practices that have dominated reading since the 1920s. Part II introduces the application of theoretical concepts about validity to the practice of assessment. The first chapter in this section, chapter 3, focuses on a critique of multiple-choice standardized tests used in the early 1990s. Chapter 4 critiques individualized assessment measures. For both chapters, two critical frameworks for analyzing the tests as artifacts are applied—one from the field of psychology and one from reading theory. Inadequacies in both multiple-choice standardized and individualized assessments are found as a result of the application of the critical frameworks.

Part III examines the validity of standardized tests from the perspective of their use. In chapter 5, Patrick Shannon presents a brief but positioned view of the history of the use of standardized tests in the United States. Shannon points to the ideological underpinnings of tests and argues that tests are about the scientific management of schools, the management of who succeeds and who fails, and the entrenchment of the system of values represented in the tests—the entrenchment of the status quo. Using voices of early reading psychologists like Gray, Thorndike, and Cubberly, Shannon provides evidence that tests resulted in the reification of White, Anglo-Saxon, middle-class values. His work further suggests that the ideologies underpinning tests extend into reading instruction and reading curriculum (e.g., K. S. Goodman, Shannon, Freeman, & Murphy, 1988; Shannon, 1989, 1990).

In chapter 6, Peter Johnston describes the injustices and misuses of tests today and thus amplifies Shannon's claims. Johnston suggests that norm-referenced, multiple-choice standardized reading assessments have multiple consequences. First, the identities that teachers and students can make for themselves become altered as a result of certain test uses (see also S. Murphy, 1997). Next, the altering of teaching and curriculum to meet the demands of tests results in a narrowing of educational experiences. Continuing the theme of ideological bias introduced by Shannon, Johnston provides numerous exemplars demonstrating the severe, long-term, and inappropriate consequences of the uses of these tests in schools.

Part IV critically considers the evidence and values underlying non-dominant reading assessment practices. In chapter 7, Jane Hansen raises the question, "If we don't use traditional tests to assess reading, what indicators would we use?" By interviewing school children, their parents, teachers, and the administrators of their schools, Hansen undertook to provide more complexly textured evidence for reading. These interviews authorize different voices to make arguments about reading—voices rarely given authority by schools. Life experiences are at the core of the perceptions of the interviewees. Their reading is not just about texts: It is about the people they read with and for. It is about how they regard themselves, and it is about the emotional involvement they have with text. These perceptions remind us that reading in contemporary society is a social act that is part of everyday experiences. The vision offered in these interviews suggests that reading is not the individual act that most tests construct it to be. Rather, tensions exist between an individual's disposition and how reading is arranged in schools, and no one is blind to these facets of reading. Yet, some interview participants felt compelled to talk about tests. For them, tests have resulted in self-doubt about personal, detailed, and multicontextual knowledge of reading. As the cultural ethnographer F.A. Hanson (1993) put it, "Power has become refined indeed when people demand that they be subjected to it" (p. 306). Nevertheless, the positions put forth by interviewees raise questions about the degree to which any reading act can stand for reading because it is influenced by so much and is often interpreted so little.

Chapter 8 looks to an alternative assessment strategy in reading, developed and refined during the last 30 years, for guidance on reform initiatives in assessment. Miscue analysis is an individualized observational tool used to make inferences about readers' use of cuing systems (graphophonic, syntactic, and semantic) and strategies in reading. The insights that miscue analysis provides to assessment include heightened awareness of the distinction between description and interpretation, knowledge of the developmental nature of assessment reforms, the tendency to use some practices of the past as a transitional device to move towards substantial reforms, and the fact that assessment is a social construct affected by situational specificity. Miscue analysis reminds those in the field of assessment that definitive assessment is more myth than reality.

Part V examines the surge of reform initiatives in assessment and considers where these reforms leave us. Chapter 9 introduces the three terms most associated with these reforms—authentic, performance based, and portfolio—and highlights the similarities and differences among them. A sampling of recent reform initiatives in reading is used to generate a listing of the tasks typical of these assessments and the interpretive stances (anthropological, psychological, hybrid) that are used. The reformed assessments raise new issues about their consequences and the evidence proffered.

Finally, chapter 10 considers what really matters in assessment. Assessment needs to "make room" for order without conformity and for individual dispositions that move toward literacy ideals. Such assessment asks those involved in assessment to always ask: "Whom is assessment for?" Even those who believe that educational assessment focuses on accountability of the system must acknowledge that at the base of this argument is the premise that assessment is for students. Consequently, revisioning of assessment toward practices that "make room" means that schools themselves must take up the challenge of reforming, or perhaps remembering, their ethic of responsibility to students. The technologies of assessment used toward this goal should not become an end in themselves but a path toward possibility for students and teachers.

ACKNOWLEDGMENTS

All the authors would like to acknowledge grants received from the National Council of Teachers of English Research Foundation and the Faculty of Education of York University, Toronto, Canada. In addition, special thanks to Christine Pappas, who introduced me to Naomi Silverman, the editor of this volume. Naomi's encouragement and support of this project were unknowingly timely. Her editorial expertise, collegiality, and effort to get to know her authors are exemplary. Appreciation is also extended to the anonymous reviewers of very early drafts of this manuscript, to Sally M. Oran of Northern Arizona University and to an anonymous later reviewer of a substantially revised version. Their thoroughness and expeditiousness in making discerning comments on the manuscript are greatly appreciated. Finally, thanks to Deborah Britzman of York University who, together with Alice Pitt, at a coffeehouse on a cold winter evening in Toronto, helped me come up with the title of the book.

—*Sharon Murphy*
York University, Toronto

ENDNOTES

[1]The story of the California assessment debacle of the mid-1990s is told in the press clippings of the day (e.g., Colvin, 1995).

[2]*Testing* and *assessment* have been used in different ways by different writers. In this text, *assessment* is used as a generic term, and *testing* is used for assessment instruments or procedures that refer to themselves as tests.

Part I

Introduction

In this section, the concept of evidence is explored. Initially, the legal system, as represented in popular culture, is used to think about the provision of evidence and the underlying question how the validity of claims is assessed. This is followed, in chapter 2, by a consideration of how everyday actions require us to weigh evidence to make decisions.

This discussion leads to descriptions of the consideration of evidence in educational assessment. In particular, several relatively recent, key publications are described. These publications suggest that educators should be using a more complicated view of evidence and validity than has been used in the past.

1

What Counts as Evidence of Reading?

The ability to read is considered essential in contemporary society. Indeed the ability of the citizenry to read is considered of such importance that discussions of literacy have often been folded into larger political debates about economic competitiveness and the press of globalization.[1] These discussions have not presented a harmonious view of reading. Both academic[2] and popular arguments have raged over the reading[3] competencies of children and adults. Not only have recent newspaper headlines about education shown this, but the message to the public from these headlines is that schools are not doing what is necessary to enable all citizens to read.[4] Despite the disputability of this claim,[5] it is undeniable that a message of inadequacy has seeped into popular notions of students' reading abilities.[6]

---

[1]See, for example, Milner (1991).

[2]One example of the debates in the field of reading occurred with the release of *Beginning to Read* by Marilyn Adams (1990), a document not without political influences, but which, nevertheless has been the focus of considerable discussion. Discussion of this text was considered of such import that nearly entire issues of *Language Arts* (Teale, 1991), the flagship journal of elementary school teachers in the National Council of Teachers of English, and *The Reading Teacher* (Baumann, 1991), the flagship journal for elementary school teachers who are members of the International Reading Association, were devoted to it.

[3] The focus on reading is not to deny the importance, politically and educationally, of writing, but simply to make the task somewhat manageable. Brodkey (1991) reminded us that literacy is often equated solely with reading and made the claim that this equation is deliberate. She suggested that when literacy is linked with writing, it is also linked with agency. In other words, in writing people find their voices and in doing so can begin to argue with the system that controls them.

[4]Examples of headlines include: Phonics Is Best Aid for Reading, Study Shows (Colvin, 1995), Governors Agree to Set Higher Goals for Nation's Schools (Woo, 1996); Half of Cal State Freshmen Needed English, Math Help (Chandler, 1996); Don't Retreat on School Standards (Gerstner, 1995); Scientific Progress, Reading Lag (1994, Aug. 20).

[5]For a recent example of a critique of the assumption that schools are failing, see Berliner and Biddle (1995).

[6]A recent, generally respected, public affairs television program (20/20), which aired a critique of language arts policies in California and promoted a "back to the basics" alternative, when examined about the degree to which the researchers behind the program had investigated their sources and counteropinions about the reading method they were promoting, was found to be quite lax (Routman, 1996). This laxity seems to emphasize the deep pervasiveness not only of assumptions about the failure of schools but of nostalgic remedies that harken back to a time when things were perceived as being less complicated. When journalists fail to query, the myths that have been created about schooling are indeed entrenched.

All these debates, whether in popular magazines or academic journals, are undergirded with different assumptions about personal agency, culture, and the interplay between individuals and culture in reading. What has unified these debates is the fact that they are debates—they call on adversaries to present evidence of reading, and they stress the consequences of being or not being recognized as a reader. Because schools are a major societal arbiter of naming people as literate, the evidence that they proffer should be particularly open to analysis and scrutiny as well as highly defensible. In contemporary society, with all its technological and epistemological advances, evidence that someone is a reader can be imagined as relatively straightforward, solid, and irrefutable—but is it?

This book is an exploration of the fragility of the evidence surrounding reading assessment. Briefly, it studies of the tenuousness of evidence as it relates to past and present practices of reading assessment. In particular, the delicacy, or weakness, of evidentiary arguments is revealed in an analysis of standardized multiple-choice and individualized tests. Also considered are the deleterious effects of making judgments about reading based on scant or biased evidence. Finally, current moves toward reconceptualizing what counts as evidence in reading and how this evidence is valued are discussed. First, however, the concept of evidence itself is explored—initially, as a popular conception of a culturally accepted form of considering evidence, the legal system. In chapter 2, everyday notions of evidence are linked with theoretical conceptualizations derived from measurement and reading theory.

The legal system is an arena of social practice in which the term *evidence* is used explicitly. Indeed, the term evokes the criminal justice courtroom, replete with prosecutors, defense attorneys, judge, and jury, perhaps with memories of the television series in which the lawyer extraordinaire, Perry Mason, confronted a witness during the last five minutes of the program. Using superhuman logic and a fair bit of badgering and supposition, Mason invariably extracted a confession from the most devious and intractable criminal. Viewers were left with the satisfaction that order was preserved and that justice prevailed. Of course, recent real-life trials, such as that of O. J. Simpson, have dashed many romantic notions of heroic lawyers and last minute confessions. Despite its tarnishing through real-life and fictive teledramas, the legal system shows how evidence gets to be called evidence and how fragile the process leading to judgments based on evidence is. This discussion opens the way for other considerations of evidence and argumentation in fields such as educational assessment in general and literacy assessment in particular.

WHAT COUNTS AS EVIDENCE?

The evidence of today's legal system is framed by a call to reason. Our culture has abandoned the evidence of signs and portents characteristic of some of the witch trials of Salem. Instead, in contemporary courts of law, evidence is of two kinds—testimony and artifact. Testimony is oral evidence—people's descriptions, perceptions, and interpretations of the passing of time and the events that surround it. Testimony is bound up in the identities of the witnesses—who they are, their credibility to speak to an event or about an artifact. Artifacts are the physical evidence—they remain as they are, relatively impermeable to time, but always open to interpretation.

So the matter of evidence in the legal system seems relatively straight-forward, but it is not. Evidence in courtrooms is a delicate matter, the subject of judgment and interpretation before it ever enters the courtroom. The admissibility of evidence is governed by long-established practices. An example of what appears to be a reasonable practice is that of safeguarding physical evidence to avoid tampering.[7] As with any socioculturally con-structed practice, conventions can be out of step with societal wishes or can reflect societal trends that ultimately beg the question of justice. The relevance of evidence is a particularly debatable issue. An example might be the admissibility of a woman's sexual history in rape cases. In Canada, the courts at one time, allowed for the admissibility of sexual history; at another time admissibility was restricted (probably because of the influence of the women's movement), and recently, in the conservative climate, the pendulum is swinging back. Clearly, what counts as evidence is not hard and fast but is itself a process of interpretation.

Similarly, what counts as evidence in the act of naming someone as a reader is a complex and multifaceted process. As in the courtroom, schools can present evidence in the form of artifact and testimony. Over much of the past century in North America, however, only certain types of evidence of reading appeared admissible and as a consequence, a more complex and thoughtful consideration of the process of naming a person as a reader got lost. Heavily influenced by the technical and scientific appeal of the disci-pline of psychology, much of education turned to the kinds of evidence that

---

[7]Typically, once a piece of evidence is discovered, a chain of evidence must be maintained. For example, records must be kept of the whereabouts of a piece of evidence and who had possession of this evidence. If this chain is broken, the evidence can be ruled inadmissible.

this newly emerging field provided. The artifact traditionally given signifi-cant weight in school and public spheres is large-scale standardized assess-ment—whether norm referenced, criterion referenced, or some of the recently developed performance-based or portfolio assessments. Many other artifacts can be considered evidence of reading in and out of schools—book reports, magazines/newspapers/paperbacks purchased, oral reading per-formances, the amount of reading done, teacher and parent testimonials, the time devoted to reading, classification of the different genres read, the responses to readings, the amount of writing done (as the act of writing requires writers to read), texts read in "content-area" subjects, notes passed, bulletins posted, the amount of time engaged in literacy activities,[8] and on and on. Yet reports describing the growth of literacy materials in the homes of the United States over the past 100 years (see, Kaestle, Damon-Moore, Stedman, Tinsley, & Trollinger, 1991) have seldom made headlines as evidence of reading and are not considered in schools as evidence of reading. Indeed, when readers and those around them were asked to identify signifi-cant indicators of their reading (as Jane Hansen does in chap. 7), the variety of indicators presented reveals a world of information largely absent from any discussion of what counts as evidence of reading.

What types of evidence do standardized multiple-choice or individual-ized tests of reading provide? Although reading assessment does not use the same precedent system as law, it is possible to use an informed lens to consider the evidence that these tests offer. For example, when theoretical principles of measurement or reading are used to review a sampling of norm-referenced, multiple-choice standardized tests, do the tests hold up to the principles by which they should have been developed? If not, what principles do they reveal?

An examination of this type, an examination of artifacts as evidence, was conducted on a sampling of standardized multiple-choice tests and indi-vidualized tests. The results of this analysis, reported in chapters 3 and 4, raise questions about the kind of evidence that the sample of tests offers. Although the tests hold fast to psychometric principles in some areas, in other areas they are left wanting. On matters such as presumed background

---

[8]The types of activities documented by A. B. Anderson and Stokes (1984) include daily living—pay-ing bills, grocery shopping, washing clothes; entertainment—fiction, doing puzzles, the television guide, rules for games; school-related activities—practice books that came from school or were purchased in support of school; religion—bible studies; work related; literacy techniques and skills; interpersonal communication; storybook time. Other researchers such as Heath (1983) and Taylor and Dorsey-Gaines (1988) provided contextualized examples of numerous reading activities occurring outside of school settings.

knowledge and culture, clarity and lack of ambiguity, individual problematic test items force the question of the robustness of these tests as a means to identify readers. Further, the way that test developers have argued their case that the tests assess reading seems rooted more in procedures driven by traditional psychometric models than by thoughtful analyses. What is particularly troubling about individualized tests is that they are used to place students in remedial and learning-disabled classes even though the tests have been viewed as technically inadequate and as providing much the same results as their multiple-choice group counterparts (Steele & Meredith, 1991). The tests were also found to be limited in the view of reading they portrayed. In short, there was little connected text (passages of text) to read on the reading tests, and a considerable emphasis was placed on the reading of words or word parts rather than on reading connected text. This limitation leaves open the much larger question of the absent evidence that could make a difference in an assessment.

Recent attempts to solve the problems inherent in standardized multiple-choice and individualized assessments have included measures that supposedly bear a closer resemblance to daily reading engagements. One of the earliest and most established of these, miscue analysis (see chap. 8), has provided insights into how evidence must sometimes be shaped to have credibility for the context in which it is presented and has revealed the importance of the social context of assessment. Since the 1980s, a wide range of alternative assessment initiatives have been developed (see chapter 9). These have attempted to answer some of the critiques of the past by incorporating, for example, more text, a greater similarity of tasks to those of school or real life, and more variety in response modes, but the evidence that these reform efforts have offered is also fragile. Sometimes the fragility has been but an echo of the concerns raised in the past, and at other times, new critique has emerged. This new move in assessment may lead to a more pervasive understanding that evidence is tenuous, nondefinitive, and open to interpretation. The goal is to put in place procedures that recognize this fact and to work to create defensible portrayals of reading.

PRESENTATION OF THE EVIDENCE

Another theme that cuts through this book is that part of creating a defensible portrayal of reading rests in the way in which the evidence is presented. In the courtroom example, it is clear that evidence is presented through lawyers. Their skill in situating the evidence in a thesis of guilt or innocence is pivotal to many cases. Because the legal system is an adversarial system,[9] lawyers position evidence as bifurcated—that is, evidence is presented in prosecutorial or defense contexts as *for* or *against* an overall argument of guilt or innocence. Inevitably, in the course of a trial, the distinctive demarcations such as *for* or *against* are the idealized backdrop against which a hearing proceeds. The overall story of the case is created through evidence and the interpretive arguments of lawyers. The same evidence is explicitly acknowledged as having varying meanings.

In the case of standardized multiple-choice and individualized tests used in the past, the typical representation of reading was that of a statistic, and the presenters of this information were test specialists. Reform initiatives have used a statistic or a more complex representation of reading such as written descriptive summaries or portfolios. Statistics seem more difficult to argue with as they represent so much but communicate so little about readers. Statistical reports are usually underpinned by assumptions about how they are generated and what they mean, but an articulation of such assumptions is typically missing from most presentations of statistics as evidence of reading.

A public example of the problems inherent in presenting statistical information occurred in the late 1980s with what became known as the Lake Wobegon affair.[10] The Lake Wobegon affair refers to the results of an enquiry produced when a conservative educational group analyzing state reports of performance on standardized tests found that the states were reporting above-average average scores (Cannell, 1988), a logical impossibility. Although flaws were found in Cannell's analysis (Drahozal & Frisbie, 1988), a replication study (Linn, Graue, & Sanders, 1990) generally confirmed the central finding that almost all states were reporting test results above the national median. Educational measurement specialists generated lengthy, highly plausible, and psychometrically sound lists of explanations for such a phenomenon (e.g., Shepard, 1990). The sheen of norm-referenced, multiple-choice standardized testing was tarnished, however, because the assumptions undergirding these tests revealed their limitations to a public that had considered tests to be solid indicators of reading. Some psychologists

---

[9]Recently, there have been some small moves away from the adversarial nature of the courtroom. In Canada, these originated with aboriginal groups who worked toward consensus building. One adopted variation is a sentencing circle. Although not dealing with evidence, it does change the dynamic of justice away from individualism toward a collective response.

[10]Lake Wobegon refers to a mythical town featured in the radio broadcasts of Garrison Keillor, in which all of the children were above average.

said that their tests could never do all that people imagined they did. Unfortunately, this standard disclaimer was never uttered quite as emphatically before the Lake Wobegon affair as after.

Assessment reform initiatives have been struggling with issues relating to the presentation of evidence. Some efforts have held fast to a psychological orientation. Others have used an anthropological approach, and yet others have worked with some combination of the two. The latter efforts have yielded contradictions. For example, once complex assessment data from the daily activities of classrooms have been collected, assessment developers have found it difficult to come up with underlying statistics such as reliability figures that bolster the results in the psychometric community (see chap. 9).

INTERPRETERS

The complexity of data presentation in reading assessment raises the issue of how interpreters work with the information they receive from tests. In the courtroom example, the central figures are the interpreters—judges and juries who listen to and view evidence to arrive at a decision of guilt or innocence. Testimony and artifact may be mediated by the skill and resourcefulness of lawyers, but the judges and jurors ultimately decide what the evidence means. The judicial system recognizes the partiality of interpreters through a variety of review processes, but screenings such as the jury selection process cannot eliminate partialities; they simply reduce or constrain partialities to particular types. Although the O. J. Simpson trial is often used as an exemplar of juror dispositions, countless trials have likely occurred in which different sets of partialities were at stake—partialities such as class, gender, sexual orientation, race, or religion. The evidence becomes even less fixed as it moves from the orchestrated performance of courtrooms into the minds of jurors and judges, who weigh it to come to a decision. Sometimes in a criminal case, the jury is free to consider degrees of guilt (e.g., manslaughter vs. murder), which can affect the sentence rendered. Apart from this possible variation, the jury is asked to make a decision that is beyond the shadow of a doubt. If doubt surrounds a case, then jurors must return a verdict of not guilty.

The legal system's usefulness as a model for thinking about literacy assessment begins to fall down in the area of interpreters: The identification of interpreters is not quite as demarcated in reading assessment as it is in the courtroom. In the case of schools, interpreters can be wide ranging and sometimes unidentifiable. Sometimes those who present a case are the interpreters—those who render the decision of whether the evidence for the case at hand warrants that the individual is certified as a reader of, perhaps, a certain type or level. Technically, anyone who looks at the data or summation of data yielded by an assessment of reading is an interpreter, but in schools not everyone has the authority to pass judgment on the implications of assessment results for a student.

To some extent, the culture of schools presupposes a certain acceptance of the numerical data from assessment reports of standard scores, percentile ranks, or grade equivalents that make an interpreter unessential. Alternatively, the categorical reporting accompanying these scores, in and of itself, seems to remove the need for interpreters: When a score is reported as average or in relation to averageness, the decision has been rendered. The endgame of the standardized test, then, with its seeming definitiveness, demands that the question of the nature of the evidence produced be scrutinized closely. For initiatives such as miscue analysis, the separation of interpretation from description is one of the hallmarks of a descriptive system for reading analysis (see chap. 8). In such a system, the focus is on what the reader does rather than where the reader stands in relation to other readers. In recent initiatives, psychological, hybrid, and anthropological perspectives yield new problems for interpretation (see chap. 9). New developments in theorizing about validity and reliability (e.g., Moss, 1994) yield strong claims for the authority of a community of interpreters making defensible judgments about skills—judgments that are contestable and whose contestability is not considered in the complex machinery of some of the past envisionments of reading assessment (e.g., norm groups, standardization of procedures, item statistics).

CONSEQUENCES

The assessment industry is largely impotent unless consequences flow from it. In a way, the approach taken by the psychology industry over the past century has kept the industry separate from test uses, but both conceptually (in terms of validity theory as discussed in chap. 2) and ethically, the time for such a separation has long passed. In the courtroom example, the consequences of the verdict of guilt or innocence in the dramatic criminal cases of television had palpable consequences. In Perry Mason land, the downtrodden, wrongly accused person is freed to go on with his or her life, and the deceptive crook is snared by the justice system to face, viewers can only presume, a life behind bars or perhaps the extinguishing of life itself. The consequences of real-life criminal trials can be as dramatic as those of television. Execution and incarceration are tremendous penalties. For the innocent and the guilty, even the association with a trial can incur long-lasting effects on employability and reputation. For all concerned, the consideration of evidence in a trial becomes a much more complex activity than looking at a smoking gun. It is a multilayered process of interpretation with enduring consequences for all those involved.

Recognition that assessment has enduring consequences has forced measurement theorists to put aside their indifference to the practice of measurement and consider consequences as part of the argument about what counts as evidence (see chap. 2). After all, when tests are unused, they remain harmless artifacts. With use, no longer are the abstractions of theory at issue. Instead, the pattern of human lives is at stake and the consequences of assessments provide yet another reason to consider evidence as tenuous, fragile, contestable, and open to interpretation.

Some might argue that the standardized testing of the past century has been relatively blind to its consequences, perhaps an unwitting accomplice in the effects of its use. As Patrick Shannon has argued in chapter 5, this view is naive. From the outset, the developers of multiple-choice standardized tests realized that the tests were instruments of societal sorting, for maintaining a status quo in which the privileged maintained their affluence and the less privileged struggled with the hope that the seemingly egalitarian system of "objective" testing offered. The positioned history presented by Shannon provides the backdrop for considering how norm-referenced, multiple-choice standardized tests work today.[11]

Part of the critique of norm-referenced, multiple-choice, standardized tests, which began to emerge in the mid- to late-1980s, came from the field that gave birth to these tests—psychology, with the emergence of the field of cognitive science in psychology (Gardner, 1985). Cognitive science yielded new insights into human learning and revealed it to be complex. Norm-referenced, multiple-choice, standardized tests appeared to be less than adequate means by which to assess complex cognitive processes. Although key figures in the field of educational measurement had previously questioned the efficacy of many published tests (e.g., Buros, 1977, p. 10;

---

[11]See, for example, Murphy (1997) who discussed how standardized multiple-choice tests continue to be used as instruments that impact on the identities not only of students, but also of the teachers who teach them and the psychologists who administer them.

1972, p. xxvii), the collective shift toward cognitive science amplified the critique so that it influenced action. Comments by researchers such as Chittenden (1987) were prototypical: "While the cognitive sciences have added substantially to our understanding of reading, of mathematics learning, and so on, the paradigm for achievement testing, constructed in the 1920s, has remained essentially unaltered" (p. 390).

Despite this critique, much has remained stable about testing practices, and their consequences continue to be pervasive. Johnston's examination of the contemporary consequences of standardized testing, in chapter 6, echoes the themes of injustice and misuse found in Shannon's overview. First, the identities that teachers and students can make for themselves become altered as a result of certain test uses (S. Murphy, 1997). The pressures to do well on these measures often require teaching-to-the-test. When curriculum becomes tied to tests, which themselves tend to be built on the basis of past tests, a cycle of regressive education results. Impoverished educational experiences then become a demonstrable effect of high-stakes, norm-referenced, multiple-choice testing. The narrowing of curriculum is not the only consequence of the use of tests. Because these tests are norm referenced, they, by definition, categorize and rank students. The assumptions underlying the rankings and the uses of categorizations have more severe and long-term consequences than these relatively minuscule samplings of reading behavior should warrant. For instance, ranking categorization can lead to retention and placement in special programs—educative solutions that themselves are reported to have limited efficacy and that appear undue "punishment" for failing to successfully complete a relatively limited number of multiple-choice questions. Cultural biases inherent in the tests disadvantage some students before they even put pencil to answer sheet. It is perhaps an understatement to suggest that large-scale achievement tests have been overextended beyond the bounds of the kinds of evidence they supply and beyond the bounds of the consequences that should result from such measures. Hansen's interviews with readers and those who know them drive home the power of tests because some of her participants were compelled to talk about the impact of tests on their perceptions of themselves as readers despite being instructed that tests were not on the agenda (see chap. 7). In fact, this final element is the most compelling piece of evidence to support a thesis of the controlling influence and consequences of tests (Hanson, 1993).

Assessment reforms have not been in place long enough to begin systematic study of their consequences, but already some ironies are apparent. Many reforms retain the desires of the past—the desire to standardize, to speak with one voice about reading. Yet they aim for insights into the complexity of the process—by trying to relate to the everyday tasks of classrooms, by providing for natural data collection, by planning data collection at multiple times across the school year. Unfortunately, in some implementations, the desire to simplify and standardize wins out and is manifested as numeric labels of quality assigned by raters who are trained to rate in the same fashion. As a result, the complex evidence possible in portfolio assessment, evidence that reveals divergences and convergences, is distilled into a category that somehow numbs, if not nullifies, the entire process. The subtleties of the meaning potential in the evidence gathered are lost, and the consequences of the absence of these subtleties remain an unknown. In addition, cultural differences in the data collected and the interpretation of these data remain largely unstudied as educators struggle with controlling the procedures used in reforms. The history of psychological assessment over much of this past century has revealed the danger of reverting to procedures rather than to careful argumentation about the gathering, interpretation, and consequences of evidence.

Some assessment initiatives continue to have high stakes for students, teachers, schools, and school districts involved—stakes that go well beyond the bounds of sensibility. In fact, when the life-long impact of these assessments on stakeholders is considered, especially in relation to the demands that a social system like law places on both evidence and the weighing of evidence in relation to consequences, reading assessment comes up short. The shortfall should be considered neither a mark of failure nor of despair as long as teachers, educators, and assessment developers continue to work toward the goal of learning from other social systems and inventing new systems to find principled and ethical ways in which to assess reading.

SUMMARY

In this chapter, the legal system was used as one way of thinking about evidence and reading assessment. The legal system is a means to introduce the fragility of evidence, the way evidence can be presented, the interpreters of the evidence, and the consequences of the evidentiary arguments presented. Many of these themes echo throughout the subsequent chapters, which present more traditional ways of thinking about the evidence of reading and its consequences.

2

Evidence, Validity, and Assessment

THE EVERYDAYNESS OF VALIDITY

Claims about the evidentiary basis for reading or any other competency are arguments about validity. In chapter 1, a sketch of a codified system for thinking about evidence was used to raise issues about educational assessment. It is important to recognize that, in the common, everyday sense of the word *validity*, validity arguments have probably been around as long as people have been around. Everyday questions of validity are raised in many different ways and under many different circumstances. Some examples of the validity questions and the circumstances in which they might occur include:

Validity question: "Can you convince me of what you are saying?"

Example: A parent and teenager arguing about whether the teen can watch certain television programs.

Validity question: "How do you know that this is the case?"

Example: Disputes over the depletion of the ozone layer.

Validity question: "How can you convince me that your knowledge is even thinkable in this situation?"

Example: Debate over the segregation of AIDS victims as a means of controlling the disease.

Validity question: "Even if your way of conceptualizing things *is* thinkable in this situation, are the consequences of thinking this way more than society wishes to bear?"

Example: Discussion that one means of population control is the regulation of the number of children a family can have.

If these examples are considered, it becomes clear that to validate, or to answer the validity question, means to substantiate a position; to make sense of information and bring arguments forward to support the scope and depth of the interpretation. This sense making or interpretation does not occur in a swirl of facts and logic alone, but is enveloped in and constrained by social and moral ethics that relate to the application of an interpretation in particular situations. In daily living, these practices and assumptions about validation and the role of evidence in validation are routine. We know that we are trying to make sense of things. We know the way that we see things may not be the way someone else sees them—in other words, even though we may feel we have validated something, it is conceivable that to someone else our validity arguments are insufficient. We also know that sometimes, even though there seems to be a sound, underlying logic to one way of seeing things, this vision may not be morally or socially reasonable in specific circumstances.

These everyday notions of validity are both the starting and the ending points for contemporary educational assessment perspectives on validity. They are the starting point because they begin at the source of a general, socially grounded, everyday approach to validity. They predate the way validity was constituted in the psychometric assessment movement of this past century. These notions are also the end point because measurement theorists have returned to these concepts after nearly a century of dealing with validity in a way that intentionally or unintentionally set it apart so that it became less a sense-making process and more a procedure. A glimpse into this century of procedure is instructive in coming to terms with today's concepts of the nature of validity.

A GLIMPSE AT A CENTURY OF TEST VALIDATION

In the field of educational measurement,[1] there is a desire to hold firmly to the contention that, even though validity has been written about in many different ways and with varying kinds of language, ultimately "Validity data were generally developed to justify a claim that a test was useful for some particular purpose" (Anghoff, 1988, p. 19). The essence of validation, its marriage with purpose, often got lost in a focus on an orthodoxy of procedure that developed through much of the 20th century and only recently was disturbed.[2]

---

[1]During much of the past century, the validation of tests has been emphasized; only relatively recently has discussion focused on broader and more varied samples of performance. Consequently, the use of the term *test* throughout this discussion merely reflects the emphasis of the field.

[2]I am not arguing here that procedure is unimportant. I am suggesting that when procedure becomes so much the focus that there is a risk of uncoupling it from the heart of validation (which is to provide argumentation that an interpretation of a data set is reasonable), then it is time to step back and consider the manner in which validation has been occurring.

The beginnings of educational and psychometric assessment are rooted in the earliest days of the formation of the field of psychology, a new field desperate to separate itself out as a science, a field eager to throw off the mantles of both philosophy and introspection and to set itself apart through an emphasis on the definable and objective.[3] In what might be considered a counterpoint to DeSaint-Exupéry's (1971) poetic phrase, "What is essential is invisible to the eye" (p. 70), early developments in the field of psychology were focused on the visible or on making the invisible visible in an attempt to render alternative explanations improbable.

Early efforts toward these ends can be found in the mid-1800s in Germany in the laboratories of perceptual psychologists like Wundt, Weber, and Fechner.[4] These psychologists worked to ensure accuracy and precision in the directions and conditions for experiments. In essence, they were attempting to eliminate competing explanations for the results of their work—they wanted to build evidence for the argument that their results were valid.[5] This desire to control conditions to support the inferences from experiments is a forerunner of the standardization of instructions in the administration of tests. This desire also reflected the elevation of mechanical procedure over dynamic process: In many cases, the procedures became so constrictive that there was difficulty in generalizing to circumstances beyond the restrictive conditions of the tests.

In the late 1800s, Galton applied statistical techniques of the normal distribution (based on the work of De Moivre, Pierre-Simon, Gauss, and Quetelet) to psychological test data. In doing so, he posited that mental abilities might be normally distributed. Once performances came to be measured against this distribution, the normal distribution became a type of validity argument, a way of categorizing people's behavior, or, as Hacking (1990) wrote, a way for "making up people" (p. 6). In early 20th-century testing practice, it was assumed that behaviors were normally distributed and test developers no longer made the normal distribution of behaviors an

---

[3]The concept of psychometry itself is an interesting one to consider in relation to the knowability of something. The fiction writer, Jeanette Winterson, gave one type of historical insight into the term: "Psychometry is the occult power of divining the properties of things by mere contact" (1995, p. 130). Although Winterson used the term *psychometry* in a discussion of the power that the first editions of books held over her, the idea of the divination of the extent of reading ability through the administration of a reading test (without giving sufficient weighting to the idea that the test was a mere sample) is an idea that took hold in the early part of the 20th century.

[4]This brief overview is based on Crocker and Algina (1986, pp. 8–11), Minium (1978, pp. 107–110).

[5]In contemporary educational debates, it is recognized that the precision and control of test conditions are often restrictive of the generalizability of the results because the restrictive conditions exist nowhere but in the test situation itself.

explicit part of a validity argument. This assumption is another example of the orthodoxies of practice or the mechanization of procedure that resulted in a fossilization of validation arguments.

In the United States of the early 1900s, psychologists such as Thorndike, Termen, Yerkes, and Thurstone began to implement intelligence tests that built on the work of French, British, and German researchers' validity arguments. Echoing the desire to establish a science of psychology, Thorndike's seminal text on test theory (initially published in 1904 and reissued in 1919), well captured what he referred to as the distinction between subjective and objective measurement in his discussion of "the essentials of a valid scale" (p. 11).

From these beginnings, the first half of the 20th century witnessed a variety of developments around the concept of validity.[6] Often with statistics as the undergirding, concepts such as the following were put forward in the delineation of validity: A test is valid if it correlates with another measure of the skill that the test is intended to measure; a test is valid if it predicts future behavior; a test's validity rests on the degree to which it correlates with an infallible measure of the skill in question (in this case, the infallible measure refers to what is referred to in statistics as the "true" scores of the test, and true scores are defined statistically).

Until about 1950, there was a general understanding that test developers could demonstrate the validity of a test by providing evidence that the test was useful for its designated purpose, that it "measures what it purports to measure" (Garrett, cited in Anghoff, 1988, p. 19). Often this evidence amounted to obtaining correlations with other measures of the skill in question. As early as 1927, however, voices cautioned test developers against getting caught up in the mechanical procedure as opposed to the dynamic process of validation. Truman Kelley (cited in Anghoff, 1988) warned of the jingle and jangle fallacies. In the jingle fallacy, it was assumed that, if two tests were named tests of a specific skill, they actually measured the same skill. The jangle fallacy described the situation of two tests that were named as measuring different skills, but that measured the same skills. Underpinning Kelley's critique was the presumption that test developers had been quick to focus on the procedures of validation by finding tests with similar names, calculating a correlation, and then claiming validity for their tests when these test developers actually needed to explore the question of validation at much deeper levels.

The 1940s and 1950s marked the beginnings of discussions that suggested that tests could be valid for some purposes but not others. This period also

---

[6]This discussion of the history of the concept of validity is based on the work of Angoff (1988).

saw the emergence of the categorization of different types of validity. The fact that providing validity arguments was still considered the job of test developers however revealed that validity was still being thought about in fairly narrow procedural ways.

In the period from the 1950s to the 1980s, test developers focused on three types of validation processes:

Content validation: In content validation, the goal is to determine whether the items used in a test represent the larger domain of interest. In the case of reading, an example would be how well a phonics subtest represents the range of situations that exist in the domain of reading and the relative weighting given to phonics in the overall domain of reading.

Criterion-related validation: Criterion-related validity is of two sorts: Predictive validity, which measures how well a test predicts future performance, and concurrent validity, which measures how strongly the test scores correlate with those of other measurements administered at the same time as the focal test. An example of predictive validity might be the degree to which a score on a general achievement test, of which reading achievement is a subtest, correlates with grade point average in college. An example of concurrent validity would be how well test scores from one reading test correlate with those from a different reading test.

Construct validation: In construct validation the behavior of interest is the psychological construct, and no defined set of content has to be measured. Instead, the goal is to make the inference that the behaviors sampled can be grouped under the name of the construct in question, in this case, reading. A variety of methods can be used to argue for construct validity: Correlations can be calculated between the reading test tasks and related areas such as school performance;[7] a comparison can be made among the scores of people who are expected to differ in reading ability; studies can be conducted in which the aim would be to improve the reading ability of participants; factor analytic techniques can be used to determine whether responses to questions cluster in predictable patterns (e.g., performance on vocabulary questions on a test should correlate more highly with performance on other vocabulary questions than with performance on comprehension items); and a multitrait–multimethod matrix can be calculated in which the goal is to provide evidence that the reading test reliably measures performance and correlates well with other measures of reading but correlates minimally with measures of different constructs (e.g., math; Crocker & Algina, 1986; Thorndike, 1982).

Today, however, "the 30-year old idea of three types of validity, separate but maybe equal, is an idea whose time has gone. Most validity theorists now say that content and criterion validities are no more than strands within a cable of validity argument" (Cronbach, 1988, p. 4).

---

[7]The rationale here is that even though these tasks are not identical, they should share some relation.

Not only is validity now seen as a more complex and interpretive task, but the burden of demonstrating the validity of a test has now shifted from the test developers to the test developers and test users. After decades of working with the various conceptualizations of the three types of validity, test theorists now emphatically state that "one does not validate a test, nor even the scores yielded by the test, but the interpretations and inferences that the user draws from the test scores, and the decisions and the actions that flow from those inferences" (Angoff, 1988, p. 24).

This conceptualization of validity is much more dynamic than were past models. By focusing on inferences and interpretations, the concept of test validity is more of a social process—a process that requires deliberation rather than mechanical compliance, a process that is open to contestation, a process in which all the parties need to be given room for their voices. In fact, in this newly emerging conceptualization, the orthodoxy of practice in test validation has to some extent been challenged. Validation has been released from its procedural shackles and conceptually returned to the basics of everyday validation, because validation is a process of providing evidence for an argument.

This new concept of validation has taken some time to take hold despite its appearance in several documents that provide substantive argument in support of it. While the world of test–assessment practice is shuffling to keep up with theoretical changes in concepts of validation, recent writing takes these newer concepts of validity even further.

CONTEMPORARY VIEWS OF VALIDITY

The climate for a change to newer ways of conceptualizing validity has been depicted as evolutionary among some writers (e.g., Angoff, 1988). Others have argued that the field of tests and measurements had stagnated and not kept up with research and writing in fields such as reading theory, cognitive science, and sociolinguistics (e.g., Chittenden, 1987; R. Glaser, 1986; Linn, 1986; Valencia & Pearson, 1986, 1987). Throughout the 1970s and 1980s, in the field of reading, critics called for assessments that were more "authentic"[8] in nature. This type of conceptual evolution as well as the burgeoning

---

[8]The term *authentic* is somewhat problematic. Derived in a fashion somewhat similar to *marked* and *unmarked* elements in linguistics, the term *authentic* actually arose to describe materials and instruction that were a contrast to large-scale multiple-choice assessments and the curriculum generated in response to such testing. The term *authenticity* breaks down as it begins to be used across the school curriculum.

of new theories of learning led those working in the field of measurement to significantly change how both assessment and validity are considered.

Three documents are key in describing the academic community's consensus about validity and its relation to the assessment of reading in particular: *The Standards for Educational and Psychological Testing* (American Psychological Association, [APA] 1985), the *Code of Fair Testing Practices in Education* (Joint Committee on Testing Practices, 1988), and *Standards for the Assessment of Reading and Writing* (IRA/NCTE Joint Task Force on Assessment, 1994).

The Standards for Educational and Psychological Testing

The Standards for Educational and Psychological Testing (*SEPT*; American Psychological Association, 1985) is significant partly because, as a document endorsed and published by the APA, it has credibility among the practicing psychologists who make up the membership of APA. In other words, the concepts articulated in the document survived the theoretical debates among academics and represented a consensus for practitioners. In *SEPT*, the APA suggested that the focus of validation should not be on tests but on the inferences derived from test use. This new emphasis meant that a test should no longer be considered valid in and of itself. Rather, test validation should be thought of as a "process of accumulating evidence to support such inferences" (p. 9). This focus on inferences in validation implicates all parties, from test developers to test users.

Since the publication of *SEPT* in 1985, there has been further movement in the measurement literature on how validity is to be conceptualized. Tests and measurement specialists, such as Messick (1988), Cronbach (1988),

---

For instance, in the primary grades, the term is often associated with the reading of published trade book literature of high quality as opposed to the reading of artificially constructed tests that might be found in a basal reader (e.g., Goodman, Shannon, Freeman, & Murphy, 1988). It is also associated with instruction in which students and teachers co-construct purposes for inquiries they might make around questions of interest (e.g., Harste, Short, & Burke, 1995). Yet, if the term is applied consistently across the grades, two things become clear. First, the authenticity operates with a particular cultural model of literacy in mind. It is an open question as to whether this model is operating on a singular prototype of literacy that may exclude literacy models of nondominant cultural groups (e.g., Gee, 1990). Second, the typical liberal arts education in the higher grades of school often involves a level of detail of study and critique of literature that probably is not typical of society's relation to literature in general. This is not to argue that a liberal arts education is inappropriate. Rather, it is to ask whether the term authentic captures the issues that need to be considered in raising the questions of the kinds of work schools need to do, the assessment that flows from this question and the relation schooling and assessment have with what happens outside schools. Nevertheless, the term has been used liberally and widely in the literature on assessment, and an introduction to some of the practices developed in the name of authentic assessment is presented in chapter 9.

and Moss (1994), further expanded the concept of validity. Messick (1988), in particular, developed a line of argumentation in which he asked those involved in assessment to consider the evidential and consequential bases of both test interpretation and test use. For Messick it was no longer sufficient to provide arguments about the inferences to be made from an instrument; those who validate tests must consider the implications or consequences of both the use of a test and the interpretation of its results. Messick's (1988) four facets of validity can be posed as questions to be asked about the validity of any test:

1. Have arguments and evidence been provided to indicate that the test discriminates among examinees on the variable of interest and provides evidence similar to that of other measures of the same construct? This question suggests that a test should be able to differentiate between, for instance, highly proficient and less proficient readers. It also suggests that the pattern of findings on a test should be reasonably comparable with the pattern of findings on another assessment tool that assesses the same competency. These types of evidence strengthen the plausibility of the inferences that can be made about performance on a test. If a test cannot differentiate among examinees in relation to a particular quality, it appears difficult to consider how the test can be a measure of this quality.[9] It also seems logical to assume that findings from the assessment of a competency like reading should bear some relation to other indexes that assess the same competency.

2. Have the value implications of the test been assessed? The value implications of a test can be considered in relation to the value inherent in the meaning of the competence being assessed and the value that the test is given in particular circumstances. In the first instance, the construct or competence in question may be framed to value particular culture-specific aspects. For instance, in some cultures, reading done in school is not valued while other kinds of reading are valued (e.g., Heath, 1983). In such a case, the value implication might be that the test should be used only with cultures that hold the same value for reading as the value held in the test. In the second instance, the use of the test in particular contexts (such as in placement of students or with particular populations of students) might assign it more significance or value than it ought to have in view of the decisions being made.

---

[9]The way in which assessment is discussed here derives largely from a linear concept of measurement. That is, the skill in question is considered analogous to something poured into a measuring cup. Some have a lot of the skill, and others have less. This concept of competency still remains fairly narrow as competencies are much more likely to be qualitatively distinctive. A few examples illustrate this. The first uses knowledge of phonics. Being taught more and more phonics does not solve the problems of children who do not seem to see the relation between graphemes and sound. There are many documented cases of children who can produce high-quality phonics worksheets of the relation between graphemes and sound but who cannot read. The point is that a qualitatively new level in reading occurs when graphophonemic knowledge is orchestrated in the context of reading as opposed to the context of phonics activities. The second example relates to the reading of a complex text like a novel or book-length essay. Readers who have difficulty interpreting these texts do not need "more interpretation" but a different way to read the text; this issue is a qualitative, not quantitative difference.

3. Have argumentation and evidence been provided supporting the relevance of the construct being assessed and the usefulness of the scores in the particular application being considered? Relevance and usefulness, both considerations of the context of assessment, seem obvious considerations for validation. Relevance in a reading assessment might have to do with the relationship between the types of tasks used on an assessment and the literacy tasks in the broader environment. It is, for instance, irrelevant to include in a functional literacy test information about the daily city bus schedule if the rural people that a test is being administered to have no need to use such information. In this example, the information is also not useful because functional literacy should relate to the contexts of literacy use. Similarly, a test that incorporates items that relate to middle class may not be relevant to lower class examinees. Relevance is intimately tied to usefulness, and test results based on items that have little relevance to the examinees should be considered of limited usefulness. In cases where items are relevant, the question of usefulness should still be asked. For instance, it may be relevant to assess knowledge of the reading of bus schedules for some urban populations but in the overall scheme of literacy knowledge this information may be of limited usefulness in thinking about what makes a person literate because it relates to a very narrow concept of literacy.

4. Has there been an appraisal of the potential consequences for the proposed use of the tests, and will there be appraisals of the intended social consequences of the use of the test? These questions are analogous to the conduct of an environmental impact study for a development project in an ecosystem (IRA/NCTE Joint Task Force on Assessment, 1994). In other words, if a treatment or test is applied, does it damage the place or people involved? If, for instance, rural people are classified as illiterate as a result of tests that do not account for their literacies, this classification, in a larger societal context, may bar them from particular jobs, academic advancement, and social opportunities. In such instances, although the intended social consequences may have been beneficial, the potential consequences can lead to an even further calcification of opportunities for some test takers.

These elements written about by Messick (1988) echo points made about the everydayness of validation. Elements of such thinking are evident in another document produced not only for psychometric practitioners but for the public at large.

The *Code of Fair Testing Practices in Education* and Related Developments

The *Code of Fair Testing Practices in Education* (Joint Committee on Testing Practices, 1988)[10] resulted when several organizations, concerned about fair

---

[10]The organizations included the American Educational Research Association, the American Psychological Association, and the National Council on Measurement in Education. Their work in the

testing practices, converged to form the Joint Committee on Testing Practices. The joint committee's code was produced in a format intended for wide circulation. The code echoed much of what had been written a few years earlier in the *SEPT*, but it did so in language intended to be understood by the general public. The code, which refers only to educational tests, is divided into four areas: developing and selecting appropriate tests, interpreting scores, striving for fairness, and informing test takers. For each of these categories, parallel sections are included for both test developers and test users. Of particular note is the section on guidelines for the provision of information to test takers. After nearly a century of testing, the test takers were considered as more than passive participants; they were seen as people who had a right to know about the procedures being administered to them.

Validity discussions have developed even further in recent years. Moss (1994), in her discussions of the relation of validity and reliability, has argued for a conceptualization of validity that is socially situated and marked by an awareness of its own situatedness. Moss suggested that questions of reliability are questions of validity. Drawing on the hermeneutic tradition, Moss suggested that, unlike past practices in which reliability was established by examining consistency of performance across independent tasks, a hermeneutic approach would aim for:

> a coherent interpretation of collected performances, continually revisiting initial interpretations until they account for all of the available evidence. Inconsistency does not invalidate the assessment. Rather, it becomes an empirical puzzle to be solved by searching for a more comprehensive or elaborated interpretation that explains the inconsistency or articulates the need for additional evidence. (p. 8)

In an application of this approach, the assessment of several oral reading performances might consider genre, readers' background knowledge, or textual features as elements that would account for variation in performance across different tasks and might see familiarity with a particular text as an explanation for why a reader would perform differently on a second reading.

---

joint committee was also sponsored by the American Association for Counselling and Development, the Association for Measurement and Evaluation in Counselling and Development, and the American Speech–Language–Hearing Association. The code is available on request from the National Council on Measurement in Education, 1230 Seventeenth Street NW, Washington DC, 20035. Single copies of the code are free.

Moss (1994) further argued that the goal of attempting to generate similar ratings by independent raters of a performance can also be considered in a hermeneutic framework. In this instance, she drew on Scriven's work to argue that achieving consensus does not accomplish objectivity. Instead, one might consider consensus no more than a mutually agreed-on subjectivity; even then, the question must be asked as to what was suppressed to achieve the subjectivity. Moss proposed a hermeneutic approach to assessment:

> [This approach] would involve holistic, integrative interpretations of collected performances that seek to understand the whole in light of its parts, that privilege readers [i.e., performance assessors] who are most knowledgeable about the context in which the assessment occurs, and that ground those interpretations not only in the textual and contextual evidence available, but also in a rational debate among a community of interpreters. (p. 8)

This approach echoes SEPT's concept of validation as an interpretive act and an everyday task. Of course, this approach raises questions about who can participate in the act. Instead of a process largely controlled by test developers, Moss (1994) argued for the inclusion of stakeholders such as students and teachers. The immediate question raised is how to avoid prejudice. Here, Moss suggested that the process be one in which decisions are "warranted through critical, evidence-based review and dialogue" (p. 10).

The Standards for the Assessment of Reading and Writing

The Standards for the Assessment of Reading and Writing (SARW; IRA/NCTE Joint Task Force on Assessment, 1994) is the third major document that deals with validity, but in this document, the discussion is particularized to reading and writing assessment. The SARW was spawned through the joint efforts of the International Reading Association (IRA) and the National Council of Teachers of English (NCTE), associations that represent a considerable constituency of literacy educators both at the school and university levels. This document too speaks with the authority of these associations to the practitioners in the field.

Validity, as embodied in the SARW, takes its direction from an articulation of the nature of assessment, language, language learning, and language assessment. The authors were particularly sensitive to the fact that in the areas of reading and writing, "language is not only the thing being assessed, but also part of the process of assessment itself" (IRA/NCTE Joint Task Force on Assessment, 1994, p. 5). The *SARW* argued for the importance of considering the cultural and personal histories of individuals in any assessment and posited that language assessments in particular must allow for a multiplicity of interpretations to be taken from texts. The *SARW* suggested that valid assessments "would allow for and encourage multiple interpretations of reading selections and make provisions for allowing students to demonstrate their ability to construct meaning through multiple response modes such as writing, drawing, speaking, or performing" (IRA/NCTE Joint Task Force on Assessment, 1994, p. 44). The *SARW* also connected valid assessment to a "valid curriculum" (IRA/NCTE Joint Task Force on Assessment, 1994, p. 44) and to the consequences of this assessment.

The *SARW*'s first six standards all involve validation:

1. The interests of the student are paramount in assessment.
2. The primary purpose of assessment is to improve teaching and learning.
3. Assessment must reflect and allow for critical inquiry into curriculum and instruction.
4. Assessments must recognize and reflect the intellectually and socially complex nature of reading and writing and the important roles of school, home, and society in literacy development.
5. Assessment must be fair and equitable.
6. The consequences of an assessment procedure are the first, and most important, consideration in establishing the validity of the assessment. (IRA/NCTE Joint Task Force on Assessment, 1994, p. 3)

Following these statements are another four that deal with the implications of these goals.

The statements contained in the *SARW* are informed by a sense of assessment practices in reading and writing over the past century. This history of practice, which is presented in chapters 5 and 6, is a history that the *SAWR* suggested resulted in the production of assessment results that narrow curriculum, are not used to inform teaching and learning, are used for gatekeeping and certification purposes, involve students as passive test takers, impose a narrow definition of reading and writing, are based on a singularity of perspective, and often do not produce useful information. These critiques are all arguments about both what assessment should do and what the processes of reading and writing involve. In particular, these principles take seriously arguments about consequential validity, one of the four validity types described by Messick (1988). Consequential validity demands that assessment tasks take into account sociocultural differences among those being assessed by bringing multiple perspectives to bear on assessment data. It demands that the decisions of test users reflect that each test is only a single sampling of behavior on a single assessment instrument; and it demands that a test be useful to those being assessed so that their participation is neither a waste of time nor an exercise in self-implication.

The SARW inevitably raised questions about who should be involved in assessment. Like Moss (1994), the SARW called for the involvement of students, teachers, parents, and the educational community. The SARW challenged the categorization of teacher observations as "informal" and "subjective" and test results as "formal" and "objective." Instead the IRA/NCTE Joint Task Force asked its readers to consider that "the knowledge constructed…[from assessment] would be quite different from that constructed in a discussion in which teachers' observations were described as 'direct documentation' and test results as 'indirect estimation'" (IRA/NCTE Joint Task Force on Assessment, 1994, p. 12).

SPECIFYING THE INTERPLAY BETWEEN EVIDENCE AND VALIDITY IN READING

The net result of the evolution of the concept of validity in the fields of measurement and literacy is the recognition that validity is a complex interplay between evidence and values. No longer sufficient are the practices of running correlations between two tests that claim to test the same thing, using tests without considering their validity in specific circumstances, or using tests without considering the consequences of their use. Instead, there is a call to return to the principles of validity as a process of argumentation. Although, as Cronbach (1988) suggested, traditional psychometric practices may be a part of this argument, they remain but a fraction of the kinds of evidence and argumentation that need to be put forth.

Questions of validity arguments for assessment in general are complicated in the field of reading by the question, "What is reading?" For instance, one assessment tool may use specific procedures to assess reading according to a definition of reading that others either might not even recognize or might deem insufficient.[11] One illustration of diverse concepts about reading can be found in *Theoretical Models and Processes of Reading* (Ruddell, Ruddell, & Singer, 1994). In this text, articles are grouped into categories that could be considered theoretically contrastive: A section on Comprehension is followed by a section on Reader Response; Social Context and Culture can be juxtaposed with Metacognition; and the section on Models of Reading and Literacy Processes reflects a heavy weighting toward Cognitive-Processing Models (of which there are six exemplars), followed by one each of the following models—Sociocognitive-Processing Model, Transactional Model, Transactional-Sociopsycholinguistic Model, and Attitude-Influence Model. Discussion of the process of reading is sometimes difficult because of the diversity of and disparity among assumptions and assertions framing theoretical views.

Even more compelling is the lack of recognition of theories about reading in some discussions of reading. Noticeably absent from Ruddell, Ruddell, and Singer (1994) are contributions from postmodern or phenomenological theorists (e.g., Ricoeur, Iser, Barthes, or Derrida). This absence reified McCormick's (1988) claim that theories of reading exist in relative academic solitudes. The absences also suggested the need for conversations to broaden the concept of reading to be held not only in the academic community but also in communities engaging in the development and use of assessment protocols.

Because reading can be conceptualized so variously, any assessment protocols of reading should be informed by validity arguments about reading itself. In this way, the construction of reading exemplified in an evaluative moment should map onto not only a satisfying theoretical description of reading but also a lived experience of reading. As with assessment itself, the degree to which a practitioner or theorist aligns with a particular concept of reading reflects the degree to which this individual believes the arguments around the position to be valid. Contrary to popular desires, there is no absolute truth in concepts of reading or assessment; both come down to judging or valuing an interpretation.[12] One possible way to characterize some of the major distinctions among concepts of reading is to consider what counts as data or evidence of reading. Data gathering and the data themselves are interpretive moments in that choosing from all the potential

---

[11]Even the examples used in the discussion of validity earlier in this chapter rely on certain assumptions about reading some might contest.

[12]In making this assertion, as well as through some of the examples presented earlier in the chapter, I have revealed my predisposition toward conceptualizing reading in terms of a sociotransactional framework.

sources of information available and naming the choices as data signify sets of assumptions about reading. The following questions may be useful in distinguishing among theories of reading:

What counts as text? On the basis of the theory used, the answer to this question can range from the graphic images of popular culture to the traditional essay or piece of fictional work to the morpheme or even grapheme. Many theorists would probably agree that connected written discourse has the possibility of being a text. Many, however, also push for consideration of text in its surround: If the surround includes pictures, moving images, and so on, then it must be drawn into discussions of the reading. There remains a group of theorists who have argued that reading is different for beginners; they have maintained that for beginning readers sub-word-level units count as text, whereas for experienced readers text is connected discourse.

What is the relationship between language and text? Language is common to oral and visual text whether the text be image based or written. Some theorists have begun to consider how the visuality of text lends itself to certain kinds of readings but more often the relation between language and text is restricted to the relation between written and oral language. Even though there is general agreement that oral and written language share a lexicogrammatic system, differences between these forms of language are also acknowledged. These differences get played out in judgments about reading. For instance, dialect influences in oral reading may be considered as faults in some descriptions of oral reading performance whereas in others they are not judged negatively as long as meaning is preserved; such influences are considered part of the expected process of working with two forms of a language.

What is the role of text properties? Among the catalogue of textual properties are the layout and arrangement of text on the page, the relation of illustrated text to written text, the genre, lexicogrammatical features (including word choices, cohesive devices), and length (Pugh & Ulijn, 1985). Some theories stress that the text is a potential influence over how a reading occurs. Others pay less attention to specifics especially if the focus of the theoretical position is on reading words rather than text.

What are the relative contributions of individual psychological processes and social collective processes?[13] Because of the heavy early influence of psychology in reading theory, it is not surprising that one family of theories locates its focus on the psychological processes of reading and tends to restrict interpretations to a microcosmic world of interaction between the text and the reader. Other families of reading theories emphasize reading as a social act informed by cultural practices

---

[13]All theories typically lay claim to both these aspects. Because language is a social construction that occurs when individuals are in interaction with other individuals, it can be safely assumed that both these aspects come into play. The point of this question is to consider which one of these aspects is emphasized in explanations of how reading occurs.

and knowledge about how to read, what it means to read, and the uses of reading. Other theories work with both these aspects in relative balance.

How fixed is the meaning of text? The words *comprehension* and *interpretation* exemplify the distinctions that might be made about the openness of the meaning of text. Comprehension, which typically refers to understanding the text, can be used to mean a fixedness of the meaning of text.[14] Interpretation suggests that there is considerable room for considering the potential textual meanings a reader might create. Some theories operate with an understanding that both of these are part of reading—that is, there is a degree to which certain departures from text cannot be justified as readings of these texts, in which case there is a claim toward, not a singular interpretation, but a bounded collection of possible interpretations.

Despite the demands to reflect on how a test or assessment procedure can be "theoretically pure," the real tests of validity ultimately occur in the contexts of the activities being assessed—in the school, workplace, home, and on the street. These contexts are the lived world of reading, and reading theories merely attempt to capture how we negotiate the print in this world. The remainder of this book is about how well past and present attempts capture and document reading, the fragility of the argumentation that underlies these attempts, and the struggles to improve on them.

---

[14]I am aware that the term *comprehension* is used by many to also mean "interpretation of text." Its history of association with comprehension questions is indicative of the type of use that I am getting at in this discussion—a use that claims a singularity of the meaning potential of the text.

Part II

The Validity of Standardized Tests From a Traditional Psychometric Perspective

In this section, I review group and individual commercially published standardized tests from the perspective of traditionally recommended practices for establishing validity. The fundamental goal of this section is not to critique these measures from outside the field but from within the field in which they were developed.

I approach this task as an analysis of artifacts. In other words, I am interested in how the artifacts reveal themselves, how the artifacts speak about the principles underlying them, and the degree of match between these revelations and basic tests and measurement principles.

By taking this approach, I am not necessarily claiming an affinity with these traditional principles, but I am considering the measures on their own terms.

3

Multiple-Choice Standardized Reading Tests in the Early 1990s

The mounting disaffection with large scale multiple-choice standardized assessment[1] that occurred toward the end of the 1980s was intensified for multiple-choice tests of general achievement. Not only did incidents like the Lake Wobegon affair raise suspicion in the public about standardized[2] general achievement tests, but the psychometric community began to work

---

[1]Large-scale assessment is used to refer to the jurisdictional scope of the assessment. For instance, state-wide assessments or national assessments are both large-scale assessments. The jurisdictional scope of the assessment has implications for the depth, breadth, and form of the assessment. Typically, large-scale assessments have several characteristics: They provide a sampling of items that represents a common instantiation of the construct; there is a struggle to ensure that the commonality does not represent a generality that is meaningless; in an effort to make the tests discriminate among examinees, there is also a danger of creating idiosyncratic items with minimal relevance to the construct being assessed. Ultimately, these assessments are the source of competing desires that become enacted on those assessed sometimes with detrimental effects (see chap. 6, this volume).

[2]Echoing their roots in turn-of-the-century psychology, standardized tests have two principal characteristics: They attempt to maintain a uniformity of procedure in the way the test is administered and scored, and they base the judgment of performance on the test in relation to established norms for the test (Anastasi, 1982). Both these characteristics utilize the everyday concept of *standards* as a set of common minimal levels, but they do so in slightly different ways.

In the first sense of *standards* in standardized testing, the focus is on ensuring *sameness* or the identicality of the testing situation. There should be as few differences as possible in such things as the ways directions are given to students, the interaction between the person administering the test and the people taking it, the order and sometimes speed in which tasks are completed, and the criteria for marking the individual items (questions) as correct or incorrect. The second sense of *standards* in standardized testing focuses on *differentiating* among the examinees who take the test—naming who did better or worse on the test. This differentiating process is similar to many other categorization processes in that there are criteria created (either through statistics or words) to distinguish among the members of a group at any one time. These criteria are like those for any category system—they are arbitrary. In other words, there is no inherent value in the criteria except the value we assign them. For instance, manufactured products that would have been considered "Grade A" 20 years ago might not pass today's criteria because our values about relative safety standards have changed.

The goal of the standardization of administration and marking procedures is to strengthen the *inference* that differences in performance on a test are due to the abilities or knowledge of a person taking the test and not to testing-situation variations that could have affected performance or the marking of performance. This concept is directly traceable to the influence of experimental psychology on assessment (Crocker & Algina, 1986). Since the onset of experimental research in psychology, data have accumulated to show that experimental control of human participants is not as simple as it initially emed. Subtle cues like voice inflection, facial expressions or pauses, and race of the examiner can

more vigorously toward alternatives that had been discussed for some time by reading theoreticians and cognitive researchers. For example, as part of an edited collection of essays called *Construction Versus Choice in Cognitive Measurement: Issues in Constructed Response, Performance Testing, and Portfolio Assessment* (Bennett & Ward, 1993), both Bennett (1993) and Snow (1993) proposed schemes for the ranking of types of assessment. Both ranked multiple-choice assessments toward the lower end of their scales, which favor more complex assessments. Yet, despite these emerging conceptualizations and burgeoning doubts (e.g., Berliner & Biddle, 1995; Cannell, 1988; Chittenden, 1987; Harman, 1991; Johnston, 1984a; Linn, 1986; Mislevy, 1993; Pearson & Valencia, 1987; M. L. Smith, 1991; Stake, 1991;

influence the performance of test takers (Anastasi, 1982; S. Murphy, 1997). Standardized directions are part of the imagined controllable context of the human experiment, but in practice the controllable context must remain an imagined one. This limitation of always being in a context that may depart in minor or major ways from the initially conceptualized context should be acknowledged whenever test users are considering a test for use.

Standardized marking procedures seem more clear-cut, but they are just as complicated. In multiple-choice tests with standardized marking procedures, one response or option in an array of responses or options is the *keyed*, or correct, response. The scorers of tests do not interpret the correctness of a response but simply check it against the keyed response. Furthermore, with the machine scoring of most tests, scoring biases and errors seem to be avoided, but masked by this seeming definitiveness are all of the assumptions built into defining what constitutes the correct or keyed response. For instance, if the decision to name a response as correct is based on cultural values, it is possible for the keyed response to be implausible to some students taking the test. Consequently, even though correcting a test seems free from bias, it may not be.

Referencing student performance on a test to a set of norms is regarded as one way to strengthen the inferences made about student performance on the test. Norms are really the transformed scores of a large "representative group of persons." The norm group's scores become the reference points for all other individuals taking the test. The transformed scores begin as raw scores (which is the simple count of the number of items correct), and they are converted into other formats. Among the general kinds of scores reported on the standardized tests examined in this chapter are grade equivalents, standard scores, and percentile ranks. Of these three, the grade equivalent score has been repeatedly criticized in the measurement literature (e.g., Crocker & Algina, 1986) because of the possibility of misleading nonmeasurement-trained interpreters of the score.

The standard scores are not always clearly understood by the layperson, but the percentile rank on which standard scores are based is more easily explained. A percentile rank indicates the percentage of the norm group who achieved a raw score lower than the raw score of the individual being examined. In other words, a person with a raw score of 36 might be at the 50th percentile rank. That is 50% of the people in the norm group obtained a score lower than 36. A host of other scores are available depending on the test. For instance, the MAT provides stanines, achievement–ability comparisons, item p-values, percentage achievement of performance indicators, Informed Reading Inventory (IRI) reading levels, and Higher Order Thinking Skills (HOTS).

Anyone who takes a norm-referenced test is compared to the norm group's performance on the test. This pattern means that a key emphasis in interpreting norm-referenced tests is on the phrase "representative group of persons." The less a person currently taking a test can be situated in relation to the characteristics of the normative group, the weaker the inference is that the person's score falls at a particular percentile rank. Issues of representativeness are often raised around racial, gender, cultural, and class differences (S. Murphy, 1997) which question the usefulness of the data from a test as evidence of reading. The standardized multiple-choice tests used in the 1990s build on these two facets of *standard*'s meaning.

Taylor, 1990a; Valencia & Pearson, 1986), several large commercial publishers continued to publish standardized multiple-choice reading tests that were put to a variety of uses by schools (Steele & Meredith, 1991)[3] in school district assessments and in special education placement and programming decisions. By focusing on a sampling of these widely used, commercially produced multiple-choice tests, the evidentiary arguments they use are assessed for their robustness and clarity.[4]

SELECTING EXAMPLES FOR ANALYSIS

The relative size of the test market can only be imagined. A glimpse into the Ninth and Tenth Buros *Mental Measurements Yearbooks* (Buros, 1992, 1993) revealed that some 168 tests that in some way deal with reading are indexed. Some of these are traditional achievement tests, others neurological tests, others simple word-reading tasks. Some are standardized and others clinical. An indexing of tests in the Buros yearbooks means that the tests continue to be published, but the listing does not provide information on the frequency of use. Standardized test usage information has been reported in studies by Afflerbach (1990), Steele and Meredith (1991), and

---

[3]Many states continued to utilize their own state-developed multiple-choice reading tests as a large part of their assessment initiatives (Afflerbach, 1990). These tests are not the focus of this chapter for several reasons: The generation of these tests by individual states means that their use is fairly restricted, whereas commercially produced tests are available and used widely; tests produced by state or provincial departments of education can sometimes change with each administration, so that comparability of performance across tests may not continue to be useful. (Innovations in some states' implementation of assessment are dealt with in chap. 9.)

Several reasons for the continuing use of standardized tests, whether commercially available or state developed, are that policy initiatives, rewards, and student placements remain tied to tests in many jurisdictions (McGill-Franzen & Allington, 1993). This practice may be a case of lagging behind developments in tests and measurements, or perhaps the culture of testing that has seeped into the school system for over a decade is so pervasive that it takes time to change.

[4]The approach taken in this chapter and the next one is to look at tests from two vantage points. The psychometric vantage point was chosen as it seemed sensible to consider whether the tests lived up to their own "rules of evidence." This argument was felt to be compelling as it judges the tests by their own rules. The second vantage point was from a limited perspective on reading—a perspective that suggests that reading tests should include connected discourse (i.e., multisentence texts) and that these texts should begin to resemble the complexity of the texts encountered in everyday reading both for pleasure and functioning in contemporary society. Here again a crude index (number of words per text) was used. As is demonstrated at the end of this chapter and in chapter 4, both these indicators in their very crudeness show that the reading assessments reviewed in these chapters are even cruder. Ultimately, they reveal an impoverished view of reading. It is acknowledged that there has been considerable discussion about the ways in which tests negatively affect students (e.g., chaps. 5 and 6; S. Murphy, 1997) and that the model represented by standardized multiple-choice and individualized tests has often been one in which students get labeled and assigned to remediation, giftedness, or averageness. This discussion of the consequences of the uses of tests continues in later chapters.

Hall (1985), who identified commercially produced tests used in either state assessments or in achievement assessment for special purposes such as remedial reading and learning disability placements.[5] More recent unsystematic indicators of test use can be found in press reports (e.g., D. L. Brown, 1995; Toy, 1995). These latter indicators suggest that despite the groundswell of reform in the educational community, standardized tests continue to have currency in many jurisdictions.

Six tests[6] commonly commercially available in 1992 and used in either special education placement decisions or large-scale school district or state level assessments[7] are the California Achievement Tests (1992), the Gates–MacGinitie Reading Tests (MacGinitie & MacGinitie, 1989a, 1989b), the Iowa Tests of Basic Skills (Hieronymous, Hoover, Frisbie, & Dunbar, 1990; Hieronymous, Hoover, Oberly, Cantor, & Frisbie, 1990), the Metropolitan Achievement Tests (Prescott, Balow, Hogan, & Farr, 1986, 1988), the Stanford Diagnostic Reading Test (Karlsen & Gardner, 1986), and the Test of Reading Comprehension (Brown, Hammill, & Wiederholt, 1978).[8] These tests are all fairly widely used. Some are general achievement tests with a reading component and others are specific to reading. In considering the evidence that test developers advanced for their tests, it is useful to cluster the evidence into two types, explicit and implicit. Explicit arguments about the validity of tests are those that test developers stated as a signification to others of the strengths and limitations of the test. Implicit arguments are those that are built into the test itself without any outward acknowledgment or discussion.

[5]Ten percent of the respondents in the Steele and Meredith (1991) study had to report using the test for it to be considered here.

[6]These tests were the versions available from publishers in mid-1992. Some have recently undergone revision. This cyclical revision is always the case with the evaluation of any commercially published material: A lapse in time occurs between the date the material was acquired and the published date. It must be pointed out that the current analysis is an analysis of tests at a particular time—after nearly 100 years of use. Even though some changes have been made to revised editions of tests, in cases where tests were revised and data are available, reviews of revised editions yielded patterns of findings remarkably similar to those contained in the present analysis (Harp, 1995; K. Smith, 1995).

[7]The tests used were those that were the most current at the time of their purchase for analysis. The authors of the test usage studies named tests that may have had earlier publication dates on the basis of the time that they conducted their research.

[8]First-, third-, and fifth-grade tests were selected where grade level designations occurred. Where no grade level designations were provided, all items were analyzed. This limitation of the number of items occurred for two reasons: to provide information on the early years of reading as that is the distinguishing period for many concepts about reading and to provide a reasonable limit to the number of items worked with. The following total numbers of items were worked with for each test: CAT5 = 288; Gates–MacGinitie = 337; Iowa = 310; MAT = 319; Stanford Diagnostic = 621; TORC = 185. The number of items analyzed was 2,060. Tests used were those available from publishers when orders were placed in 1992.

EXPLICIT VALIDITY ARGUMENTS

Explicit validity arguments in standardized multiple-choice testing are typically based on psychometric tradition.[9] Three methods are popular:

- Comparing the scores of subtests as a way of arguing that the common element underlying them all is reading. For instance, scores on reading vocabulary and reading comprehension subtests should be more alike than scores on reading vocabulary and a math calculation test.
- Comparing the test scores of one test to those obtained on a different test that assesses the same thing. If scores on the two tests are similar, then it can be concluded that they measure the same thing.
- Comparing scores on the test across different age groups on the assumption that reading skill increases with age and should follow a developmental pattern.

These comparisons are all done statistically. The statistical test typically used in all these cases is correlation. In this procedure, the goal is to see whether scores on tests or subtests covary—that is, if students do well on Test-Subtest A, they also do well on Test-Subtest B, or if students do poorly on A, they do poorly on B. The inference underlying correlation is that if two performances are positively correlated, then the reason is due to a common element—in this case, reading.

Similarity of Subtest Scores

Arguing the validity of a test by presenting intercorrelations of subtest scores is a kind of statistical introspection. It is looking inside the test with the hope that there is enough similarity to argue that all the subtests measure the same thing. Because the subtests are subtests, each usually measures something a little different from the others. So the dilemma is how to interpret the correlational statistics.

This dilemma is magnified in an examination of the tests under review. Test developers of the Test of Reading Comprehension, Brown et al. (1978),

---

[9]For instance, if the selected tests are evaluated in terms of other categories of assessment, they might fare differently. In Bennett's (1993) categorization of the response type required of examinees, only the TORC provided any items that are not multiple-choice tasks (multiple-choice items are low-complexity items in Bennett's conceptualization), and even in the case of the TORC only 11% of items fell into more challenging response types. Less than 1% required selection–identification tasks where examinees must select from such a wide variety of responses that guessing is probably not a successful test-taking strategy; 9% required examinees to reorder or rearrange items into a sequence; and 3% required construction of a response.

argued that intercorrelations among subtests should be neither extremely high nor extremely low (the range is from .36 to .72[10]). This range of intercorrelations, they suggested, demonstrates that some subtests measure very different things while others very similar things. For the Gates–Mac-Ginitie (MacGinitie & MacGinitie, 1989b), no interpretation is provided for intercorrelations that range from greater than .55 to .88. In Brown et al.'s (1978) reasoning, intercorrelations as high as .88 could be a sign that the subtests are not really measuring different constructs. Alternatively, is a correlation of .36 (which suggests that only 12% of the variance between the subtests is shared) indicative of shared variability in regard to reading? Perhaps the shared variability is related to test-taking skill, background knowledge, or other variables.[11] Clearly, even though statistics suggest hard evidence, there is considerable latitude in how these statistics are interpreted. Such latitude indicates that other evidence is necessary to bolster these validity arguments.

Similarity to Other Test Scores

A favored way of asserting that a test measures a construct like reading is to correlate it with scores on other tests that claim to measure reading. The following listing of the correlations of tests with other tests is typical: The Gates–MacGinitie is correlated[12] with the Iowa Tests of Basic Skills, the Tests of Achievement and Proficiency, the Comprehensive Tests of Basic Skills, the California Achievement Tests (CAT), the Metropolitan Achievement Tests (MAT), the Survey of Basic Skills, the Preliminary Scholastic

---

[10]A correlation is a measure of association. A perfect measure of association is ±1.00. For a perfect positive correlation of +1.00, when Score A goes up, Score B also goes up and if A goes down, Score B also goes down. Scores that do not covary would have zero correlation. In a perfect negative correlation of -1.00, one score goes up while the other goes down. One way of interpreting correlations is in terms of the Score A variance that is associated with changes in Score B. To calculate the variance accounted for, the correlation is squared. So correlation of .88 indicates that 77% of the variability in Score A is associated with changes in Score B.

[11]For instance, Johnston (1984a) reported that a significant amount of the variability in reading comprehension as measured by questions on text explicit or implicit passage information could be accounted for by background knowledge. Another competing explanation for the common variance included the influence of test-taking skills. In a meta-analysis of the literature, Scruggs, White, and Bennion (1985) reported that, on average, .10 of a standard deviation could be accounted for by relatively short test-taking training programs of 4 to 20 hours in length. Even though the amount of variability accounted for in these studies is relatively small, it appears to add another dimension to the interpretation of intercorrelations.

[12]In this section, the phrase "is correlated with" specifically means "is significantly positively correlated with." The shorter form has been used for ease of reading.

Aptitude Test, and the American College Testing Program; the Metropolitan Achievement Tests are correlated with the Otis–Lennon School Ability Test; and the Test of Reading Comprehension (TORC) is correlated with the Peabody Individual Achievement Test (PIAT).

The list of correlations demonstrates that contemporary test validation is, in part, a nepotistic process: The "family" of popularly used measures becomes a venue for demonstrating "commonality." For instance, the Gates–MacGinitie test is correlationed with versions of the CAT and MAT that were no longer in use because they had been revised. Herein lies the conundrum. If correlations between tests are to be used to argue for validity, then test developers must avoid departing too much from old models of reading assessment for fear of failing to obtain the desired positive correlations. This "correlation with the past" means that psychometrics participates in a tradition that resists change because correlations with the past are an important part of validity argumentation.

The inevitable question that results from considering the pattern of statistical nepotism is: "If correlating tests with published tests is a regressive procedure, then what are alternatives?" This question again returns to the heart of the validity question and can be answered only by another question: "What arguments best make the case that any measure is valid for a particular circumstances?" Even if there are high intercorrelations between tests, it is important to remember that "these *are* all tests" (Thorndike, 1982, p. 190). The relation of performance on these indexes must always be considered in relation to nontest indicators. Ultimately, unless tests relate closely to the actual behaviors they are intended to sample, they are by and large useless. To revert to the analogy of legal evidence, a test that does not relate closely to the behavior of interest is like a witness who testifies about a crime (and maybe even a defendant) unrelated to the case before the court.

Age-Related Patterns of Development

In the TORC and Gates–MacGinitie, the argument of a gradual increase in performance in relation to age is used to suggest the developmental nature of reading, but this argument assumes that reading is a developmental skill. On the basis of the demonstrated impact of background knowledge on reading performance (Pearson & Fielding, 1991), it would seem difficult to disambiguate the impact of knowledge and experience about what is read from reading itself. Consequently, this argument seems to need bolstering by studies demonstrating the developmental nature of reading.

An Absence of Validation Information

Despite professional, competitive, and ethical injunctions to include argumentation about the validity of tests, some test developers have failed to provide such information even though the tests are readily available for purchase. For instance, the California Achievement Tests were available for purchase during the time that the present test analysis was being conducted; yet the technical material that accompanied them in the form of their first technical bulletin contained no validity arguments.[13] The Stanford Diagnostic similarly has provided no validity arguments, nor did any additional material listed in the order catalogue appear to contain such information. In instances such as these, test users must ferret out arguments to be made for and against the possibility that the test is an appropriate measure of reading in the context in which it is used. Even in instances where validation arguments have been posited, it is important to continually visit the question as to whether any alternative explanations for performance on the test suggest that the test could be assessing something other than reading.

An Overall Assessment of Explicit Validity Arguments

With a couple of exceptions, test publishers have provided traditional psychometric arguments. The limitations of these arguments are not particular to the tests assessed but can be applied in general. Most problematic of all are situations in which publishers have failed to provide any validity arguments. Perhaps these publishers desire to be "out the door first" with a new product, but a competitive market edge should be balanced by consideration of the ethical call to inform test users. Alternatively, perhaps information for ordering technical manuals is not contained in general test order catalogues. If so, it seems puzzling because this kind of ordering information should be easily attainable so as to optimally serve test users. In cases where explicit validity argumentation is not available, test users must turn to the implicit validity argumentation contained both in technical manuals and in the test items and questions themselves.

---

[13]The fact that validation information was not ready for release even when the tests were being sold likely shows the competitive pressures under which manufacturers of large-scale achievement tests operate.

IMPLICIT VALIDITY ARGUMENTS

Technical manuals that accompany tests typically contain several categories of description that can be considered implicit validation arguments. These include descriptions of the statement of purpose of the test, item development procedures, item review panels used to evaluate bias, and item discrimination procedures. All these represent a validity argument as they involve some investigation into what the test is to be used for and how well it accomplishes this task.

Statements of Purpose

A common starting point for all test developers, whether articulated in written form or not, is the creation of some statement of purpose for their tests (Crocker & Algina, 1986; Thorndike, 1982). The statement of purpose is an envisionment of the uses to which a test is put. Ultimately test users must judge the appropriate use of a test, but the statements of purpose can be the first messages that test users receive about a test's potential uses. In this way, test developers become implicated in test use.

The language contained in statements of purpose can create heightened expectations in test consumers. Even a seemingly bland statement like the test is "designed to measure achievement in the basic skills commonly taught in schools throughout the nation" (CAT5, 1992, p. 1) creates an expectation that may or may not be warranted, depending on the way in which this statement is read. When the statement is contrasted with the listing of over six purposes in the Gates–MacGinitie (MacGinitie & MacGinitie, 1989b, p. 9), its promises seem to pale by comparison. Statements of purpose often include terms like "diagnosis,"[14] or "strengths and weaknesses," or an equivalent, and, occasionally (e.g., CAT5) imply that the test can assist in programming for students.

Statements of purpose seem generic and the language of these statements is likely to be psychometric. Terms such as *measure, basic skills*, or *achievement* are to be read psychometrically. In such a reading, for instance, *measurement* means "sampling behavior," *basic skills* means using a particular set of items

---

[14]The language of diagnosis also harkens to a medical model of education in which a test is administered, the disease is discovered, and a treatment is administered. An alternative medical model would be a wellness model in which the focus is on well-being or competence. Psychometric models tend to follow the former model.

(which may or may not be closely aligned with the curriculum in a particular region) that have been determined to correlate to other measures and to discriminate among students taking the test, and *achievement* means how well a student performs on this sampling of behaviors relative to others who take the test (the norm group). In everyday use of the terms, *basic skills* can mean all the skills needed to read effectively, *measurement* suggests an accuracy similar to the seeming accuracy of linear measurement with a ruler, and *achievement* suggests general overall competencies.

This potential confounding of a psychometric reading with an everyday reading of the statement of purpose means that naive test users may assume that a test can do much more than the test developers think they are saying. These assumptions demand a different kind of validity evidence than that provided by most test developers because the scope of what is read into the statement of purpose is much broader. Because the statement of purpose is the first step on the path toward validity argumentation, an obvious reform step for test developers would be to reframe their statements of purpose. The goal of this reform should not be to make the language more technical but to safeguard against obvious misinterpretation of terms by test users and ultimately to provide test users with explicit information about the purposes of the test.

Descriptions of Item Development Procedures

In test theory, one recommended stage for test developers is that of the design of a table of specifications for the items (or questions) on the test (e.g., Crocker & Algina, 1986). Tables of specifications take the form of a grid outlining the specific content to be assessed and the complexity at which it is to be assessed. Test developers plan the proportion of items they wish to cover in each area and at each level of complexity. Such tables can be invaluable for test users who want to figure out whether the test is a good match to local curricula.

Tables of specifications are another way of assessing the purpose of the test. They are a specific layer of argumentation about what terrain the test intends to capture and can be a powerful source for building up evidence to support the claims that a test assesses reading. Yet, none of the tests reviewed provided tables of specifications.[15]

---

[15]I reviewed the materials that were available to any consumer of the tests who ordered them in 1992. For instance, at the time of this study, no technical manual was listed in the catalogue from which the Stanford Diagnostic was ordered. If one did exist, it seems unusual for it not to have been listed. The manuals provided with the test were more like administration manuals than technical manuals.

The fact that material has been published since then or that technical manuals are available now but were not then is not the point. The point is that if consumers of tests had to make a decision about what tests to buy in 1992, they would have had available to them what I had available to me. I suspect that matters are not much different now; publishers compete to get their products out fast and may tend to push some parts of their materials into production earlier than others to gain market share. In the meanwhile, violations of the Code of Fair Testing Practices (Joint Committee, 1988) seem to be a secondary concern at best.

It could be argued that reading is not a construct that lends itself to a grid outlining content and complexity but no such argument was made. Test developers for the tests reviewed do however provide lists of quasispecifications. For example, the CAT5, Gates–MacGinitie, MAT6, and TORC refer to graded word lists, dictionaries, readability formulas, and a variety of curriculum guides that were used to develop test items. Absent from the presentation is a discussion of how these listed items were used in the construction of test items. If, as Cronbach (1988) suggested, one task of test user-"validators" of assessment instruments is to compare local curricula to test specifications, then the task set out is made difficult by test publishers because of the general way in which information about item development is presented.

Descriptions of rules for writing items (e.g., Use only one-syllable words in a word recognition subtest) can also be a valuable source of information indicating what a test developer believes important in the assessment of reading and ultimately in what constitutes reading (e.g., Bormuth, 1970). Unfortunately, little if any information is provided by test developers in this regard. The Gates–MacGinitie provided detail for the specifications for generating distractors[16] for items on *one* subtest, while the Iowa provided a general description of considerations in item writing. Only occasionally, as in the case of the non-multiple-choice items on the TORC, is the choice of a particular format for administration discussed. Here again, test developers have overlooked an area that could provide not only relevant important information to test users but also evidence about the construct of reading

---

[16]In multiple-choice tests, examinees are presented with several options as possible answers to the question presented. The item that has been designated as correct by the test developers is called the keyed response, and the remaining items are termed distractors (from the idea that there are pieces of information contained in them that may contain some partially correct or erroneous information and this information distracts examinees into not opting for the keyed response). In recent years there has been criticism that one of the problems with distractors is that partial information is not credited (Tierney, 1990). When some knowledge is weighted the same as no knowledge, an inaccurate portrayal of the examinee results.

and ultimately about the inferences any test user might consider making regarding student performance on these tests.

Item Review Panels

Traditionally, test developers have used item review panels as one way to argue that a test has been reviewed for systematic biases. Usually, these panels are composed of teachers and consultants with expertise in reading or with knowledge of or membership in a particular cultural or linguistic group. Such a panel is asked to review the content of a test to evaluate whether cultural bias in individual items can be identified.[17] Less typical would be the case in which a panel is asked to comment on the portrayal of reading inherent in the tests. All test developers, except for the Stanford

---

[17]Each item contained in a test is the result of a multiplicity of efforts. These efforts range from those involved in conceptualizing the test domain to be assessed, to those involved in writing items and manuals accompanying the tests, to those involved in scrutinizing items, to those of layout and graphic artists, to those of teachers in schools participating in item tryouts, to those involved in computing statistical information pertinent to items and the norming group's performance on the final set of items used. In many respects, all these persons are charged with executing their tasks to the best of their ability in view of the parameters in which they operate. Throughout the lengthy process of the development of a test, many of those involved, either consciously or unconsciously, use certain principles to guide them in their task. These principles, which may range from the use of simple logic in evaluating an item to the application of specific criteria, represent the values of the tests and measurement community. In following this shared set of principles, the participants in the collective task of creating a test are all engaged in an exercise that converges on one thing–the elimination of competing explanations for performance on the test. These collective actions all impinge on issues of the validity of the inferences made as a result of use of the test.

The description of test development procedures in classic tests and measurements in graduate-level textbooks provides one framing argument for the validity of a test. The degree to which test developers follow these procedures strengthens or weakens their arguments (from a psychometric perspective) that a test has the potential to be a measure of reading ability. One example of the expectations appropriate in test development is found in Crocker and Algina (1986, p. 66):

1. Identify the primary purpose(s) for which test scores will be used
2. Identify behaviors that represent the construct or define the domain
3. Prepare a set of test specifications, delineating the proportion of items that should focus on each type of behavior identified in step 2
4. Construct an initial pool of items
5. Have items reviewed (and revise as necessary)
6. Have preliminary item tryouts (and revise as necessary)
7. Field-test the items on a large sample representative of the examinee population for whom the test is intended
8. Determine statistical properties of item scores and, when appropriate, eliminate items that do not meet established criteria
9. Design and conduct reliability and validity studies for the final form of the test
10. Develop guidelines for administration, scoring, and interpretation of the test scores (e.g., prepare norm tables, suggest recommended cutting scores of standards for performance, etc.).

Similar guidelines are offered by Thorndike (1982).

Diagnostic,[18] made use of panels at some point in the test development process, but several questions have implications for the validity arguments that can be made through the use of such panels.

First, the question must be raised as to how panels are selected. In other words, the credibility of expertise is of interest. More often than not, test developers simply provided a list of reviewers' names with school or university affiliations. The job titles and geographic areas in the lists imply breadth although no specific discussion was presented about whether breadth was a criterion for panel membership. Even if this discussion were present, test developers have been silent on "the nature of expertise."

This issue leads to another: "What criteria do panelists invoke to judge items?" Typically, panels were asked to review items for cultural diversity. Occasionally, specific attention was given to a feature. For instance, in the Gates–MacGinitie, Jane W. Torrey was asked to examine Subtests 3 and 4 of Level PRE to determine whether any items were potentially problematic to speakers of "African American vernacular English" (MacGinitie & MacGinitie, 1989b, p. 10). The task assigned to reviewers might substantially affect the identification of items. Absent too is any discussion of whether panelists were provided opportunity to comment on the way reading was operationalized—the concept of reading embodied in the test.

The vagueness of the role and impact of judges is all the more problematic in view of O'Connor's (1989) assertion that the use of judgment panels made up of minorities for the purposes of judging bias in items has not worked because the biases of some items are not always socioculturally or linguistically transparent. Here again, an opportunity to bolster arguments that the tests assess reading was underdocumented in the selected reading tests.

Item Tryouts and Item Discrimination Indices

All standardized tests usually go through one or more trials. These trials are used to refine the processes of administering the tests to examine the way one or more samples of students reacted to the tests, and to evaluate the clarity and discriminatory effectiveness of individual test items. All these refinements work toward building the validity of the test. The stringency of procedures for administering the tests is an attempt to eliminate competing explanations for student performance by subjecting everyone to the same procedures. The discriminatory effectiveness of items is tied to the idea that

---

[18]See previous note.

if a test is supposed to test an ability, then items should discriminate between test takers with more or less of this ability. The table used for converting raw scores into a normed score is another type of validity argument. Tests excelled particularly in the area of providing statistical evidence in validity argumentation. Detailed item discrimination[19] information was given for the CAT5, the Gates–MacGinitie, the Iowa, and the MAT6. All tests presented norm tables and some information about the groups on which the norm tables were developed.

An Overall Assessment of Implicit Validity Arguments

In the provision of implicit validity arguments, the tests used in the early 1990s were mixed. Test developers provided statements of purpose that can easily be misinterpreted. They excelled in providing item analysis information but seemed lax in providing conceptual information relating to item development and review procedures. One remaining source of implicit validity argumentation remains open to test developers, and that is the test items themselves.

TEST ITEMS AS VALIDITY ARGUMENTS

The crux of making an argument about whether a test assesses reading lies partly in the elimination of competing explanations for a student's performance. One way to handle this task is statistical, as in item discrimination procedures. Another way is qualitative—through an item-by-item analysis of the tests.[20] A qualitative analysis can raise questions about whether the

---

[19]The goal of most standardized tests is to discriminate among the individuals assessed in terms of the criterion of interest. In other words, on a reading test, the goal would be to differentiate among the students taking the test in terms of their reading abilities. Item discrimination indexes are statistical indexes that provide information on how well each item distinguishes between those who score relatively high on the test versus those who score relatively low. As Crocker and Algina (1986) suggested, "The goal is to identify items for which high-scoring examinees have a high probability of answering correctly and low-scoring examinees have a low probability of answering correctly...we would be suspicious of an item on which both high and low scorers were equally successful. Such an item would not seem to measure the same construct as the other items" (pp. 313–314). Several statistical parameters are used as indicators of the effectiveness of items to discriminate among test takers of different abilities.

[20]Only a few items are implicated in each of these categories. When this type of information is presented to some in the tests and measurement community, they revert to statistical defenses and discuss the fact that the contribution of one or two items to an overall test is fairly limited. This defense is unacceptable when the flaw could have been avoided, when tests are being used for placement purposes (the life paths of students may be at stake) even though test developers may not identify this as a purpose, and when the aggregation of several different types of errors may create a significant difference in the raw score attained.

quality of test item design hinders the argument that the items (and ultimately the tests) assess reading. Several clusters of competing explanations for performance on some of the items of these tests are reported next.

Variability of Administration in Subtests

Standardization in administration of the test is a classic method of reducing one possible source of variability in test performance. Typically, standardization is taken to mean that all tests should be administered in the same manner, but administration can also be a source of variability that confounds the performance of any task. In this view, changes in the mode of administration in a subtest, even though they are applied uniformly across tests, can introduce a source of variability that affects the construct being assessed. In the tests surveyed, this variability occurred in the Gates–MacGinitie Use of Sentence Context subtest. In this subtest, for five items the teacher read the sentence and the options; for seven items only the sentence was read by the teacher; and for three items nothing was read by the teacher. Even though this procedure is consistent across students taking the test, it creates a possible source of variability in the subtest because each small cluster of items could be argued to constitute a slightly different task.

Ambiguities

Ambiguities are obvious sources for competing explanations of performance on items. In the tests reviewed, three categories of ambiguities were uncovered: ambiguous illustrations, ambiguous and unusual language in texts, and ambiguous language in the test–option choices.

In the primary grades, illustrations are often used in tests in lieu of words. The illustrations are intended to capture concepts, to stand for particular words, or to supplement the limited text. Consequently, their clarity cannot be underestimated. Even though all the tests reviewed used illustrations in at least one level, only the MAT6 and the Stanford Diagnostic Reading Test contained problem items. An example of a problematic item would be the ambiguous rendering of the illustration of a "cake" on the Word Recognition Subtest of the MAT6 (Primer Item 11). Arguably, the teacher's instruction to name the illustrations in this subtest should eliminate the ambiguity, but students eager to complete the task may move ahead of the teacher. In such cases, student failure to follow directions (which has more to do with

personality and adherence to authority than with reading) and the subsequent misidentification of the ambiguous illustration may produce a
performance that has little to do with reading however it is defined.

Unusual language features, which included verb tense disagreements in
a set of questions, ambiguity of pronomial reference, and the use of archaic
forms, occurred much more frequently than did ambiguous illustrations.
Five of the six tests contained subtests with unusual language features: the
CAT5 Comprehension subtest, the Iowa Vocabulary, Pictures, Sentences,
Stories, and Reading Comprehension subtests, the MAT6 Reading Com-
prehension subtest, the Stanford Diagnostic, and the TORC Syntactic
Similarities and Paragraph Reading subtests.

The following example, from the CAT5, illustrates the type of problem that
careless excerpting from children's trade book material can cause. The text for
Items 12 to 17 was prefaced by an introduction indicating that a boy and his
grandfather were inspecting fences on the grandfather's ranch. The text then
began: "Suddenly he saw a...". Because the preceding text focused on both
male characters, there was no clear referent for the "he." Indeed, the referent
did not become clear until the second sentence when the "he" said, "Look,
Grandpa." Cataphoric reference (in which the direction of the pronoun
reference is forward in the text rather than backward) is unusual in elementary
texts, and this arrangement of text forces the elementary student to operate on
the assumption that this is a cataphoric form of reference. What makes this
text even more problematic is that if students do not read the preamble to the
text, it is quite possible that they would read the first paragraph as though there
were three characters—the unnamed "he," the grandpa, and Justin. Similar
problems were documented in MAT passages by Fillmore (1982), yet these
passages still remain in the MAT6.

A different language problem occurs on the TORC Syntactic Similarities
subtest. The examinee is presented with the following options and is asked
to pick the two that mean the same thing: (a) He wants to go slowly; (b)
He goes slowly; (c) He had gone slowly; (d) He will go slowly; (e) He went
slowly. If the examinee chooses the keyed response, c and e, the aspectual
feature of language would have to be ignored.

Ambiguity in the test–option language use resulted in two different sets
of possibilities. In once case, even though there was a keyed response (i.e.,
a response that the test developers had marked as correct), a respondent
might justifiably consider that none of the options presented plausibly
answered the question. In the other case, the respondent might justifiably
consider that two of the options were correct.

One or two problematic items with no correct response were found on the Iowa Vocabulary, Pictures and Comprehension subtests, the MAT6 Reading Comprehension subtest, the Stanford Diagnostic Reading Comprehension subtest, and the TORC General Vocabulary test. Typically, for these items, the only way in which a respondent could arrive at the keyed response was to eliminate all the totally implausible options and select the remaining one because it had something to do with the text preceding the question even though it was *not*, at face value, a correct answer to the question. An example from the Iowa Primary 2 Reading Comprehension Subtest (Text IV) is illustrative. The story is told of Max who daily passed a house that, he suspected had a dark and scary interior and also had a ghost in it. One day he tiptoed to the front door to have a look. Item 17 posed the following question: When Max went toward the house, he was: (a) laughing, (b) running, (c) worried. We know that Max was very likely neither *laughing* nor *running* because the text described him as *tiptoeing*, and *tiptoeing* suggests that laughter would disrupt the silence. The option of *worried* does not fit either. If Max was worried, then why did he bother to go to the door at all? A more likely option would have been *nervous* or *tense*, but neither of these was presented, so none of the options is really satisfactory.

In contrast to items that contained no response, there were also items that contained two or more plausible responses. In multiple-choice assessment, it is usually recommended that all options have a degree of plausibility "so that a person who does not know the answer might reasonably choose it" (Thorndike, 1982, p. 43). But five of the tests reviewed (CAT5 Vocabulary subtest, Gates–MacGinitie Sentence Context subtest, Stanford Diagnostic Reading Comprehension subtest, and TORC Paragraph Reading subtest) included one or two items in which two or more responses could be considered plausible enough to be the keyed response. An example of items of this type comes from the CAT5 Vocabulary test. The item is:

The passengers were all _____ and ready to go.
•*asleep*   •*famous*   •*aboard*   •*captured*

All options, except perhaps *famous*, are possible. The item developers appeared to be cuing "willing participation" by the term *ready*, but "willingness" and "readiness" are not semantically identical. For instance, if the passengers were all former escapee convicts on a prison ship, the term *captured* would signal a readiness to go on the journey.

Design Variabilities

Two sources of variability resulting from design features were found in the tests under review. The first relates to the use of multiple formats for items in subtests. The second is variability in what appears to be a template for generating items in some subtests.

Minor changes in item formats can yield differential performance on tests. For instance, research on the cloze procedure indicated that typographic modifications such as altering the length of lines for blanks affects performance (Hartley & Treuman, 1986). Because of such effects, it would seem reasonable that, at least in the subtest for a particular area, test developers would retain the same item format throughout a subtest so that the extraneous sources of variance created by different item formats would be eliminated. Unfortunately, this was not the case.

Three standardized tests surveyed contained subtests in which the format of the items changed within the subtest. These tests are: the CAT5 Comprehension subtest, the Gates–MacGinitie Initial Consonants and Consonant Clusters, Final Consonants and Consonant Clusters, Vowels, and Vocabulary; and the TORC Reading the Directions of Schoolwork subtest. An example from the Gates–MacGinitie Initial Consonants and Consonant Clusters subtest (Level R) is illustrative of this problem. In the first part of this subtest (four items), students were presented with an array of four pictures and a letter prompt and then asked to select the picture that begins with the same letter as the letter prompt. In the second part of this subtest (five items), students were presented with an array of four words and one illustration that is named by the teacher and then asked to select the word from the array. The tasks are different, and consequently a question can be raised as to whether differences in performance relate to task variability or to reading.

Following the logic of psychometric design, test developers should follow a procedural plan or use a template for designing multiple-choice times. The template should ensure, among other things, that the items are on the content–process area assessed, the options from which examinees choose are based on criteria relating to the content–process area assessed, and the options do not systematically discriminate against specific populations. In the present survey, the *inferred* pattern or plan for generating options within any subtest was named the option template. The use of the term *option template* assumes that test developers attempted to minimize competing

explanations for performance on a subtest by producing items that share a focus on the skill assessed and that do not introduce new sources of variance into an item set.[21]

One or two option template problems were found in every test: CAT5 Vocabulary and Reading Comprehension subtests; Gates–MacGinitie Final Consonants and Consonant Clusters subtest, Initial Consonants and Consonant Clusters subtest, and the Vocabulary subtest; Iowa Word Analysis and Vocabulary subtests; MAT6 all subtests; Stanford Diagnostic Auditory Vocabulary, Auditory Discrimination, Phonetic Analysis, and Word Reading subtests; and, TORC General Vocabulary and Mathematics/Social Studies/Science Vocabulary subtests. Examples run all the way from including a multisyllabic word as an option in one item of a subtest when all other options for all other items of the subtest contained one-syllable words, to an unsystematic approach for generating words on word meaning tests, to including poetic text in a subtest in which all other items were nonpoetic.

Here is an example from the Iowa.

Someone who steers a car is a _____ .
• racer • driven • rider • driver (Iowa, Item 29, Level 7)

This item includes an option that can be eliminated on the basis of syntactic unacceptability. In other words, the word *driven* can be eliminated because it does not grammatically fit with the rest of the sentence. Yet the options presented for all but two other problematic items on this subtest were restricted to those that were syntactically acceptable in the context of the sentence. Consequently, for three items on this subtest, one new source of variability is introduced which could differentially affect performance.[22]

Failure to Consider Dialect

In tests of reading, there are several ways in which dialect can affect performance. One of these occurs when very young readers are asked to

---

[21] The use of such criteria for the analysis of items may be regarded as quite stringent, but these criteria fall well within the boundaries of what should be reasonable psychometric practice in making inferences about a content area as solid as possible.

[22] In terms of the present analysis, a criticism could be raised that if options are designed too tightly, there is a possibility of creating a response set in which, once the pattern has been determined, the whole subtest can be answered relatively easily. Such a criticism is unwarranted under the assumptions of the model implemented because tests *must* take into account both *what* is being assessed and *how* it is being assessed. Response set problems can be avoided with careful design as the previous analysis suggests.

match the sounds they hear to specific graphemes. This process is especially problematic for vowel sounds, which are typically involved in dialectal differences. The second area is in oral reading performances of students.

Three standardized tests reviewed (the Gates–MacGinitie, the CAT5, and the TORC) appeared to contain no items that might differentially affect performance on the basis of dialect,[23] but dialect did seem to be a potential factor on the Iowa and the MAT6. For these tests, dialectical lexicogrammatical features result in the possibility of items having two correct options. For instance, on the MAT6, for Primer Form L, Word Recognition Item 20, the item had a keyword *tooth* and the student had to identify the item with the same final sound from among the options *peanut, earth, wolf*. This item would prove ambiguous for children who would pronounce *tooth* as *toof*, as is the case in some regions of the United States (Milroy & Milroy, 1991, p. 167).

On the Stanford Diagnostic Reading Test, the stated strategy for dialect was to avoid words influenced by dialect. Needless to say, the test developers were unlikely to be successful (nor did they indicate the criteria they used to gauge what would be considered dialect). Even with their claimed avoidance, in Green Item 8 of the Phonetic Analysis subtest, the word to be matched in sound is *tree* and the choices are *third, try, throw*. As Milroy and Milroy (1991, p. 161) indicated, in many areas, the initial *th* when followed by an *r* is pronounced as though it were *tr*.

Lack of Passage Dependency of Items

All sets of questions about a passage rely, to some extent, on the background knowledge and experience of the reader. In reading tests, "Test items are considered to be passage-independent if reading the passage makes no difference to performance on the item" (Johnston, 1983, p. 45). In the present review of tests, the researcher read all test items before reading the passages. If the keyed response to an item could be derived without the reading of the passage, that item was deemed to be passage independent.[24]

---

[23]This assertion is made from my own general knowledge of dialect. I am certain that there are many dialect possibilities that I am not aware of, and my inability to identify dialect issues in these tests does not necessarily mean that they are free from these issues.

[24]Arguably, this approach to passage dependency provides an adult's view of the text. The only alternative would be to conduct large studies with groups of children who would answer the questions without reading the texts. Even here, the results would be subject to the background knowledge the children brought to the texts.

There are several varieties of passage independent items. For instance, items could often be answered on the basis of simple logic alone. For expository text passages, many questions could be answered without reading the passage if the reader had background knowledge on the topic. In any case, items of this type clearly put into question whether what was being measured was "reading" or "general knowledge."

All tests surveyed contained items that were not passage dependent. Unlike other instances of poor test design in which only one or two items were problematic, for this category several items per subtest were typically involved.

Item Interconnectedness

A key element in developing items for tests is item independence. Item independence presumes that each item is a separate measure of the skill being assessed and is not dependent on the performance on other items. A feature related to item independence is that of item interconnectedness. Item interconnectedness occurs when, by reading preceding or following questions, test takers can obtain the keyed response to another item. This pattern typically occurs in question sets that follow reading comprehension passages. Both the CAT5 (Vocabulary subtest), and the Iowa (Stories subtest) contained interconnected items. In the CAT5, there were some Double Item Cloze tasks—items in which two words have been deleted in the same sentence. In this instance, for some of the items (e.g., Items 29 and 30 of Level 13), if the student chose one of the incorrect options for the first cloze blank, then he or she could use this knowledge to eliminate options for the second blank of the sentence.

Assessment of Test Items as Validity Arguments

In reviewing the pool of test items, finding one or two problematic items per test across different categories of validity issues seems insignificant, but the number of items is not the point. These items suggest a less-than-careful adherence to psychometric design principles. Because multiple-choice tests contain a relatively small number of items, the peppering of flawed items throughout tests suggests that student performance on the tests may be partly due to some design flaw and that tests are fragile evidence indeed. Ultimately, however, the question is whether these tests are tests of reading or of some other patched-together assortment of skills that represent a particular view of schooling. The last area of the validity investigation of reading tests is just what is there to read on these tests?

CONCEPTUALIZING READING
BY THE AMOUNT OF TEXT TO BE READ

One way to explore whether a test assesses reading is to consider how much reading of what sort is done on the reading test. This process of evaluating reading materials in terms of the amount of text read has been used in other studies (e.g., Freeman, 1986; Goodman et al., 1988) and was modified into the following analytical categories for application to the tests used in the early 1990s:[25]

- Nonword focus—items with no print graphemes.
- Subword focus—items that focus on the manipulation of graphemes or phonemes in a word and do not use syntactic and semantic cues beyond a morphological basis.
- Word focus—items that focus on the manipulation of or interaction with words and that may use syntactic and semantic cues at or below the lexical level.
- Phrasal focus—items that focus on the manipulation of or interaction with phrases and that may use syntactic and semantic cues at or below the phrase level.
- Sentence focus—items that focus on the manipulation of or interaction with sentences and that may use syntactic cues at or below the sentence level.[26]
- Discourse focus—any items that have as their focus the manipulation of or interaction with chunks of text of two or more sentences and that may use syntactic and semantic cues at or below the discourse level.

As Table 3.1 illustrates, the tests reviewed did not contain a lot of reading material. None of the standardized tests surveyed contained half their items at the discourse level. In fact, as Table 3.1 illustrates, on the Stanford Diagnostic, TORC, and Gates–MacGinitie, more than 50% of items were at or below the word level. Two tests, the CAT5 and the MAT6, were close to 50% level for a focus on discourse, but even this percentage seems small for tests of reading. Furthermore, as Table 3.2 indicates, only in the CAT5 did the text length exceed 250 words at the upper grade levels of the tests reviewed.[27] Such texts seem much shorter than the typical short stories, or the novels, that fifth graders would be reading.

---

[25]Subtests were coded using a simple coding scale. They were coded Yes if they wholly or partially focused on the target aspect of text and No if they did not.

[26]The reading of directions was not coded.

[27]Not all test levels were reviewed. The tests levels reviewed were those that most closely approximated first, third, and fifth grades in their grade level assignments. In cases in which no grade level assignment was designated, the whole test was reviewed.

TABLE 3.1

Percentage of Items With a Specific Textual Focus for Tests Reviewed

Test	Nonword	Subword	Word	Phrase	Sentence	Discourse
CAT5	0	23	4	10	16	47
Gates–MacGinitie	0	13	40	0	21	28
Iowa	0	16	13	23	9	39
MAT6	0	27	0	0	25	48
Stanford Diagnostic	2	44	23	0	7	24
TORC	0	0	54	14	11	22

TABLE 3.2

Range of Passage Length in Tests Surveyed

Test	Range
CAT5	23 to 401 words
Gates–MacGinitie	5 to 149 words
Iowa	35 to 203 words
MAT6	49 to 190 words
Stanford Diagnostic	11 to 244 words
Test of Reading Comprehension	30 to 119 words

These tests seem not to operationalize reading of continuous discourse but have an alternate concept in mind. This concept is somewhat troubling because discourse was defined as text made up of only two or more sentences. As Table 3.2 illustrates, for some of these tests, two sentences consisted of five words. Clearly, the standardized tests of the early 1990s appear to be operating with a very restricted definition of reading, a definition that has more to do with reading of very small text units like parts of words, words, or single sentences than it has to do with reading of connected discourse. Ironically, it is at the level of conceptualizing what reading is all about that the arguments provided by test developers are at their weakest even though there does seem to be a definite concept underpinning their products.

EVIDENCE AND ARGUMENTATION IN THE STANDARDIZED TESTS OF THE EARLY 1990S

Overall, the standardized tests used in the early 1990s left much to be desired in terms of providing validity argumentation, whether explicit or implicit. At best, the strength of argumentation provided can be considered quite varied. These tests were particularly strong in areas utilizing statistical indexes (describing items, subtest intercorrelations, correlations with other measures, and age-related correlations) and particularly weak in areas demanding a theoretical and conceptual approach to the question of validation. Design fragilities recurred through tests but did not occur in every item. In fact, it is a moderately positive sign that, for the most part, design problems occurred only for a few items in a test. Nevertheless, these items when aggregated with others could potentially lead to several problematic items for each test. In most of the tests reviewed, raw score differences of several points could well make a difference in the classification assigned to a student's reading and, as such, should be taken seriously. The test developers clearly have taken a procedural approach to validity, rather than a process approach, and even on the procedural approach, they were, at times, lax.

Additionally, there is the compelling problem of little text to read on these reading tests, particularly at the lower levels of these tests. Thus, either test developers are operating with implicit theories of reading that they have failed to acknowledge or they simply have wedded test development so much to the past that little seems to have changed in tests across the past century. Generalizing from these measures to reading tasks that involve the reading of connected discourse is problematic.

If test developers are going to continue to build tests within the tradition of psychology, they need to make evident elements that they are now leaving for test users to guess at or ignore because of the pressures of time and money. The ethical obligations of test developers as indicated in the Code of Fair Testing Practices (Joint Committee, 1988) clearly call for considered action in making background information about tests explicit so that test users can evaluate the tests appropriately. As they stand, the arguments made by test developers for the tests reviewed do not inspire a great deal of confidence. The choices facing test makers are obvious. They must significantly modify test development practices so that they are at least in keeping with good psychometric practice (regardless of what we may think of that practice) and ideally should move to keep pace with current validity theory. The preferable path would seem to be to abandon these test development practices in favor of the development of alternatives. Surely we can now do better.

4

Individualized Assessment

Like norm-referenced group assessment, the history of individualized assessment, particularly individualized assessment in reading, is rooted in the discipline of psychology. In this sense, the framing of validity arguments launched by developers of individualized assessment is similar to that of multiple-choice tests. Popular individualized reading assessments branch into two distinct paths: norm-referenced tests and criterion-referenced tests. To consider how argumentation about the validity of the variety of individualized measures is presented, it is important to consider some background to these individualized assessment measures.

Norm-referenced individualized measures, like other norm-referenced group measures, draw on the work of researchers like Binet, Termin, and others who developed the early intelligence tests (Crocker & Algina, 1986). These measures are concerned with controlling extraneous variables that might offer competing explanations for a reading performance; they compare performance on the test to that of a norm group.[1] Individualized standardized measures may differ from group standardized measures in the nature of the tasks required of the student.[2] Multiple-choice, fill-in-the-

---

[1]The assumption behind the inferences made about the comparability of an individual's score to that of the norm group is that the norm group sample is either a random sample or a stratified random sample. Every member of the population has an equal chance of being a member of the norm group if random sampling is used. Characteristics on which population members might differ are randomly dispersed throughout the sample when random sampling is used. Consequently, the sample should be unbiased, but in most standardized tests, some form of stratified sampling is used. In this type of sampling, specific population characteristics are delineated, and then efforts are made to sample from within these. For instance, geographic region might be an identified characteristic. Consequently, students would be randomly sampled from within the geographic areas identified (e.g., Northeastern United States, Southeastern United States, Northcentral United States, Southcentral United States, Northwestern United States, and Southwestern United States). The more categories of stratification that are identified as important to sample from, the more difficult stratified random sampling becomes.

[2]Individualized standardized tests are especially popular in the field of special education (Steele & Meredith, 1991), probably because they seem to build on the technology of group achievement tests, which are a part of school culture and have been for some time. In special education, this culture is reinforced by a bureaucracy related to the provision of special education that requires assessment of children (Milofsky, 1989). By offering a seemingly narrower definition of the domain of assessment (e.g.,

bubble (often machine-scoreable) forms[3] common to group tests are usually displaced by an examiner who presents tasks to students and writes down the student response. There is often an expectation that the specialized attention of individualized assessment allows for more diversity of tasks presented and of the depth of the assessment.[4] In individualized assessment, the potential error from a student accidentally filling in the wrong bubbles is replaced by different sources of error—accuracy of the examiner's perceptions of correct performance and annotations of the performance. Consequently, it is not unusual for examiners of some tests to take accreditation courses to ensure standard administration practices.

Criterion-referenced tests can be either group or individualized measures. Unlike their standardized counterparts, which rate student performance against the performance of the norm group, criterion-referenced tests rate students against the content being assessed (Anastasi, 1982).[5] Typically, the content is subdivided into smaller units, which are then defined in performance terms. In tests of reading, the "content" amounts to a conceptualization of the process of reading. For instance, one example of an objective

---

reading versus general achievement), there is an appearance of specialization. Like their group counterparts, many developers suggested that their tests provide a diagnostic function, and as Steele and Meredith (1991) pointed out, many teachers believe that the tests perform this diagnostic function. Special educators, caught by the demands of individualized programming, tend to choose tests based on their ease of scoring and attractiveness (Connelley, 1985) rather than on psychometric rigour. Adding to this problem is the mistaken idea that the tests provide more precision than do general achievement tests. Connelly (1985) suggested that the use of some of the "screening" devices is redundant as "most schools administer school-wide achievement batteries, and information about a referred student's achievement levels in various skills is usually readily available from the regular classroom teacher" (p. 154).

[3] Some measures required written responses. The TORC, for instance, required writing.

[4] In comparison to their multiple-choice norm-referenced counterparts, standardized individualized tests presented a greater variety of response types for examinees. Bennett (1993) presented a hierarchical classification of assessment tasks: multiple choice, selection-identification, reordering-rearrangement, substitution-correction, completion, construction, and presentation. In this hierarchy, multiple choice represents the low end of the continuum and presentation the high end. If popularly used individualized reading measures are assessed, the Durrell has 4% multiple choice, 66% identification, 14% completion, and 16% construction items; the PIAT-R has 35% multiple-choice items, 30% items involving identification, and 35% items requiring completion of an item; the WRAT has 100% of its items at the identification level; and the Woodcock has 65% items at the identification level and 35% items at the completion level. Consequently, individualized assessments are not taking advantage of the individualized performance setting to sample at a more complex level the behaviors of interest. Part of the reason may be that these tests tend to provide validity argumentation in the form of correlational evidence with other measures such as group tasks. The more the individualized assessment is unlike these other measures, the more likely it is that any yielded correlations are lower and, as a result, might impinge on the validity argumentation. This pattern might provide just reasons for reconsidering this form of argumentation in testing.

[5] Content organized into grade-equivalent sequences amounts to a backhanded norm referencing as ultimately someone's performance deemed the material in the test to be of a certain grade level. This backhanded approach to norm referencing in criterion-referenced testing is not often discussed in the psychometric literature.

for a criterion-referenced test might be: "Immediately recognizes words with a regular C-V-C pattern." Criterion-referenced tests typically use *mastery* as a heuristic to talk about performance. Mastery refers to control over the area being assessed and is usually designated in terms of the percentage of correct responses (e.g., 80% correct). Validity argumentation in criterion-referenced testing addresses the interrelated issues of the number of items needed to obtain a reliable estimation of performance and the rationale for deciding the cutoff level for mastery. As with any sampling of behavior, the larger the sample of behavior (i.e., the more items there are), the more likely that the measure is a reliable indicator of performance.[6] In criterion-referenced testing, the number of items is especially important because mastery of a skill is decided by how many items are correct. As for how the cutoff point for mastery is established, Anastasi (1982) described a variety of statistical procedures for developing satisfactory mastery levels. Like their norm-referenced individualized reading assessment counterparts, criterion-referenced reading measures are popular with special education teachers (Steele & Meredith, 1991) who have to document student performance and develop individualized educational plans for children.

To help ferret out the ways that these tests frame the evidence they put forth about reading, several tests were chosen (based on the same test usage studies presented in the previous chapter[7]): Durrell Analysis of Reading Difficulty[8] (Durrell & Catterson, 1980), Gilmore Oral Reading Test (Gilmore & Gilmore, 1968), Peabody Individual Achievement Test–Revised (PIAT-R; Markwardt, 1989), Wide Range Achievement Test–Revised (WRAT-R; Jastak & Wilkinson, 1984; Wilkinson, 1987), Woodcock Reading Mastery Tests–Revised (WRMT-R; Woodcock, 1987), Brigance Diagnostic Comprehensive Inventory of Basic Skills (Brigance, 1977), and the Brigance Diagnostic Inventory of Basic Skills (Brigance, 1983).[9] As the

---

[6]Simple logic supports this idea on several grounds. First, the more items there are, the greater likelihood that less information is excluded in the sampling. Second, errors are less costly to examinees if there are more items. For instance, one error out of a possible four items is much more costly to an examinee than one error out of twenty items.

[7]A discussion of the selection of tests from test usage studies is presented in the previous chapter.

[8]This measure is a hybrid individualized and group measure. It has a number of characteristics, most notably the scoring and some of the administration procedures, that make it more like an individualized measure. Therefore, it was categorized as an individualized measure.

[9]The norm-referenced standardized tests in this group are the Gilmore, PIAT, WRAT-R, and WRMT-R. The Durrell might be considered a type of hybrid standardized–criterion-referenced test as it has many of the stylistic features of group standardized tests but uses grade equivalencies without norm tables as its reporting mechanisms. Both versions of the Brigance are criterion referenced with a mastery level ranging from 75% to 100% for the Brigance Diagnostic Comprehensive Inventory of Basic Skills (Brigance, 1977) and 80% to 100% for the Brigance Diagnostic Inventory of Basic Skills (Brigance, 1983).

listing indicates, these tests are not recent and are dated in comparison to the group tests. This pattern likely reflects that large-scale group tests are generally competing against other tests for large-scale markets such as entire school districts or states. Because purchases of these tests are done on a large scale with significant monetary implications, there is considerable pressure to maintain whatever market advantage possible. A relatively recent publication date is one advantage because assessment professionals know that some sources of competing variance in test scores are reduced when the dates of norming are closer to the dates of test administration. Individualized tests, on the other hand, are typically not chosen by whole states but by individual educational assessment professionals or by school districts. Because these tests focus on individual students rather than on the population at large, the same pressure cannot be exerted to ensure that individualized tests have up-to-date norms. For instance, the Lake Wobegon crisis did not raise issues about individualized assessment despite the fact that these tests can be critical for the individuals concerned (e.g., Taylor, 1990a, 1993). Ultimately, educational professionals are faced with using what is available, what they know, and what they feel is appropriate for the cases under consideration. On the basis of the publication dates of these individualized tests, what is available is not very recently published material, material available in schools, or material that these professionals had used when they were trained in assessment courses. The continued use of these measures reveals the slowness of educational change and highlights how difficult it can be to change evidentiary practices in relation to reading assessment.

EXPLICIT VALIDATION ARGUMENTS
PRESENTED BY TEST DEVELOPERS

The evidentiary practices used in individualized assessments are much like those of standardized multiple-choice norm-referenced tests. For explicit arguments, the typical concepts of content, and concurrent and construct validity, in the form of age-related arguments, were used.

Individualized measures provided a mixed bag of arguments in relation to content validity. For instance, the Durrell presented little in the way of validity information. The WRMT–R scope and sequence charts could be considered an argument supporting a particular concept of reading, but detail on the sources for these charts was not provided. Claims about the "real-life" nature of the items in the WRMT–R were not supported with documentation. For the PIAT–R, item development statistics were the focus of the discussion. And for both versions of the Brigance, one would expect a great deal of documentation about the development of the test content because, for criterion-referenced tests, this subject forms the backbone of the validity argument. Both versions of the Brigance, however, provided lists of published school texts as the sources for many of their subtests but did not provide much detail about exactly how the final set of items was derived. Finally, the WRAT–R noted that initial items were selected by the test developer from a dictionary but did not reveal how the selection occurred; subsequent items built on this initial set.

For concurrent and construct validity, the typical mechanism of providing tables highlighting correlations with other measures was used. Some test developers also referred to or discussed studies that contain such information. The Gilmore presented a good example of this approach. Scores on the Gilmore were correlated with the Gray and Durrell; the first-grade study by Bond and Dykstra was cited as additional evidence that there are reasonable correlations among the Gilmore, the Stanford Achievement Test, and the Gates Word Pronunciation Test; and a journal article is cited to support correlations between the Gilmore Accuracy scale and the WRAT.

As the following list demonstrates, the tests continued the almost nepotistic arrangement for claiming concurrent validity except that their correlational evidence extended to group tests:

> The Gilmore was correlated with the Gray, the Durrell, the Stanford Achievement Tests, and the WRAT.
> The Test of Reading Comprehension (TORC) was correlated with the PIAT.
> The WRAT–R was correlated with the Woodcock Johnson–Reading, while the WRAT was correlated with the California Achievement Test, the PIAT, and the Stanford Achievement Test.
> The Woodcock Reading Mastery Tests were correlated with the Woodcock Johnson.

Factor analytic evidence was also presented for the PIAT–R.

Age-related validity arguments, which depend on a gradual increase in performance in relation to age, were presented for the PIAT–R. These arguments remain prey to the same problematics identified in chapter 3 and should be considered only one aspect of a validation argument.

The limited discussion of validity is somewhat surprising for these tests, especially because their individualized administration seems to bring with it the expectancy of added depth in all aspects. In comparison to group measures, the evidence provided was quite uneven and at times relatively unsophisticated. Discussion ranged from traditional tables of item development statistics, to reports of correlations with other tests, to listings of curricular materials, to, in one instance (the Durrell), a statement that the test was valid because it has been used a long time (the test originated in 1932; Durrell & Catterson, 1980).

IMPLICIT VALIDATION ARGUMENTS PRESENTED BY TEST DEVELOPERS

As with the large-scale group measures described in chapter 3, consideration is given to implicit validity arguments. These focus on elements of test design and development including item development.

Statements of Purpose

Like norm-referenced multiple-choice tests, the statements of purpose for criterion-referenced tests can be as grand as they are ordinary; they made frequent use of the term *diagnosis* or some equivalent. The use of the latter term can be particularly seductive for individualized assessment users.

The competing pulls of marketing pressures and psychometric principles create a contradictory set of purposes for individualized assessment measures. As an example, the PIAT–R has been described as "an individually administered achievement test providing wide-range screening in six content areas" (Markwardt, 1989, p. 1). The author even mentioned that the PIAT–R may help in the selection of a diagnostic instrument and implied that the PIAT–R is not such an instrument. The generality of the PIAT–R was emphasized by the following statement:

> The items on the PIAT–R were not selected to sample the curriculum of any individual school system, but instead represent a cross section of various curricula in use across the United States. Therefore, although the PIAT–R allows meaningful comparisons to be made between the subject's scores and the mainstream of United States education, the examiner must consider the specific curricular background of any given subject when interpreting his or her results. (Markwardt, 1989, p. 4)

Yet when uses for the PIAT–R were presented, they ranged from individualized assessment for gaining insight into strengths and weaknesses, to planning of programs, to counseling, grade placement, student grouping, follow-up evaluations, employment screening, and research.

Of additional note is the toning down of the statement of purpose for the WRAT, which in 1978 read as follows:

> The Wide Range Achievement Test…[is] a convenient tool for the study of the basic school subjects of reading word recognition and pronunciation, written spelling, and arithmetic computation…the method of measuring the basic subjects was advisedly chosen to achieve the following ends: (1) to study the sensory-motor and coding skills involved in learning to read, spell, write, and figure, (2) to provide simple and homogeneous content, (3) to avoid duplication and overlapping with tests of comprehension, judgement, reasoning, and generalization studied by means other than reading, spelling, and arithmetic tests, (4) to free diagnostic inferences from common confusions due to operational semantics, and (5) to permit validity analyses by the method of internal consistency. (Jastak & Jastak, 1978, p. 1)

The authors noted that the WRAT has been found to be valuable in applications ranging from determining the instructional level for school children to "the selection of personnel at various occupational levels for promotion in business, industry, and the National Services," to "study[ing] the degree and nature of loss of reading, spelling and arithmetic ability as a result of brain injury and other physical disturbances" (Jastak & Jastak, 1978, p.1).

Even though the test has not substantially changed, the most recent edition sported the following statement of purpose:

> The purpose of the WRAT–R is to measure the codes which are needed to learn the basic skills of reading, spelling, and arithmetic…When used in conjunction with a test measuring general intelligence which has the same standard deviation units as the WRAT-R, it can be a valuable tool in the determination of learning ability or disability….One can then determine precisely where the individual is having difficulty and can then prescribe those remedial/education programs which will target treatment for the specific defect. (Jastak & Wilkinson, 1984, p. 1)

Like their norm-referenced multiple-choice standardized cousins, individualized assessment measures have some way to go in ensuring that their statements of purpose do not misrepresent their claims. In the exemplars under study, it would be extremely difficult to assign all the suggested purposes to tests; many statements were likely produced by assessment professionals who exaggerated what the test does. The tests merely allow the professionals to speculate and hypothesize about the sample of work collected. But if this is the case, are individualized tests really needed when samples of classroom work would suffice?

Tables of Specifications

As with group standardized tests, the documentation practices for individualized measures did not appear to include tables of specifications. Only the PIAT–R presented test specification charts. Other indexes of content may have been provided in lists of curricular materials consulted, but by and large the detail necessary to map this information onto a particular curriculum for the purposes of determining local validity was absent. If a table of specifications were imagined for most tests, it would simply be some composite of decoding, word identification, and comprehension.[10] Little information was given about the theoretical underpinnings of these areas in relation to reading.

Generation of Items

When information is provided about how items are generated (as was the case for the Brigance Diagnostic Comprehensive, the Brigance Diagnostic, the Gilmore, the PIAT–R, and the WRAT–R), it was, for the most part, general. The Brigance developers presented detailed information for the generation of items for some tests and scant information for others. For instance, on the Brigance Diagnostic, the Functional Word Recognition test enumerated 11 criteria for the selection of words, some with subcriteria; for Direction Words eight text series were listed, and the exact mechanisms used to generate the words were not described. The PIAT–R developers provided some information indicating that items from the first edition of the PIAT were critiqued and noted that revisions resulted. Tying the information to the PIAT makes the PIAT–R only as good as the arguments presented for its predecessor and requires an analysis of that instrument to determine how items were generated.

---

[10]The WRAT–R would not fit in all these categories but would be only a test of word recognition.

For most tests, even though lists of words, basal readers, and the like were referenced, it could not be discerned how these materials were used to generate the set of items used in the test. Even general information is more than that provided by the Durrell Analysis of Reading Difficulty, which listed no resources for the development of items. In fact, Durrell and Catterson (1980) commented that "our proposals for devoting more space to test rationale and remedial suggestions were generally rejected [in a survey requesting feedback]. Clearly what was wanted was an updating of the familiar *Analysis*, with verbiage and expense kept to a minimum" (p.1). Although Durrell and Catterson followed the letter of this statement, other test developers followed the spirit by taking a general rather than specific approach to presenting evidence to bolster their claims that a test assessed a particular domain of reading processes and skills.

Item Review Panels

Information about item review panels was also limited. For the PIAT–R, WRMT–R, and two versions of the Brigance, panels of teachers or consultants were called on to perform item reviews or to have some input into the test. Like norm-referenced multiple-choice group tests, little detail was presented on the procedures relating to these reviews. Nevertheless, these tests did present some information, while the Durrell, Gilmore, and WRAT–R did not present information about such reviews.

Item Tryout Information

When it was presented (as for the PIAT–R), item-tryout information was adequate. Statistical information about item discrimination was provided for the PIAT–R and the WRAT–R. Only occasionally (as for the PIAT–R) was the choice of a particular format for administration discussed.

Norm Tables

For the norm-referenced tests (the Gilmore, the PIAT–R, the WRMT–R), norm tables were presented. It is surprising that tests like the Gilmore, with a standardization sample dating back over 25 years (to 1967), is still in use. Ultimately this fact is a criticism of test users who continue to use outdated material but if test publishers publish outdated material, they too should examine their practices.

Cutoff Points for Criterion-Referenced Tests

Both versions of the Brigance provided cut-off scores and were organized according to grade levels. In a sense the Durrell operated like a criterion-referenced test in that raw scores were converted into grade equivalents, but the Durrell did not attempt to exhaustively sample areas in the same way as the Brigance tests. In this sense the Durrell is limited as a criterion-referenced test. None of these tests included any information about how the number of items in each subtest or the item cutoff points were derived.

TEST ITEMS AS VALIDITY ARGUMENTS

As noted in chapter 3, the key to inferring that what an item tests is reading lies, in part, in the elimination of competing explanations for a student's performance. In examining the tests under review, several sources of competing explanations for students' performance were identified. Many of these parallelled explanations for group tests, but there were some differences. Many of the following points do not apply to the WRAT–R simply because the test is nothing more than a list of words.

Ambiguity or Variation in Administration and/or Scoring Directions

Standardization in administration and scoring is one means by which test developers attempt to reduce one possible source of variability in test performance. Ambiguities in administration or scoring directions were evident in the Durrell (Listening Vocabulary and Sounds in Isolation subtests), the PIAT–R (General Information and Reading Comprehension subtests), the Woodcock Reading Mastery–Revised (Visual Auditory Learning, Word Identification, and Word Attack subtests), the Brigance Diagnostic Comprehensive Inventory of Basic Skills (Word Analysis—Reads Words With Vowel Diagraphs and Diphthongs, Reads Words With Phonetic Irregularities, Reads Suffixes, Reads Prefixes, Functional Word Recognition—Warning Labels, Food Labels), and the Brigance Diagnostic Inventory of Basic Skills (Oral Reading, Substitution of Initial Consonant

Sounds, Ending Sounds Auditorily, Short Vowel Sounds, Long Vowel Sounds, Initial Clusters Auditorily, Phonetic Irregularities, Vocabulary—Context Clues).

The problems encountered were varied. One type of problem was unnecessary complexity that got in the way of successful performance rather than allowing for it. For instance, on the Durrell, students were told the name of an attribute associated with a depicted item, and when presented with several options, they were to select the item that matched the named attribute. Such directions were unnecessarily complex.

Ambiguous language in directions was another source of problems. For example, implicit in many of the questions of the PIAT–R Information subtest was the idea of eliciting a general name for something even though the question did not explicitly ask this. An example analogous to those presented in the test would be "What do we call the name of the building where students go to learn?" If students give a specific response (e.g., J. S. Smith School), they are to be probed by a question like "What do we call that kind of place?" If the keyed response was "school" and the student said "day care" or "university," then the student is asked, "Tell me another name for a building where students go to learn." In other words, despite the correctness of student responses, the goal is to probe for the general response even though the test developers did not explicitly signal this aim. An exception is Item 24 where the supplementary clarification question is raised as "Yes, that happens, but *in general*...."

In other cases, examiners were told to perform certain actions during the administration of a test but were not provided with guidelines to evaluate the actions they were monitoring. For instance, in the Woodcock Reading Mastery–Revised Word Identification and Word Attack subtests, examiners were asked to ensure that the examinees generated a "natural" reading performance, but no criteria were specified to describe this task, and examiners were not told how to proceed if a natural reading did not occur.

Unusual or Ambiguous Language

Only the PIAT–R (Reading Comprehension) contained any items that had unusual language features where unusual conceptual density of items at upper levels was problematic. The items would not survive any editor's pen and would be unlikely to occur in everyday speech or good literature.

The PIAT–R (Reading Comprehension) was also the only test containing an item in which the ambiguity in the language used might have resulted in an examinee's deciding there was no correct response. The item language focused on some "animals" being "in" the bed; in the illustration only one animal is "in" the bed by virtue of being under the covers, and the other animal is "on" the bed by virtue of being on top of the covers.

Layout Problems

The impact of the form and organization of reading materials has only relatively recently become a focus of interest (e.g., Mosenthal, 1990/1991; Waller, 1991). Layouts that seemed confusing were found in two subtests (Initial Consonant Sounds Visually and Oral Reading) of the Brigance Diagnostic Inventory. The following problem from the Oral Reading (for accuracy) is illustrative. Students were presented with a series of short fictional passages for reading aloud, but the texts' unusual formatting might have been the source of some reader miscues. The texts were all flush left and generally followed a pattern of one sentence per line, with the exception of the occasional lengthy sentence completed on the subsequent line. This visual display pattern accustomed the reader to expect of one sentence per line and (as previous research has indicated) could be the source of miscues at the line boundary mark of the lengthier sentences (D. Menosky, personal communication).[11]

Design Variabilities

Item formats and the option template (see chap. 3) are examples of design variabilities. Only the PIAT–R (General Information and Reading Recognition) and the Brigance Diagnostic Inventory of Basic Skills (Reading Comprehension subtest, for primer and lower and upper first grade) contained items in which the format of the items changed in a subtest. For instance, in the Brigance, some questions were posed to which the student must generate a response; for the other levels assessed, the items were multiple choice, and the student chose from an array of responses. The variability of response format introduced a new competing explanation for performance.

---

[11]It should be not be inferred that all texts should be presented in a single line for each sentence type of format. Instead, research on line boundaries indicated that highly controlled texts implicitly teach readers to expect a pattern in print that exists only in primary basals—that of highly controlled sentence–line features. If, through textual encounters, readers learn that lines do not necessarily mean the ends of sentences, then they have learned that line length is not a cuing system of the printed language.

Option template problems (see chap. 3) were found in the Durrell–Visual Memory of Words, Identifying Sounds in Words, Syntax Matching, and Identifying Letter Names in Spoken Words and the WRMT–Revised–Passage Comprehension. Typically, only a few problematic items were found in each subtest. This was not the case with the criterion-referenced tests. For the Brigance Diagnostic Comprehensive Inventory, eight subtests were involved, whereas for the Brigance Diagnostic Inventory five subtests were involved.

Failure to Consider Dialect

Dialectal variation is very likely to be revealed in the oral reading performances of students or examiners. Oral reading formed a component of all the individualized reading tests. For the Durrell, the PIAT–R, the Woodcock Reading Mastery–Revised, and the WRAT–R, pronunciation guides were provided for some subtests, but no substantive discussion of dialect was provided. For the Gilmore, dialect was not addressed. For the criterion-referenced tests, the patterns were similar: Little direction was given on the two versions of the Brigance as to dialect.

Lack of Passage Dependence of Items

All tests surveyed, with the exception of the WRAT–R, which measures only word recognition, and the Woodcock Reading Mastery–Revised, which also has limited text, contained items that were not passage dependent. Unlike other instances of poor test design in which only one or two items were problematic, for this category several items per subtest were typically involved. In general, the relative percentage of problematic items was lower at the first-grade levels, perhaps because of the underemphasis on comprehension at these levels. Examples of items from the Gilmore that can be answered independent of the passage included: "Name another area of study besides psychology in which specialists are studying problems of human relations" (Question D-10). "How will the guidance counsellor be of help?" (Question C-8).

The PIAT–R test was included in this category of analysis even though it did not include passages presented for reading comprehension. Because passage dependency is really concerned with the relation between the examinee's background knowledge and the keyed responses for items, it was decided that the General Information test operated on the assumption of a particular form of background knowledge with a definitive cultural focus.

In a sense, unless the examinee was of the assumed cultural background, then he or she would have difficulty answering many items on the General Information subtest. Examples included everything from the naming of a typical animal that produces milk to specific knowledge about Western fairy tales. Fifteen items of this type were identified in the PIAT–R.

Item Interconnectedness

The Durrell (Listening Comprehension), the Gilmore (Comprehension subtest), and the Brigance Diagnostic Comprehensive Inventory of Basic Skills (Reading Comprehension) contained items in which response to one question affected another.

Nonfunctioning Format for Item Presentation

In the construction of tests, it would seem reasonable to suspect that the textual environment in which the items are presented should have something to do with the completion of the items. Because test theory includes items that are distractors (provided to distract the respondent from the keyed response), even these serve a function in the broader context of the multiple-choice test situation. Consequently, when elements appear to serve not even as a background to the focus of the task at hand, it can be argued that these elements may be construed as having a purpose and could mislead respondents.

For the standardized tests, only the Durrell contained items in which the general format seemed divorced from the task at hand. In the Naming Letters–Lower Case test, the examiner reads the student a sentence that is accompanied by a visual representation of the sentence. The student's task is to name the letters in words that are pointed to by the examiner. This task appears to be a token attempt at using context, but the context serves no apparent function in the testing task. A similar situation occurred for the Writing Letters subtest and the Writing From Copy subtest.

Assessment of Test Items As Validity Arguments

Like their group counterparts, individualized tests of reading were peppered with items suggesting that competing explanations for performance might explain attained scores. Like their group counterparts, only a few of these exist on specific subtests, but the aggregation of these problems could account for significant performance variations leading one to question whether what was being assessed was reading. To further examine the reading on the reading test, I turn to the question of the amount of text on the reading test.

CONCEPTUALIZING READING BY THE AMOUNT OF TEXT READ *OR* HOW MUCH READING IS ON THE READING TESTS?

Group tests have the problem of being survey tests. It can be argued that we should not expect much of them because they are really not intended to do all that much. Individualized tests, however, seem to give the impression of depth and attention to detail, areas that one might expect are overlooked by the group survey measures. Consequently, expectations for the amount of reading done on individualized reading tests is likely to be quite high even though, as others have already pointed out, these tests are probably unable to deliver much more than their group counterparts.

The criteria for determining the amount of text read identify whether items have a nonword, subword, word, phrasal, sentence, or discourse focus. As Table 4.1 illustrates, by and large most items for all tests emphasize the word, subword, or nonword level. Only the Gilmore, which is a standardized oral reading inventory, focuses at the discourse level. This is a fairly generous interpretation in that the Gilmore does have a word focus in the counting of errors made in oral reading. Because of the focus on the tests as artifacts, a count of errors could not be made for the Gilmore as the errors depend

TABLE 4.1

Percentage of Items or Subtests of a Specific Textual Focus for Tests Reviewed

Test	NW		SW		W		P		ST		D	
	I	S	I	S	I	S	I	S	I	S	I	S
Brigance Diagnostic	0	0	45	63	49	27	3	7	0	0	3	7
Brigance Comprehensive	0	0	26	59	70	38	0	0	0	0	4	3
Durrell	0	0	54	65	36	24	0	0	0	0	10	11
Gilmore	0	0	0	0	0	0	0	0	0	0	100	100
PIAT-R*	35	33	6	33	30	33	0	0	29	33	0	0
WRAT-R	0	0	17	50	83	50	0	0	0	0	0	0
Woodcock	0	0	40	43	48	43	0	0	11	14	0	0

Note: NW = No words; SW = Focus on subwords; W = Word focus; P = Focus on phrases; ST = Focus on sentences; D = Focus on continuous discourse; I = Percentage of items; S = Percentage of subtests. *The asterisk indicates that subtests for these tests fell into two or more of the coding categories. For instance, a subtest might include both subword and word items. In this instance the subtest was counted in both columns.

TABLE 4.2
Range of Passage Length in Tests Surveyed

Test	Range
Brigance Diagnostic	33 to 100 words
Brigance Comprehensive Diagnostic	33 to 100 words
Durrell	23 to 143 words
Gilmore	24 to 248 words
PIAT–R	4 to 22 words
WRAT–R	no passages
Woodcock Reading Mastery–Revised	1 to 3 sentences

on a reader's producing them. As Table 4.2 suggests, even the few discourse-based items that exist do not represent large chunks of text. In fact, the California Achievement Test (CAT5) group test contains lengthier passages than did any of the individualized tests examined.

This lack of attention to the reading of discourse in individualized tests echoes norm-referenced tests but is particularly disappointing because these tests are administered individually, at considerable expense in time and personnel, and have an aura of probing further than do the group tests.

EVIDENCE AND ARGUMENTATION IN INDIVIDUALIZED TESTS USED IN THE EARLY 1990S

The individualized tests surveyed presented even less validity argumentation than did their group counterparts. At best, the information can be conceived as poor to uneven with some tests presenting virtually no validity argumentation and others presenting information comparable to that of group tests. The distinguishing characteristic between these tests and group tests is that a multiple-choice format was not used. In this sense, the items could be considered to assess reading in a more sophisticated way. The focus of attention however, was not on reading connected with discourse but on much more limited texts.

As with their group counterparts, these tests need much improvement. The fact that these tests are often relegated to special education initiatives is even more problematic because the children in need of additional assistance in classrooms should be receiving the best that our knowledge of reading and assessment has to offer. The fragile or nonexistent validity argumentation provided in the individualized tests surveyed suggests that it is time to re-examine what is being done in the name of helping students.

Part III

The Validity of Standardized Tests From the Perspective of Their Use

As demonstrated in the chapter on validity, the psychometric field is now moving toward a much larger idea of validity than was traditionally conceptualized. This view homes in on the *use* of tests as fundamental to any validity argument.

In this section, use is reviewed from two different perspectives—from the social and ideological underpinnings of test use from the turn of the century until the mid 1960s and from the research evidence that demonstrates the recent effects of standardized tests. Both of these aspects are important considerations as both situate tests in societal and educational frameworks of use.

Like those touting the new validity theories, we believe that the uses of tests are paramount considerations in validity. They turn the artifacts of tests into tools that can liberate or suppress.

5

A Selective Social History of the Uses of Reading Tests

Patrick Shannon
Pennsylvania State University

Reading tests are modern.[1] In fact, they represent the liberal stance on education as few other artifacts can. Reading tests embody assumptions from the Enlightenment, capitalism, and cultural Darwinism; they project aphorisms such as science is progress, efficiency is paramount, and Anglo-Saxon tradition is virtuous. During their history, they have played many roles, but they have always served just one purpose—to hide the social construction of privilege behind a cloud of scientific objectivity. Since their invention just before the turn of the century to their recent invocation in the debates about the effectiveness of schooling in California, reading tests have been used to mold public education and to shape professional and popular perceptions of reading and reading education.

Ironically, during the last decade, support for reading tests among educational scientists has begun to wane. Tests were once considered the bottom line of reading programs, but their status has now sunk (Neill & Medina, 1989). For example, Richard Anderson, past president of the American Educational Research Association, wrote: "The strength of a standardized reading test is not that it can provide a deep assessment of reading proficiency, but rather that it can provide a fairly reliable, partial assessment cheaply and quickly" (R. Anderson, Heibert, Scott, & Wilkinson, 1985, p. 98). This valuation is quite a fall from the exalted heights that

---

[1]Throughout this chapter I use the term *reading tests* to refer to norm-referenced standardized reading tests.

William S. Gray set in 1915: "Standard reading tests supply information concerning all phases of instruction from broader issues involved in the course of study to the detailed difficulties encountered by individual pupils" (p. 141).

Having recently changed their minds, educational scientists have seemed confused by the continued, even expanded, use of standardized reading tests. Roger Farr (1992) tried to "solve the reading assessment puzzle"(p. 17). Jack Pikulski (1990) searched for "the role of tests in a literacy assessment program" (p. 8). To educate test users and the public, these scientists engaged in campaigns to expose the problems of reading tests and to propose alternative "more scientific goals and means for reading assessment" (e.g., S. G. Paris et al., 1992). Despite their concerns, confusion, and campaigns, U. S. students have continued to take more and more reading tests: unit tests, district tests, state competency tests, and by 1999 a national reading examination at the end of fourth grade. Neill and Medina (1987) estimated that U.S. students take over 105 million standardized tests annually.

In what follows, I explore why the public, legislators, and many educators have clung to standardized reading tests while experts have begun to question their value. To address this question, I briefly examine the history of standardized reading tests. Reading tests are not just reified psychological principles; they are social artifacts produced in the continuous curricular debates about whose knowledge is most beneficial, who is considered literate and who is not, and what roles schooling and literacy programs play in the government's and ruling class's attempts at social engineering. Reading tests exist, are written in particular ways, and are used for social and political reasons as well as academic and scientific ones. To understand why the use and valuing of reading tests do not change as quickly as academic and scientific rationales is to understand that science is in the service of political ideologies, and not the reverse. Therefore, I investigate the social and political reasons for reading tests' existence, development, and patterns of use.

Standardized reading tests were invented during the progressive era when science and business were thought to hold the answers for all social problems. During the decades at the turn of the 20th century, U. S. schools appeared unable to serve society and individuals as the United States changed from a nation primarily of small towns run according to face-to-face contact among citizens to one based on growing urban centers organized around industrial and commercial interests (Cremin, 1988). Changes in the social organization of the nation also altered traditional family life and values and further hindered children's chances of making sense of the modern world. Moreover, the millions of immigrants settling in cities added foreign languages and customs to the new cultural challenges already facing public schools. Urbanization, industrialization, and immigration forced the public and educators to re-examine elementary and secondary school curricula to prepare citizens for the 20th century.

Then as now, although most agreed that change was necessary, there was much less agreement about what these changes should be (Kliebard, 1986). Traditionalists from William Torrey Harris at the turn of the century through E. D. Hirsch today favored continuation of European content and values over tests and technique. Child-centered advocates from G. Stanley Hall to David Elkind prized development and creativity over measurement and method. Social reconstructionists from Lester Frank Ward to Maxine Greene promoted access and equity over evaluation and erudition. Educational scientists from Joseph Mayer Rice to P. David Pearson argued that science and market would objectively remake schools and would equip both individuals and society for whatever changes might follow. Reading tests are one way to track how this last position became the dominant one in U. S. schools and social discourse about education.

DISENCHANTMENT OF THE MIND

Standardized tests of reading were first used to explore the processes of perception, thinking, and learning. They were instrumental in the creation of the academic discipline of psychology and its efforts to separate the study of the mind and its functions from the field of philosophy (Venezky, 1984). Discussions of Plato's theories of remembrance, Rousseau's theories of mental transactions, Froebel's mysticism, and the like were considered too subjective to calculate the workings of the mind. Philosophical explanations of the mind required leaps of logical faith that could not necessarily be verified beyond argumentation. On the contrary, psychological investigations produced empirical data from which explanations of the mind could be built objectively:

> The judgments of science are distinguished from other judgments by being more impartial, more objective, more precise, and more subject to verification by any competent observer and being made by those who by their nature and training should be better judges. Science knows or should know no favorites and cares for nothing in its conclusions but the truth. (Thorndike, 1906, p. 265)

From their inception, reading tests connoted objectivity, precision, and power. Standardization of design, implementation, and analysis were necessary to distinguish results from typical teacher judgments, to reduce error, and to make results comparable. Following John Locke's writings about the mind, psychologists theorized that mental activity was based on perception and sensation. They designed reading tests that would first help them to investigate sensation, mental speed, attention, recall, and the basic association of ideas through formalized activities involving decontextualized letters, syllables, words, and sentences as stimuli. From such data, they sought to build explanations of how perception led to understanding. To explain understanding, reading tests used paraphrasing (Huey, 1908/1968), free recall (Romaines, 1884), and questioning (Thorndike, 1917) to glimpse what readers remembered or recognized from texts ranging in length from phrases to short paragraphs. This approach, of course, was in keeping with contemporary associationist theories and, later, behaviorist theories of reading: "When the mechanics of reading, if we may use that phrase to distinguish the process of reading from the process of understanding, are mastered, the whole attention may now be concentrated on the significance of the passage (Judd, 1914, p. 368).

Absent from these tests and psychological considerations of reading were personal engagement, critical response, or individual construction of meaning because these obvious characteristics of sophisticated reading seemed at the time to require a spiritual re-enchantment of reading behavior. To continue to study these aspects would be unscientific, emotional, and incomparable. Results of such study could not lead to true statements about either the human mind or reading. As early as 1886, James Cattell acknowledged these concerns: "The conditions of the experiments place the subject in an abnormal condition, especially as to fatigue, attention, and practice" (Cattell, 1886, p. 63). Yet, the results of the early psychological investigations of reading using reading tests were substantial enough to lead Paul Kolers (1968) to conclude that "remarkably little experimental information has been added to what Huey knew [in 1908], although some of the phenomena have now been measured more precisely" (p. xiv). Reading tests were recognized as the objective way to disenchant the mind of the spiritual notion that some things may be unexplainable, to define reading once and for all, and to determine who could read.

SCHOOL EFFICIENCY

Thorndike's faith in science carried over from psychology to school management. Reading and other tests provided measures by which administrators could make objective, rational decisions about what content and methods should be included in the school curriculum. This scientific management of schooling was patterned after the efficiency movement in business and industry, in which contribution to profit was the only acceptable rationale for introducing or maintaining any factor in production processes. Metaphorically, reading test scores became the profit in the production of literate citizens. The disenchantment of traditional, spiritual, or cultural explanations of mind was extended into school practices as teachers and students were considered factors in production equations. In this way, scientific management and reading tests were used to standardize and reduce the subjective human contribution to education.

Not all school personnel enthusiastically supported the scientific management of schooling, as Leonard Ayres (1915) reported in this retrospective:

Eighteen years ago the school superintendents of America, assembled in convention in Indianapolis, discussed the problems then foremost in educational thought and action. At that meeting a distinguished educator—the pioneer and pathfinder among the scientific study of education in America, Joseph Mayer Rice—brought up for discussion the results of his investigations of spelling among the children in the school systems of nineteen cities. These results showed that, taken all in all, the children who spent forty minutes a day for eight years in studying spelling did not spell any better than the children in the schools of other cities where they devoted only ten minutes per day to the study.

The presentation of these data threw that assemblage into consternation, dismay, and indignant protest. But the resulting storm of vigorously voiced opposition was directed against the investigator who had pretended to measure the results of teaching spelling by testing the ability of children to spell.

In terms of scathing denunciation the educators there present and the pedagogical experts, who reported the deliberations of the meeting in the educational press, characterized as silly, dangerous, and from every viewpoint, reprehensible, the attempt to test the efficiency of the teacher by finding out what the pupils could do. With striking unanimity, they voiced the conviction that any attempt to evaluate the teaching of spelling in terms of the ability of the pupils to spell was essentially impossible and based on a profound misconception of the function of education.

Last month in the city of Cincinnati, that same association of school superintendents again assembled in convention devoted fifty-seven addresses and discussions to tests and measurements of educational efficiency. The basal

proposition underlying this entire mass of discussion was that the effectiveness of the school, the method, and the teacher must be measured in terms
of the results secured. (pp. 85–86)

By 1911, scientific management was so well accepted that the National
Society for the Study of Education's Department of Superintendents
established the Committee on the Economy of Time in Education to
eliminate nonessentials from the elementary school curriculum, to set
minimum standards for each school subject, and to improve teaching
methods through the use of standardized tests. To gather appropriate data
to accomplish these tasks and to measure compliance and performance
later, ability tests had to be translated for large-scale implementation. "In
the first place, it is undoubtedly desirable that the reading ability of students
in one system of schools should be compared with the reading ability of
children in other centers. For the purpose of such a general comparison, it
is probably desirable that norm scores of standard tests be developed"
(Judd, 1915, p. 562).

Reading tests became both the means and the ends of the scientific
management of reading lessons and curricula. Advocates of scientific management began with two assumptions: that contemporary psychological
definitions of reading were accurate and complete and that objective and
precise instruments to measure that definition were possible and desirable.
E. L. Thorndike put it this way in 1914:

> It is obvious that educational science and educational practice alike need
> more objective, more accurate and more convenient measures of (1) a pupil's
> ability to pronounce words and sentences seen; (2) a pupil's ability to
> understand the meaning of words and sentences seen; (3) a pupil's ability to
> appreciate and enjoy what we roughly call "good literature"; and (4) a pupil's
> ability to read orally, clearly, and efficiently …Any progress toward measuring
> how well a child can read with something of the objectivity, precision, co-
> measurability, and convenience which characterize our measurements of how
> tall he is, how much he can lift with his back, squeeze with his hand, or how
> acute his vision, would be a great help in grading, promoting, and testing the
> value of methods of teaching. (p.1)

By 1919, W. S. Gray published *Principles of Methods in Teaching Reading as
Derived From Scientific Investigation*, which included 48 tested principles
covering skill knowledge norms for student progress throughout the grades,
suggestions for oral and silent reading instruction, even specification for the

printing of books to maximize the economy of reading. Using test score gains as the sole criterion for recommendation, Gray (1919) reported that "much reading of simple interesting material is effective in increasing the rate of reading" (p. 41), and "knowledge, while reading, that the material is to be reproduced improves the quality of the reading." He found that experiments had not shown one textbook method of teaching reading to be necessarily superior to all others regardless of circumstances; rather he maintained that instructional effectiveness varied according to how teachers used the materials, the backgrounds of the students, and the amount of materials available for instruction. Reading tests were not just to redesign the curriculum, they were supposed to redesign teaching, to produce verifiably literate students. "Tests will be most productive when individual teachers scrutinize their work carefully and record facts accurately, and reconstruct their methods on the basis of the facts secured" (Gray, 1918, p. 141).

Because of reading tests' newfound importance in managing schools, most leading reading experts and several educational psychologists produced their own versions of the tests (e.g., Buswell, Courtis, Dearborn, Gray, Judd, Thorndike, and later, Durrell, Gates, and Horn). Surveys of the reading tests began to appear as early as 1910 (see Bliss, 1918; C. Gray, 1917; W. Gray, 1916, 1917; Judd, 1914; Schmitt, 1914; Thorndike, 1914). Tests were available nationally by 1914. Competition for part of the reading test market was acute and served to reduce the variability among the reading tests being produced (Monroe, 1917). By the 1920s, reading tests became the primary tool for school improvement, program design, and judging student progress.

MEASURES OF CULTURE

Scientific management was expected to provide an objective means through which schools could be organized and run. Through the application of scientific methods, school personnel could justify the operations and outcomes to the public. Yet, the tools of scientific management in general and reading tests in particular were developed and designed by human beings, who held definite biases about society and all who inhabit it. Standardized tests encoded these biases, and an argument can be made that the tests themselves were developed and used to prove that these social biases were true. The following quotes trace these intentions from the originating premise during the Enlightenment, to the field of psychology in general, and to reading tests in particular:

God has stamp'd certain Characters upon Men's Minds, which like their
shapes, may perhaps be a little mended; but can hardly be totally alter'd and
transformed into the contrary. He therefore, that is about Children, should
well study their Natures and Aptitudes, and see, by often trials, what turn
they easily take, and what becomes them; observe what their Native Stock
is, how it may be improved, and what it is fit for. He should consider, what
they want; whether they be capable of having it wrought into them by
industry, and incorporated there by Practice; and whether it be worth while
to endeavor it. (Locke, 1705/1976, p. 67)

It may interest you to know the first [postwar] problem chosen for investigation by the Division of Psychology and Anthropology of the National Research Council is the problem of the mental and moral qualities of the
different elements of the United States. What does this country get in the
million or more Mexican immigrants of the last four years? What has it got
from Italy, from Russia, from Scotland and Ireland? What are the descendants
of the Puritans and Cavaliers and Huguenots and Dutch; and what are they
doing for America? Psychology will undertake to do its share in an inventory
of the human assets and liabilities of the United States, whenever it is asked
to do so. (Thorndike, 1918, pp. 280–281)

Reading tests to the teacher cannot help but eventually mean not only
concise and definite statements as to what she is expected to do in the course
of study, but the reduction of instruction to those items which can be proved
to be of importance in preparation for intelligent living and future usefulness
in life. It will mean, too, an ultimate differentiation in training for the different
types of children with which teachers now have to deal, and the specialization
of work so as to enable teachers to obtain more satisfactory individual results.
(E. P. Cubberley, 1917, p. xii)

Although standardized reading tests were supposed to eliminate teachers'
bias from decision making about reading curriculum and instruction, in fact
race, class, and gender biases were encoded in the theory, practices, and
artifacts of the scientific management of reading through the use of these
reading tests. Reading tests were to be the measure of success for some social
groups whose "Native Stock," "mental and moral qualities," and "types"
matched the expectations of psychologists and reading experts, and they
also were used to justify the sorting of other social groups by their lack of
the same factors to provide them "industry" and "practice" of an "ultimate"
differentiation in training. From the beginning there were more measures
of culture than true tests of literate ability. The systematic use of these tests
meant success for the few, but failure for the many.

These biases were not obvious in the tests themselves or in the rationales for testing. Whether individual or grouped, timed or untimed, reading tests employed the same formats to evaluate all readers. Because of the prevailing psychological theories, this practice seemed universally fair. Standardized directions, items, and passages, scoring procedures, and statistical scales attested to the egalitarian principles of testing. It soon became apparent, at least to some, however, that reading tests and the other standardized tests were stratifying students according to culture: "In several large cities, the school child, because of his unfavorable reactions to the school situation, comes in for clinical diagnosis. Since it is the child's reaction to the school situation which is at fault, it is well to test him along the line of the special abilities which he is expected to develop under the conditions of the school situation" (Schmitt, 1914, p. 152).

> The same biases that teachers demonstrate in grading pupils are also apparent in standard reading tests. Students of different language and experiential backgrounds score lower. For example, Italian pupils are seriously handicapped. The sections of the city in which these pupils live are such that factors other than mere lack of English in the homes are probably to be recognized as contributing to the low rank of these pupils on tests. (Jerdon, 1921, p. 111)

Even when these biases were identified, prevailing theories in psychology and education (which reflected society's faith in science, capitalism, and Anglo-Saxon traditions) found fault with cultures, and later individuals, rather than with science and scientific management. Once students were identified as "inferior," "disabled," or "deficient" (as Nila Banton Smith, 1936, labeled them in her history, *American Reading Instruction*), individual students were in line for more reading tests. "Pupils because they have had difficulties with a subject are in most need of the best possible teaching" (Gates, 1927, p. 19). To determine the best approach, reading experts began with the standard achievement test results and then applied a battery of specific subtests: standardized test records, test of attitudes and interests in reading, test of level of reading ability, test of abilities in comprehension and interpretation, test of oral and written recall of reading, test of abilities in the mechanics of reading, test of abilities related to study (see Durrell, 1939). By 1930, these batteries of tests could be constructed at any grade level with several alternative tests for each of the seven subsections of information required.

In the first book devoted entirely to remedial reading, C. T. Gray (1922) reported "a survey of the literature upon remedial measures shows that the development of methods and devices for this type of work has not kept pace with the development of methods of diagnosis" (p. 365). Shortly thereafter basal readers began to fill this void with scripted lessons designed to boost test scores. For example in 1925, William P. McCall and Lelah Mae Crabbs published a six-book series, *Standard Test Lessons in Reading*:

> The Standard Test Lessons in Reading are offered to the teachers in our school (Lincoln School at Teachers College, Columbia University) with confidence that their use will give to pupils a rate of speed and power to comprehend exceeding that yielded by ordinary methods of teaching silent reading....Every lesson is a test and every test is a lesson....Not only is every test a lesson, but every test is a standard test; that is, it shows how well the normal or typical pupil would read these same lessons. (p. xi)

These basals furthered the efforts to manage reading lessons scientifically and to measure students' culture (Shannon, 1989). The teacher guidebooks, with scripted lessons and scope and sequences of skills, directed teachers to use the principles apparently derived from experiments. At the same time, the stories and the featured skills promoted what have come to be called Anglo-Saxon middle-class values and social habits (Luke, 1988). The basals, then, provided the technical control that would enable teachers to work scientifically and culturally toward verifiably literate students capable of fulfilling their roles in society:

> Within recent years various types of organizations of materials similar to published standardized tests have appeared....The better types represent an effort to develop a comprehensive series of exercises that include in well printed and illustrated forms the best informal devices and tests that the teacher would otherwise have to prepare herself. They are organized systematically to provide learning of the basal words, word recognition, comprehension, appreciation, and study techniques and simultaneously to test and diagnose ability and difficulty. Their purpose is to provide the nearest possible approach to the policy of daily diagnosis with the least expenditure of time of the pupils and teachers. (Gates, 1937, p. 374)

By the 1950s, surveys of school practices concluded that over 90% of teachers used basal materials on a daily basis and 98% of school districts administered standardized norm-referenced reading achievement tests at least once annually (Austin & Morrison, 1963; Barton & Wilder, 1964).

This interconnection between teaching and standardized tests became law, and large amounts of federal funding were directed to schools during the 1960s (House, 1978). Senator Robert Kennedy was apparently concerned that school administrators would divert federal funding for Title I reading programs away from people who were poor, unless a "reporting" requirement was added to the enabling legislation (McLaughlin, 1975). The purpose of the requirement was to inform parents so they would have access to the facts and figures to judge their children's progress. When this legislative requirement was operationalized through the federal government's Planning, Programming, and Budgeting Systems Office, the requirement was translated into scientific management terms in which standardized reading tests used to place students in the program would also become the means by which individual and program success would be measured and reported. Echoing to Judd's remarks of 1915 and presaging current opinions, Education Commissioner Keppel argued in 1964 that public reporting would provide performance comparisons among schools, districts, and even states and would thus stimulate competition. This renewed interest in scientific management was relabeled "system analysis," but reading tests were still considered profits to be counted.

The illusions of scientific objectivity—standardization, universality, and mathematical precision—obscured cultural, racial, and social class biases encoded in the formats, procedures, and topics of reading tests. The results from these tests became self-fulfilling prophecies that produced biased treatments of different social groups under the guise of scientific truth. In this way, reading tests not only define reading and measure school and programmatic success, but they verify White middle- and upper-class superiority.

AN END TO HISTORY

In light of this selective social history of reading tests, continued support for reading tests and the testing of reading makes sense, despite recent concerns among some psychologists and reading experts. Test advocates and users have simply been following the liberal traditions of psychology which have directed schooling and educators during most, if not all, of the 20th century. Although these traditions have prepared these groups to seek more scientific tests, more efficiency in reading instruction, and more affirmation of our national heritage, they do not prepare or enable any of us to call for the abolition of reading tests and the ending of the testing of reading.

Tests and testing are embedded in the fabric of schooling—its definition, its organization, its functioning, and its public legitimacy. They have been encoded in federal legislation, state laws, and district policy during the school lives of school personnel and taxpayers. In a sense, reading tests are part of our history both as students and as educators. To deny reading tests is to deny our schooling, our teaching, our literacy, even ourselves. It takes more than a few psychologists' and reading experts' contrary opinions to end the history of reading tests and the testing of reading. Reading educators, administrators, and the public are still told:

> We must let scientific evidence answer questions about the reading process. (Stanovich, 1994, p. 280)

> America will become a nation of readers when verified practices of the best teachers in the best schools can be introduced throughout the country. (Anderson et al., 1985, p. 120)

> They often argue that the approach cannot be evaluated because it is expected to affect competencies other than those reflected by standardized measures. Fine, so identify those competencies, and competent reading researchers will find ways to measure them. (Pressley, 1994, p. 190)

> Although nationalism may be regrettable in some of its worldwide political effects, a mastery of national culture is essential to mastery of the standard language in every modern nation....Children also need to understand elements of our literacy and mythic heritage, for example, Adam and Eve, Cain and Abel, Noah and the Flood, David and Goliath, The Twenty-third Psalm, Humpty Dumpty, Jack Sprat, Jack and Jill, Little Jack Horner, Cinderella, Jack and the Beanstalk, Mary Had a Little Lamb, Peter Pan, and Pinocchio. Also Achilles, Adonis, Aeneas, Agamemnon, Antigone, and Apollo as well as Robin Hood, Paul Bunyan, Satan, Sleeping Beauty, Sodom and Gomorrah, the Ten Commandments, and Tweedledum and Tweedledee. (Hirsch, 1987, p. 30)

> We will develop American Achievement tests for 4th, 8th, and 12th graders in the five core subjects. (George Bush, national educational strategy speech, April 18, 1991)

I offer a social, not a technical, history of reading tests because it is impossible to separate human intention from the tests or the tests from the testing. Nor is it possible to separate the testing and testmakers from all the social pain that surrounds the continued scientific management of reading programs. As I have tried to demonstrate using advocates' own words, reading tests are designed to reduce reading to a psychological shell, to direct the teaching of reading, to sort social groups, and to protect the feelings of superiority of certain social groups over others. Regardless of the care given to these concerns in recent efforts to modify tests (e.g., Michigan and Illinois state examinations, the National Assessment of Educational Progress, etc.), these intentions remain in the tests and testing. Changing reading tests cannot change biased minds. Abolishing reading tests cannot abolish liberal ideology and history, which legitimate and perpetuate an unequal status quo in and out of schools. To end this history, we must wrestle schooling away from psychology and psychologists; we must deny reading education as a market to be fought over by multinational corporations; and we must stop reading education as cultural imperialism through both the forms and content we valorize. One lesson of this selective history is that we must invent postliberal reading education.

6

The Consequences of the Use of Standardized Tests

Peter Johnston
State University of New York at Albany

The last decade has seen some shifts in the criteria that are applied to the evaluation of tests. Three of these changes are most important for this chapter. First, there has been a greater emphasis on validity in all forms of assessment. Second, the concept of validity has been expanded and transformed (Moss, 1992, 1996). Validity now includes the consequences of interpretations and uses of tests as central and unavoidable aspects (Cronbach, 1989; Messick, 1989). Consequently, the validity of a test cannot be considered outside a given context of use. Although this understanding is not new, it was regularly ignored because it was not a central tenet of an integrated theory. Third, what it means to be *literate* and to *achieve* are being re-examined, along with their relation to assessment practices (Edelsky, 1996; Johnston, 1997).[1]

The increased emphasis on validity along with an elaboration of the meaning of validity has produced an interest in "authentic" and "performance-based" assessment practices. The idea is to have assessment instru-

---

[1]Other changes include: Fourth, the concept of reliability has been subsumed in the notion of generalizability. Agreement between student rankings on tests and subtests is only a part of generalizability, which also includes whether a performance on a test has anything to do with performance in "real" situations. Fifth, because of changes in our understanding of the cultural nature of literacy, there is a change in our understanding of test bias: its source, its inevitability, and its consequences. Sixth, directness and transparency are becoming increasingly valued. *Directness* refers to whether the assessment task is actually the intended outcome behavior or some indirect indicator (for example actual writing versus a multiple-choice grammar test). *Transparency* refers to the extent to which the criteria valued in scoring the assessment are clear to examinees.

ments that reflect the complex nature of literacy in the real world rather than the simplistic construction of literacy reflected in multiple-choice tests. More importantly, however, validity is now commonly seen as having two major and inseparable aspects: construct validity and consequential validity.

Construct validity has to do with the value of the constructs through which people make sense of the behavior being assessed. For example, common constructs include comprehension, dyslexia, reading ability, decoding ability, intelligence, and reading level. Responding to a cloze task is not the same as responding to a multiple-choice test, particularly one that is broken into various subskill tests, and neither of these is the same as talking with someone about a book one has read. Yet each of these assessments is likely to be described in terms of the constructs of reading and ability. "Failure" on one or more of these assessments might be interpreted as being caused by "low ability," "low intelligence," "dyslexia," or some other construct.

Consequential validity, on the other hand, refers to the value of the consequences of particular assessment practices and interpretations. For example, what are the consequences of explaining a student's behavior through the construct learning disabled as opposed to low intelligence or lack of reading experience? What are the consequences of the use of a test to hold teachers publicly accountable? The consequences of particular assessment practices are now seen as critical and are becoming well documented. When we evaluate tests, then, we cannot evaluate them out of the context of their use. Apart from anything else, the conditions under which a person takes a test are likely to change the nature of the performance and thus the construct measured by the test. The assessment practices of a school district have important consequences for what teachers and students do in their classrooms.

The focus of this chapter is on consequential validity. I review the available research on the consequences of tests and testing practices. The impact can be seen on teachers, students, and curriculum, as well as on institutional relations and matters of equity. Although the consequences for students are the most important to consider, I begin with a description of the effects on teachers because teachers mediate many of the consequences of tests. The bulk of the relevant research is qualitative rather than quantitative in nature. It is supported by a different set of beliefs about science, knowledge, and human nature from those that support standardized testing.

CONSEQUENCES FOR TEACHERS

The most prominent uses of tests in this country are, directly or indirectly, to "hold teachers and students accountable" and to classify students. These uses have been called "high stakes testing" because the consequences for individual teachers and students can be substantial. In some districts, for example, test scores are regularly posted classroom by classroom in schools or published in newspapers. Teachers' salaries can be tied to their students' test scores. The consequences of such testing practices are becoming well documented (e.g., Shannon, 1986).

The higher the stakes, the more teachers' efforts become focused on test preparation and teaching to the test to the neglect of whatever is not measured. The higher the stakes, the greater the effect (Herman & Golan, 1991), and effects are often intensified over time (J. Fish, 1988). Testing also works against the possibility of teachers' improving their instructional practices for the future. As teachers focus their efforts on the tests and the use of related worksheets and test preparation materials (each of which is often required by administrators), their experimentation with alternative instructional strategies is restricted. Indeed, teachers actually begin to lose the skill to teach in flexible and individualized ways (M. L. Smith, 1991). Stodolsky (1988), for example, found that teachers were less inclined to be innovative in their teaching when there was increased accountability pressure, and they were also less likely to collaborate, a primary means for them to learn about and expand their teaching practices. Furthermore, the feelings that teachers reported in response to the testing situation exacerbated the problem. They felt anxiety and stress, they felt as though their instructional lives were out of control, they felt shame, anger, and guilt (Johnston, Afflerbach, & Weiss, 1993; Johnston, Guice, Baker, Malone, & Michelson, 1995; M. L. Smith, 1991; M. L. Smith, Edelsky, Draper, Rottenberg, & Cherland, 1991;). None of these reactions helps them to become better teachers or better learners about teaching.

Teachers' positive self-regard and job satisfaction have also been negatively related to the accountability pressure they have felt (Herman & Golan, 1991; Shannon, 1986), and the lower their professional self-concept, the more likely they have been to experience burnout (Friedman, 1991). The pressure to produce high performance on tests has led teachers to teach in ways that conflict with their values and beliefs and sometimes to engage in "cheating," which produces anxiety and low self-esteem (Dorr-Bremme, Burry, Catterall, Cabello, & Daniels, 1983) and involves them in stressful ethical dilemmas.

Some of these dilemmas are produced by differences in stakeholders' distance from the actual assessment situation and from individual students. As M. L. Smith et al. (1991) pointed out, a teacher with an intimate knowledge of a child's learning and experience of the child taking an achievement test is considerably more sceptical about the value of test information than is a person without such knowledge and experience. Teachers with more experience are more sceptical of the value of test results. A teacher forced to make instruction conform to an instrument that he or she does not value is placed in an ethical dilemma, neither side of which allows productive feelings about oneself or one's practice.

These dilemmas are exacerbated as teachers are required to make young children take tests where scores can hold no meaning or value for them; yet those scores could dramatically influence children's opportunities in school. Teachers' distress is compounded by the traumatic effects of the tests on some of the children in their classes and often by the denial of these effects by their administrators (M. L. Smith et al., 1991) . A teacher whose experience of children taking tests includes children crying and experiencing failure cannot help but feel anger, guilt, and a range of related emotions. Indeed, the more caring and involved the teacher, the more likely are these feelings to emerge.

The use of standardized tests for public accountability purposes has serious and unfortunate effects on teachers' assessments of their students (Johnston et al., 1993; Johnston, et. al. 1995). In the long run, these assessments are most important because they form the basis of moment-to-moment instructional adaptations and relationships. The greater the press for accountability through standardized tests, the more likely it is that teachers' descriptive assessments of children's literacy development are brief, standardized, and global rather than extensive, specific, and personalized; focus on what students cannot do rather than on what they can do; are cast in impersonal, distancing language; emphasize a simple linear, technical view of literacy; exclude reference to books the children are reading. Because high-profile testing programs constrict teachers' conceptions of reading and the teaching of reading (Shannon, 1986), some of these consequences are predictable.

Aside from influencing teachers' instructional strategies, these effects have the power to influence the relationship between teacher and student, and to influence the students' assessments of themselves. For example, Deci and his colleagues (Deci, Spiegel, Ryan, Koestner, & Kauffman, 1982) found that student teachers were more coercive in their teaching when they believed that they would be held accountable for their students' attainment of standards, the same situation constructed in accountability testing. Parents, behaved in exactly the same way (Renshaw & Gardner, 1987). In other words, tests not only have the effect of stultifying classroom learning, the very thing they are intended to improve, but they also alter the relationship between teacher and student.

CONSEQUENCES FOR STUDENTS

The consequences of standardized testing practices for students have become increasingly apparent. Testing takes time, not only for the testing itself, but for test preparation and recovery (the higher the stakes, the greater the time). It has been estimated that tests consume some 100 hours of instructional time each year for each child (M. L. Smith, 1991), an estimate that is certainly conservative in schools with curricula that are focused entirely on test performance. The full consequences of this removal of instructional time are as yet not fully examined.

Aside from draining students' learning time, there are more personal consequences. Teachers have argued that children are adversely affected by the tests and suffer stress, physical illness, disruption of their community through misbehavior and fighting, and long-term test anxiety (M. L. Smith et al., 1991). Levels of anxiety differ across students in nonrandom ways; Hill and Sarason (1966) found that anxiety predicted school grades just as well as did achievement test scores. In fifth and sixth grade, the most anxious 10% of students were about 1 year behind the least anxious students in test performance and were retained at twice the rate. Test anxiety and test performance are increasingly negatively related as children get older. By 11th grade the correlation is -.60 (Fyans, 1979).

Some effects of standardized testing are less direct than is the anxiety produced by actually taking the test. A primary function of testing has been to place students into instructional groups and programs. This testing function has major consequences for students' lives. In a study of high stakes testing, Richard Allington and Anne McGill-Franzen (1992) pointed out that, although the intent of testing might be to improve instruction and to allow early identification of difficulties, the effect has been to increase the number of students retained or placed in categorical programs. In their study, by the time students reached the third-grade state reading test, as few as 36% of the entering kindergarten cohort remained. The rest had been retained, transitioned, or placed in special education. Retention has been shown to inflict substantial personal and social cost and not to improve students' performance over their unretained peers (M. L. Smith & Shepard, 1988). Similarly, placement in categorical programs is less than helpful for children's learning (McGill-Franzen & Allington, 1991).

Although children are born with a powerful orientation toward mastery learning, in this culture they become socialized to develop and identify with a comparative-competitive notion of ability (Stipek, Recchia, & McClintic, 1992). This belief system is strongly developed through schooling and is fed by the use of standardized norm-referenced ability testing. Torgeson and Fairbanks (1978, cited in Madaus & McDonagh, 1979) pointed out that students who had failed the Functional Literacy Test in Florida viewed themselves as global failures, a particularly debilitating attribution pattern as it removes motivation for any productive investment of effort or strategy (Diener & Dweck, 1978; Nicholls, 1989). Students who learn that they are, in norm-referenced terms, "unable" become essentially helpless when they face performance situations; they fail to use even those strategies that they have, let alone seek new ones (Bandura & Schunk, 1981; Diener & Dweck, 1978; Elliot & Dweck, 1988; Nicholls, 1989; Schunk, 1984). These low evaluations of competence can lead students to use problematic strategies such as setting either low or unattainably high goals and applying no effort so that no one (including themselves) can attribute their failure to low ability (Covington & Beery, 1976).

Institutionalizing a view of literacy that stresses a noncontroversial, closed view of knowledge (as is required by multiple-choice tests) reduces the extent to which literate dialogue occurs in the classroom and is likely to lead children to view themselves as "received knowers" who do not partici-pate in the construction of knowledge (Belenky, Clinchy, Goldberger, & Tarule, 1986). This situation is not only highly unmotivating, but is associ-ated with students' separation of their school learning from the rest of their lives (Nicholls, McKenzie, & Shufro, 1994).

Students' motivation is affected in other ways, too. For example, testing can reduce children's intrinsic interest in achievement tasks (MacIver, Stipek, & Daniels, 1991). Paris and his colleagues (Paris, Lawton, Turner, & Roth, 1991) have shown three trends in students' approaches to tests as they get older. They become increasingly disillusioned by the tests, and they lose their motivation to perform well. At the same time, they increasingly use strategies that do not improve their performance. The latter two changes reduce the construct validity of the tests.

Exploring the consequences of standardized testing practices for students has barely begun, and some effects can only be guessed at. For example, the act of assessing with standardized multiple-choice testing is depersonalizing. The organization of schooling around such testing institutionalizes this depersonalization and provides a situation most likely to produce the alienation that leads to dropping out of school (Mann, 1986). In the domain of special education, this depersonalizing has been made clear, particularly with respect to minority families (Harry, 1992). Similarly, in the work of school psychologists, the depersonalization is consequential and differentially distributed across race and class (Milofsky, 1989). As Edelsky (1996) pointed out, tests make it possible to treat children as objects.

Children's self-assessments are socialized, and part of this socialization is influenced, directly or indirectly, by standardized testing. As teachers' assessments of children are influenced by "objective" accountability testing, they are inclined to talk about children in impersonal and normative terms. When this talk makes its way into the classroom, it becomes part of the curriculum, part of what children learn. Tests reinforce the belief that meanings are singular and reside in the text itself. Tests help children and teachers define literacy in terms of accuracy and convention, a definition that excludes many learners. Tests are a means of arranging for both the definition and the demonstration of failure in what McDermott (1993) called "degradation ceremonies."

CONSEQUENCES FOR THE CURRICULUM

Madaus and Airasian (1977) pointed out that recognition of the influence of testing on the curriculum is not new. They quoted Holmes (1911), who noted that:

> Whenever the outward standard of reality (examination results) has established itself at the expense of the inward, the ease with which worth (or whatever passes for such) can be measured is ever tending to become in itself the chief, if not sole, measure of worth. And in proportion as we tend to value the results of education for the measureableness, so we tend to undervalue and at last to ignore those results which are too intrinsically valuable to be measured. (p. 128)

expose educational inequalities. Consonant with the American value of equal opportunity, the general idea has been to reduce the effects of personal bias on instruction and selection through the use of "objective" tests, that is, tests that are impersonal and unbiased. As with many aspects of testing, good intentions have been thwarted by unforeseen problems. Three problems are most significant. First, because of the cultural nature of literacy, it is not possible to create an unbiased literacy test; tests always privilege particular forms of language and experience. Second, tests are inequitably applied with the result that the consequences of testing so far described are more severe for some groups than for others. Third, the beliefs about language, learning, and ability perpetuated by tests have differential consequences for those deemed more and less "able."

The understanding that literacy is cultural has gradually become more widespread. Language is social, and there are cultural and situational differences in the ways people use language. These differences lead to differences in the ways people write and understand what is written, and thus it is impossible to make an unbiased test (Johnston, 1984b; Marvin, 1988). Even the makers of standardized tests are beginning to concede this point. For example, the makers of the California Achievement Test (CAT/5, 1992) noted that "no test designed to be used nationally can be completely unbiased. The best one can do is minimize the role of the extraneous elements, thereby increasing the number of students for whom the test is appropriate" (p. 25). To the extent that particular patterns of language and experience are favored by tests, these patterns are unlikely to be those of minority groups.

Because of the cultural nature of testing in general and literacy testing in particular, the test performance of those most at risk of being misjudged by testing should at least have the benefit of a wide range of observations including interviews with students and parents. These students, however, are the least likely to receive such benefit, not only in classrooms but also in the use of tests by school psychologists. Milofsky (1989) has shown that the lower the socioeconomic status (and the greater the number of Black students in the school), the greater the volume of testing that school psychologists engage in, the less time they spend consulting with parents and teachers, and the less time they spend on any individual case, often halving the case time. The briefer the case study, the more automatic, formal, and test based it is. Because the most useful information provided by testing is how a child performs as he or she does rather than sheer normative performance, the most instructionally useful information is likely to be a major and differentially distributed loss.

In addition to the cultural biases in the tests themselves, tests are not equally administered to all children. For example, accountability pressure is not equally distributed across school districts. Herman and Golan (1991) pointed out that "testing is more influential and exerts stronger effects on teaching in schools serving more disadvantaged students" (pp. 55–58). Their study showed that teachers at low socioeconomic status schools, particularly urban ones, report greater accountability pressure than do teachers at high socioeconomic status schools. The lower the socioeconomic status of a school, the greater the school attention to test scores, the greater the time devoted to test scores by the teachers, and the greater the attention teachers give to testing in planning instruction. Furthermore, the greater the pressure teachers feel to improve test scores, the lower their job satisfaction and the pride they feel in their teaching. Thus there is a systematic bias against teachers and students in low-socioeconomic status schools. This inequity is compounded by the fact that racial and ethnic groups are not equally distributed among high- and low-socioeconomic status schools. Black and Hispanic students are far more likely to attend low-socioeconomic status urban schools than are White students.

Standardized tests portray reading as a unidimensional, normally distributed ability that an individual has more or less of. Organization of schooling and belief systems consonant with this portrayal lead to differential treatment of more and less "able" students. Children entering school without the cultural capital required by testing programs are placed in exactly those situations that produce failure-oriented belief systems (Elliot & Dweck, 1988; Nicholls, 1989), which exacerbate the difference between the haves and the have-nots. Where ability grouping exists, such students are much more likely to be placed in "low ability" groups, and the differential treatment they receive does not serve them well (Allington, 1983; Hiebert, 1983; Stanovich, 1986). Furthermore, minority students are many times more likely than are mainstream students to be classified as "handicapped" and removed from classroom instruction (Milofsky, 1989), an arrangement that compounds the problem (Allington & McGill-Franzen, 1992).

This differential treatment is compounded by the combined effects of local funding of schools, free enterprise, and the use of standardized tests. Students in lower socioeconomic status schools score, on average, lower than do those in higher socioeconomic status schools. Thus the higher socioeconomic status schools are more appealing to people with the resources to make choices about where they live. Realtors capitalize on this appeal by using test scores as a marketing feature of expensive housing. This situation carries over to the location of light industry, which exacerbates the problem of differential funding.

TESTING: CAUSE AND SYMPTOM

Although research on the consequences of testing practices has barely begun to be taken seriously, the evidence is growing and consistent. Current testing practices clearly have deleterious effects on students, teachers, and the curriculum. These effects are not distributed equally across gender, race, or class. Although intended to improve teaching and learning, testing in many ways accomplishes the reverse. Although intended to improve equity, testing veils the erosion of equity.

It could be argued that the tests themselves are not to blame, that the problem is inappropriate use of reasonable tests. Certainly if the tests were not used, they would not constitute a problem. Nonetheless, as is shown in earlier chapters of this book, the tests themselves do not stand up to close scrutiny.

On the other hand, it might be argued that the tests are problematic but salvageable. Indeed, the major current reaction to the "testing problem" has been to try to build better tests (Shepard, 1989; Wiggins, 1989). It might also be argued that the uses are salvageable, for example, through more rigorous policing of testing practices in high-stakes contexts, but the pervasiveness of the consequences so far documented speak against such simplistic solutions. In any case, tests and their uses are not so easily separated. The beliefs that underlie test construction are the same beliefs that organize their uses (Shepard, 1991). Tests and their uses are bound together by the same set of cultural beliefs (Bellah, Madsen, Sullivan, Swidler, & Tipton, 1985; Schon, 1983). We might perhaps more profitably argue that the problem lies in the cultural beliefs and practices rather than in the tests per se, the tests being merely artifacts.

But the tests are not without blame: They represent the reification of the belief system. A test that offers 10 decoding subtests and one comprehension subtest reflects as well as projects a particular view of literacy, a view of a significant group of people, and once the view is sanctioned by science in the form of a test, the view has the authority to dominate a conversation. Consequently, when school psychologists bring such test scores to a meeting of a Committee on the Handicapped, alternative perspectives are not heard (Mehan, 1984). Worse, however, is that such tests direct instruction toward attempts to repair the subtest pieces, a counterproductive strategy (Allington, 1983; Church & Newman, 1985; Hiebert, 1983).

There are other consequences of the use of standardized reading tests. The format that requires simple right or wrong answers may foster a view of knowledge as the accumulation of right answers from authorities such as teachers and texts. Such a concrete, dualistic view of knowledge is nondialectic and is unlikely to foster inquiry approaches to instruction. Teachers with such attitudes toward knowledge have been shown to be more coercive, less resourceful in their teaching, less empathic to their students, and less encouraging of student independence and responsibility, than are their colleagues with more complex views of knowledge (Koenigs, Fiedler, & DeCharms, 1977; P. Murphy & Brown, 1970). As we continue to research the consequences of testing practices, we find that our efforts to improve education through testing work directly against the necessary conditions for a healthy democracy.

Part IV

Moving Toward Alternatives

In this section, two very different components of assessment are examined to inform reform initiatives. One component involves the perceptions of students, teachers, parents, and administrators about reading. The perceptions of these groups are the untapped mine of information about reading, how it is shaped, and how it is assessed as a social act. These perceptions need to be the basis of any initiatives toward reforming assessment. They start from a different point than do traditional psychometric approaches and, as a result, can lead to new insight.

The other component is miscue analysis. Miscue analysis provides another counterpoint to traditional psychometric approaches to assessment because it is both a transparent and a direct assessment of reading. Its frameworks and structures can inform innovations in assessments.

7

"Evaluation Is All Day, Noticing What Is Happening": Multifaceted Evaluations of Readers

Jane Hansen

University of New Hampshire

If teachers couldn't use tests, what would they do to evaluate their students? What would administrators say about the students in their schools if they couldn't talk about them in terms of test scores? What would parents say? What would students say?

For this chapter I interviewed students, parents, administrators, and teachers to learn about their evaluations of students as readers. I asked the students to tell me about themselves as readers throughout their lives, and I asked the other people for information about these same students and/or others.[1] Not only did

---

[1]I conducted 24 interviews in six sets, with four persons per set. Each of the six sets included a student in Grades 1, 3, 5, 7, 9, or 11. The second person in each set was a parent(s) of the student; the third person was the student's classroom teacher or English teacher or had been the student's English teacher the previous year. The fourth person was an administrator, who might be a principal, an assistant principal, or a department head. I interviewed these people in conference rooms, offices, at the end of a quiet hallway, in a restaurant, in empty classrooms, and in an empty teacher's room.

Each interview was 30 minutes in length, and I recorded my interviewee's words throughout each session. If I got behind, each one waited for me. Each person knew in advance the question(s) I would ask: For students, "Please tell me about yourself as a reader throughout your life"; for parents, "Please tell me about your child as a reader throughout her or his life"; for teachers, "On a daily basis how do you evaluate your students as readers? What is significant to you in what they do and what they say? We aren't going to talk about tests at all. I want to know what you value in regard to your students as readers." For the administrators, "On a daily basis how do you evaluate the students in your school (department) as readers? What is significant to you in the classrooms, at other places in the school, and in conversations? We aren't going to talk about tests at all. I want to know what you value in regard to the students as readers." During an interview, when my interviewee stopped talking, I prompted by asking for more information, usually about something the person had already mentioned.

they seldom mention test scores, but many behaviors they considered important go unrecognized in a test-driven evaluation system. Specifically, when I categorized my data, I found three commonalities that have implications for what we might consider when we evaluate readers and when they evaluate themselves. The three conditions that define readers are:

Readers thrive among other literate persons. Everyone talked about the influences of immediate and extended families, teachers, classmates, the overall school, and the community on the behaviors of readers. Reading was not seen as a singular accomplishment of individuals; various people contribute to readers' prowess. This overall culture is more important than a test score when a description of a reader is sought.

Readers possess individual characteristics. Everyone talked about the behaviors of individual readers. Against the backdrop of others, each reader has unique traits that go unrecognized when test scores are used to identify readers. Tests are not designed to place value on diversity. Instead, everyone is either better or worse than a standard.

Readers invest their emotions in their reading. Everyone talked about the emotional investment of readers. My interviewees used words such as "fervor" and "engagement" to describe important characteristics. This information is not identified by tests, which place no value on the affective domain. A student who hates to read and who never reads can be mistaken for a good reader if he or she has high test scores.

These findings need to be viewed in terms of the focus of this book on the fragile nature of the evidence we have typically used to describe readers. What might we use as less fragile evidence? What evaluation practices might capture the social, individual, and emotional natures of reading as described by these interviewees? Certainly, reading tests are not the answer. The competition that tests value does not promote supportive interaction among readers, an appreciation for diversity, or passion. Nor do tests promote discussion about what to do to improve evaluation processes.

I present my three main findings, with supporting data from the interviews, after a brief context for each of the six readers I interviewed.

Mike, a first grader, lives in North Conway, the town my Grade 7 interviewee and his family referred to when they talked about buying books in its bookstores. North Conway is not a large town, but it is the tourist town of New Hampshire, the hub of outlets and restaurants for the White Mountains. New Hampshire's main source of revenue is tourism, and North

Conway is the center of it. Mike started his story of himself as a reader at home. "My mom reads to me. She sits on my bed on top of my feet!" His sense of humor showed itself on several occasions throughout our interview.

Nicole, a third grader, attends the elementary school in Conway, a small town near North Conway (where Mike lives). The main street of Conway is Highway 16, a major route traveled every weekend by tourists from southern New England on their way north. Conway is busy on Fridays and Sundays, quiet otherwise. Nicole became a reader in second grade and likes to read in her bed, to her little sister, and in her classroom.

Lindsay, in the fifth grade, attends the Oyster River Elementary School in Durham, New Hampshire, the small town dwarfed by the presence of the University of New Hampshire (UNH). She began our interview with these words, "I've got a lot of books that are mine. I've got too many. I'll sell some at a garage sale. *Where the Red Fern Grows* is a really good book. In second grade our teacher read it to us. I've read it a few times since. I've got it at home."

Michael, in Grade 7, attends the middle school in Gorham, New Hampshire, a small town in the north country, the area above the White Mountains. Gorham is a company town; the major employer is, and has been for decades a large lumber–paper mill. A seemingly quiet young man, Michael started our interview with these comments, "I just finished *God's Lost Children*, by Sister Mary Rose McGready. It's about kids whose parents threw them out. They hate their kids. The kids go to Covenant House. People there help them. Some kids sold their bodies on the street to get money. Some went on drugs. Then the Covenant House planned their future, helped them enroll in college, or go to school, and they started to have a life and felt good about themselves. This takes place in New York. They have other Covenant Houses in Fort Lauderdale, Houston, Anchorage, and other places. My grandmother got the book for me at the church she goes to. She got two books. She read one and gave me this one."

Nate, a ninth-grade student, goes to Kennett Junior High in Conway, on the same campus as Nicole's elementary school. Nate is an athletic young man who is very active in both school and recreational sports, such as family soccer, Babe Ruth baseball, snow- and water-skiing. He started his story about himself as a reader in this manner: "I first really got into reading in fourth grade. I started reading *The Hardy Boys*. I really liked those novels. I read every single one. I loved to see what would happen next. I love mysteries." They read mysteries last year in eighth-grade English, and Nate enjoyed them.

Shana, as an 11th grader, attends Exeter High School in Exeter, New Hampshire, where John Irving set his book *A Prayer for Owen Meany*. A small town in southern New Hampshire, Exeter dates back to colonial times, has many stately homes, and is the site of Phillips Academy, a prestigious prep school. Shana, who seemed to be somewhat reserved, appeared comfortable throughout our interview. I introduced myself by telling her that I teach at UNH (20 miles away), and she responded with, "I think I'll go to UNH. I'm interested in children." We conversed a bit more, and then Shana started to talk about her favorite book, *A Prayer for Owen Meany*.

I now present my three main findings via data from my interviews with these students, their parents, teachers, and administrators.

READERS THRIVE
AMONG LITERATE PERSONS

No one becomes a reader or remains so in a vacuum. My interviewees talked about their interactions with various people as they struggled and enjoyed books and magazines. No one talked about themselves or students as readers without bringing in the roles of others. Reading was not seen as a singular accomplishment of individuals; various people contribute to a reader's involvement. This overall culture (Purcell-Gates, 1995) shows the complexity of a reader's behaviors and is more important than a test score when a description of a reader is sought.

After Mike said, "My mom reads to me," I asked him to tell me about a book his mother had recently read to him, and he quipped:

> Some squeezed through mail slots
> Some slipped through open windows
> Some hid in toy cupboards
> Some creeped into bed with lonely children.

What an answer! These lines are from *Ruby*, a book Mike's mother later told me she recently checked out of the town library and read to him twice. When I asked him, Mike did not know the title of the book, but when I asked him to tell me about another book she had read to him, he quoted again, "He opened the window and flew out like the wind." This, he knew, was from *Peter Pan*, a book his mother has "told" to him many times. When Mike talked about himself as a reader he placed himself with others; he did not see himself alone. In school, he pictured himself with his classmates and teacher.

When Mike and I left his classroom for our interview down the hall, I asked him to bring "two books you can read." One was *Little Critters*, and he chose his three favorite pages to read to me, each a funny one. I asked how he had learned to read the book and he said, "The teacher read it to us. We read it on a piece of paper lots of times. We read it all together. Everyone has one."

I asked Mike what he wants to learn to read next and he immediately said, *Goldilocks and the Three Bears*. What will he do to learn how to read it? "Try to read it. Do it again. Ask my mom and my teacher for help." He knew what to do (Moore, 1993; Ohlhausen, & Jepsen, 1992), and knew that learning to read involved mentors he could count on.

Similarly, Nicole talked about her mother, teacher, and friends. She enjoyed the American Girl books, a popular, relatively new series for young girls. "I read at night before I go to bed. I read at school. Sometimes I read on weekends. I just finished *Samantha's Surprise*. I've read lots of them in school. It was in the book order so I wanted to get it....Sometimes I read two chapters a day and sometimes one. In *Samantha's Surprise* they were long chapters, like 13 pages." Lots of girls read these books. Publishers and authors have capitalized on the swapping, casual chatter, and common interests of children when they create series.

At the time of our interview Nicole was also reading *The Secret Life of the Underwear Champ*, by Betty Miles. "My teacher read it to us last year and I wanted to read it because I liked it. I forgot some of it." The importance of the teacher's reading to the class came up in many of my interviews (Avery, 1993), and the likelihood that students reread the books teachers read to them interests me. I can remember the day when we hid information about books from probable readers because we did not want to "spoil" a book. In none of my interviews did a reader tell about a book's being spoiled because of information known beforehand.

Nicole confirmed this when she talked about learning to read. "My mom read books to me. After she read them to me I read to her. It was fun....The first book I learned to read I kept reading it. I really liked it. It was neat to be able to read it." Now, Nicole performs the task her mother performed with her; she reads to her little sister. "When my mom is cleaning after supper I read the books she got at the library." Books often bring readers together in families.

Michael's grandmother gave him *God's Lost Children*, the book I mentioned earlier, with the strong hunch that he would like it. Michael's father explained why this book about kids who go to Covenant House might have been particularly important to Michael. "He's interested in New York City. He went there 2 years ago with his uncle and saw the Macy's parade." His son's experience with his uncle influenced him as a reader. I heard many stories about family activities (Vogel & Zancanella, 1991) that, when isolated from the overall context of their lives, might sound as if they had nothing to do with reading.

The family connections surrounding this one book continued. As Michael talked about it, he said, "A lot of disabled people, I think, can't read. My uncle is like that. My grandma has taken care of him always. He can only read kindergarten words. He can't walk. He really can't talk. He can only mumble a few words. He can only eat if someone puts it in his hand. If both my grandparents die he won't survive unless he goes to a nursing home." Michael's thoughts about the homeless and Covenant House meandered, and led him to his disabled uncle and nursing homes. This on-task book talk (Newkirk with McLure, 1992) in which readers evaluate their relationships to others shows the influence of reading on the thinking of readers.

Frank, the chair of the English department in which Nate is a student talked about what he does in his teaching to encourage the students to use reading in this manner. "I'm trying to get beyond a teacher-directed class. I want my students to compare what each other found. In *Black Boy* they saw their own broken households. I'm looking to validate their perceptions, to see contrasts and similarities." The students' views of others, their home lives, and their friendships all have a place in the English classroom. Their "whole life" is of value to Frank. To focus on only the "student" or only the "reader" shortchanges the large picture in which students live.

Lindsay's mother talked about the family's influence on Lindsay. "When she was little I worked part time so I was always leaving the other kids notes. She loved to participate in the note writing. She'd answer the phone and write messages: MRE = Marie called. She was so proud of herself. It made her a part of the family. She's the youngest....The other children read to her." Lindsay also learned of the importance of reading from the avid reading behaviors of her parents. In talking about her father, she said he read "all the Civil War series," and her mother explained her own reading habits with these words: "Lindsay was always sitting with me at sporting events. She saw that reading is something to do to not be bored. She reads a wide variety of things."

So do the members of Michael's family. He said, "My mom likes to cook so she reads *Women's World* and *Better Homes and Gardens* magazines." I was impressed that this Grade 7 boy knows the names of his mother's magazines.

She confirmed their interests in magazines. "Dick (Michael's father) and I are not the type to sit down with a book. We're too busy. I enjoy magazines because they're short."

About his dad's magazines, Michael said, "My dad's really into cars. He reads these Corvette magazines. He has a Corvette. One night he flew down to Maryland and drove up with a white 1966 Corvette. That was maybe 4 years ago. He drives it sometimes to Berlin (the next town) and to the Dairy Bar. Sometimes he drives it in parades."

Shana referred to her mother when she talked about herself as a reader. "John Irving is my favorite author, and *A Prayer for Owen Meany* is my favorite book. Mom recommended *Owen Meany*. I made Mrs. Moher (her English teacher the previous year) read it. I like adventure, not science fiction, but I read *Anthem* last year and I liked it! Mrs. Moher got me to read it. Usually I'll read a book recommended to me by someone. In high school the teachers have encouraged me to read what I wanted but encouraged me to read others, also. Mrs. Moher convinced me to read *To Kill a Mockingbird*. I really liked it! *Fade* was good....I read a lot of Stephen King....He has a book of short stories. 'The Mist' was good. In junior high I read *Flowers in the Attic* by V. C. Andrews, and the next two or three. I read basically what everyone talks about."

The influence of friends who are readers can also be a cause of concern, as Lindsay's mother explained. "Many kids in this town are very programmed." They have lessons, clubs, and activities every day after school, in the evenings, and on the weekends. Not only do they not have time for themselves and their families, time to read is not given priority. Lindsay's family, however, is "careful about that." Lindsay explained, "I dropped some things, like swim team. I'm taking basketball, but it's only on Saturdays. Last year we had no homework. This year we have homework, so there's not as much time to read. I still try to read."

Her Grade 5 teacher has tried to keep students' interactions around books alive (O'Neal, 1991) and said, "As far as evaluation (of the students as readers) on a daily basis goes, the big thing is whether their reading...goes someplace. It's for a purpose. The area that's fascinating is what they do with the information. They teach others."

On the day of my interview the students had given the class overviews of what they had done to prepare for their research reports, with an emphasis on the processes they had used so far (Wood & Muth, 1991). Pete, the teacher, explained his reasons for arranging this class session: "I ask them what they think is important in something someone else did, not what I think is important. Having children learn from what each other has done fascinates me." Pete's intern commented at this point, "Pete models children's work from last year instead of listing lots of guidelines."

In addition to sharing ways to organize information, students shared concepts about life. Pete said, "They aren't just going to write about Hopi agriculture and where they got their corn. One student said, 'I'll get into the difference between males and females and I'll get into the spiritual area, the care they have for each other.'...When we look at skills, these kids do so much more than tests show. Respect for mankind isn't on the skill–drill lists. The more students come up with this kind of thinking, the more you use this for modeling and the more good thinking you generate."

As Pete said, "Respect for mankind isn't on the skill–drill lists," and his goals for his students went far beyond the accomplishment of itemized skills. He wanted a "just society," a change in the social order of society (Johnston, 1992; 1993; Shannon, 1992). If this is what many of us value, then a change in assessment schemes is necessary. A careful look at what our evaluations beget is in order.

The principal of Pete's school realized this. She not only supported his particular values, she wanted her teachers to share with each other their goals for their students and the assessment schemes they used to help them accomplish these ideals. She knew what each of her teachers did, but she was concerned that the different instructional and evaluation approaches were not shared among the classrooms. "Two teachers next door to each other might not talk....I want to nurture this. I can suggest to one teacher that she talk to another. Pete, for example. If I ask him about a student, he could tell me a great deal of information but he might have little in writing. Another teacher has a big notebook with a section per child. It includes what they're doing in each subject. It's extensive....Another teacher always walks around with a clipboard, always knows what each student is doing in writing. For her that works. What's important to me is that there are effective ways to document students' progress as readers. The variety is fine with me. The diversity reflects the diversity of the school."

To share with and learn from each other is not only a characteristic of readers, it is based on an underlying principle about learners. They are hungry for knowledge and new ways to do things. Teachers who are learners learn from other teachers; students from other students; students and teachers from each other; readers from readers.

Lindsay had a close relationship with her school librarian, as her mother explained, "Lindsay loves the school library....Last year the librarian recommended books to her, and she and the librarian met once a week to discuss authors. When the librarian told her she was leaving, Lindsay said, 'Will the new librarian be as nice as you? Will you tell her about me?'" This librarian has written (Jenks & Roberts, 1990) about the collaboration among herself, readers, and a teacher in her school. The value placed on the school library is an often-overlooked element in the evaluation of a school's reading program. In a school of readers, a library with a reader-librarian is the center. She suggested books, and the children did likewise. She readily admitted and appreciated that they expand her repertoire. These adults and students were readers who knew each other and took each other personally into consideration when they offered books. These teachers valued diversity among their students (Rief, 1991) and fostered it with book recommendations.

READERS POSSESS
INDIVIDUAL CHARACTERISTICS

Everyone talked about the differences among people and the importance of honoring their particular interests and culture. Each reader has a unique life story (Wolf & Heath, 1992), which is given no value when test scores are used to identify readers. Tests are not designed to show the details of rich, individual differences; they devalue diversity. Instead, everyone is simply above or below a standard. Rather than setting up a system where all educators, families, and students constantly search to establish strengths from which each person can grow, tests automatically place some readers in the bottom quartile.

Mike's mother confirmed his uniqueness, "He approaches reading much different than his sisters. What I've had to do with Mike is be an actor to get him involved. I have to put a lot of excitement into books to let him know, 'This is a whole experience here. You can get into it.' The author may use a lot of words but I paraphrase it so I don't lose his attention. If an author knew, he'd probably not like it, but it's necessary. You don't want to lose them."

"You don't want to lose them." To keep the children interested is the challenge. Children do not want to get lost, and no one wants to lose them. Sandy Ashnault, Mike's first grade teacher, watched him carefully. For evaluation, she said, "I watch and listen all day. I take notes....I have reading conferences. This morning a boy read 'green' for 'grass,' but he figured it out. I asked, 'How did you figure that out?' He said, 'He's up here in the grass.' I want them to know their strategies. They have reading folders and record sheets. The records are kept by the children and their buddies."

"They have buddies in Grades 3 and 6," an increasingly common practice in elementary schools (Segel, 1990). She continued, "I've read them some books several times, so they all have something they can read to their buddies. I keep the ones I read to them separate so they can find them more easily. It's easier to read if you've heard it before. ... I walk around during buddy time. It's a 60-minute miracle. I evaluate all day long. I know more about my students as readers than tests can ever show." As she collected information about individual readers and the strategies they used, she was on the lookout for the energy of each child.

Nate liked Stephen King. He read *Cujo*, and saw the movie, but "liked the book better. The movie went too fast." Nate's father was not so sure about Stephen King, but it was important to him to have his son read. Nate's academic history has caused some worry. In elementary school his grades were not always the best. "We attribute this to his study habits, his lack of motivation toward academics. ... We always have to remind him, 'Do you have homework tonight?' ... It's difficult to set up a study schedule at home because every other week I work days and every other week, nights. It makes it difficult for him. ... Now from 7:00 to 8:30 we have no TV or music in the house. It's homework time. ... We'll see if we can enforce it."

Stories of their children's difficulties surfaced in many parents' comments. Nicole's mother said, "I think I started to read to her when she was 2 weeks old, not because she understood it, but to relax her. When she got older, I continued to read to her at bedtime to relax her....In kindergarten they wanted to hold her in transition instead of Grade 1 because she was shy. I had the final decision. I let her get into first grade. I think they thought she'd have a hard time because she'd sit back and listen. That was a hard decision. I didn't want to push her.

"In first grade she wasn't too keen on reading. She didn't take time out for it. She was too busy. She didn't take to it as much as I thought she would. In second grade she had a wonderful teacher who pushed her more. She encouraged her to take time out for books. Now she's interested. She reads every night. She gets to watch one show. I don't watch TV and I tell them to read. I'll get a book or magazine. I'm reading all the pregnancy books I can get my hands on. In school this year they pick out their books."

Norma Alexander, Nicole's teacher, explained her classroom procedure. "Every day they have silent reading from books of their choice, and they record that reading. I save those sheets for parent conferences. They're a good tool for me. They show whether the child is reading lots of easy books, what their interests are, and whether they finish books. It's good to record what they read. After they read on their own, they write in their journal. They retell, write something they learned, ask a question, or write what it reminded them of. That's good evaluation information for me, what they get out of their books. They write about these books and the ones I choose in the same journal."

She kept records of what the children said in conferences with her and what they said when they shared books with the class. "They like to go off in threes or fours to share their reading. They love to do that. That's harder to evaluate. I go around from group to group." She traveled among the groups with her clipboard and recorded what she heard and saw. She wanted her children to interact closely, to learn from each other (Glover, 1993).

"Evaluation is all day, noticing what's happening....All of this is a little different from the basal tests I used to use! I have some in my drawer. My first year teaching reading without the basal I still used the tests." Now she no longer did, but she constantly evaluated her students and herself as she tried to create a better and better environment for reading. "Every year I do something different."

She told me about the new "continuum" the teachers created during the previous summer to document each student's growth in reading skills. "The parents want documentation. We had to rethink everything this summer. We met at various teachers' houses...talked a lot, swam, and ate! This continuum is something I'm thinking of when I teach reading." They created items such as Relates story to personal experience, Asks for help when does not know a word, and Understands verbs. "It's helpful for us teachers when a parent comes in. I talked about it when parents came in for Open House so they know we're thinking about this. We had a few vocal parents who said we threw the skills out, some skeptics."

The teachers in this school needed to be strong and to support each other as they insisted on the preservation of each child's complexity in this new continuum (Hoffman, 1991). If not used carefully, it could show which children were not as proficient as others, rather than place value on the individual histories of each child as she or he became a reader.

Their principal fostered each student's uniqueness as she meandered throughout her building. "The other day a child was reading *The Witch of Blackbird Pond*, and I said I didn't like it. The student was so surprised....I not only didn't like it, but I said so....They learn that not all adults agree about a book."

This principal read children's literature and could strike up a conversation about lots of titles. She was a reader in the eyes of the students in her school. They knew what she read and what she thought of these books (Graves, 1990). Her individuality as a reader came through, and they knew she placed value on what they thought of the books they chose to read.

Similarly, Lindsay's principal valued the students as evaluators. "I want children reflecting on their own reading, talking about their own reading...bringing their own experiences to their reading...making choices, taking risks about new kinds of reading, and writing about their reading. I think of reading as a part of the fabric of the school, acknowledged and affirmed in every way possible." Evaluation, from this perspective, is a time for a reader to take stock, to become articulate about what he or she can do, what he or she has accomplished, and what he or she might do.

All the readers I interviewed could do this (Greenwood, 1992; Short & Kauffman, 1993). Lindsay saw potential in herself as a reader (Hansen, 1994), but her life as a reader had not been perfect. "I used to not finish my books. I'd start one and find one I liked better. I had a pile this high." Then, her third-grade teacher put her foot down. Lindsay had to finish most of the books she chose to read. "Now I'm used to reading the whole book, and it seems a lot better. I usually read the whole book. Usually I read it pretty fast."

Lindsay's mother, however, was not convinced of the completeness of Lindsay's evaluations, her teacher's, or her own as a parent. Her worries may be similar to those of the parents in Nicole's school, as noted earlier in this chapter. She said, "They have no report cards at Lindsay's school. They learn to read from trade books. They do say she's reading on a certain level. It makes you a bit nervous to not have benchmarks. When my other children were younger, I checked into their achievement test scores. This year was the first time I've ever checked into Lindsay's. I got the scores from the guidance counselor. They were not as high as I predicted because she reads so much.

"Her vocabulary scores were especially low. As I recall, the other kids' scores went up and down. I don't know. Maybe it's just that one test last spring....She has an excellent speaking vocabulary when I listen to her talk with her friends....Her comprehension wasn't that good, which surprised me. She's easily distracted. Maybe she didn't concentrate....She read some difficult material on Seminole Indians and picked it apart for social studies this year....She had language arts scores, too. They were very bad in word analysis. I've seen her approach words when we go to museums and plays.

She has lots of good skills. Before kindergarten she was reading the Little Bear books....The counselor gave me an example. She and I couldn't come up with the right answer on the test!...So then I didn't feel bad. I have mixed feelings about the testing." Lindsay's mother got anxious and wanted additional information, but the tests contradicted what she knew about her daughter. The tests showed an individual's ability to perform on specific tasks in relation to other students. The test scores tended to negate the complex stories of readers.

Michael described the various aspects of himself as a reader. "My sister is in Grade 3. She really likes to read. I was never the kind of kid like my sister who really loves to read. I usually like to watch TV. I have a subscription to *Garfield* magazine. I also read Garfield comic books. They're one of my favorite kinds of books. When I was a kid I didn't want to read."

Michael's mother confirmed this. "When he was really little, Michael wouldn't sit still. Before bed I'd read bedtime stories, which he liked. We'd relax. He'd enjoy the bedtime story because he could stay up later. He never wanted to sit down and pick up books till he was much older. He wanted to be creative with his hands. He liked paints and wood. He has a good imagination."

Michael told a similar story. "I started reading more after second grade. I sort of liked reading some books but not the books the teacher picked. In Grades 3 to 6 we started reading books of our choice, but usually we read books as a class. I didn't like that. Some teacher made us read *Anne of Green Gables*, which I'd never have picked, and *The Secrets of NIMH*. I'd never have picked it, either. I didn't like all the comprehension questions. I don't like it much when we have to read a book and do these comprehension questions. Nobody does." Michael's concerns reflect those of educators. We must be careful not to use old teaching techniques, such as comprehension questions with literature (Silvey, 1989). The last thing we want to do is dampen students' enthusiasm for good books.

Michael continued, "Mrs. Jensen (his present teacher) lets us choose our own books." Michael appreciated being able to choose what he read and not having questions to answer about the literature, but it was difficult for Michael to find books he liked. His mother said, "The school library doesn't have many books, and in the town library they (her children) don't find many books they like. In school they get book club order forms. I order books they like. The book clubs are cheaper than the bookstore. When we go to North Conway (the town where Mike lives, 30 miles on the other side of the mountains, the closest town with good bookstores), I buy a book of their choice, but with three kids that's expensive." Michael concurred with his mother: "I don't really go and get books at the library. They don't have books I like. They've just opened a minilibrary here at school. The town library really doesn't have anything, either. I usually get my books from the book club or bookstore. Also, kids swap. A kid said after I'm done with this one he wants to read it." The book Michael referred to is *The Face on the Milk Carton*, by Caroline Cooney. The book reflects the caring and social awareness (Garrison, 1990) that I heard expressed earlier when Michael talked about *God's Lost Children*.

Kids swapped books. Books became a currency for relationships, friendships, common interests. Michael's current teacher and his new principal believed that these junior high students could become readers, and wanted them to become so. It was hard, though, even with a principal who read. As he said, "I am an avid reader. I read all the time. I can't tell you how important it is in the age of media for kids to read. Reading makes us think. TV puts us into a catatonic state, but when I came up to the north country, to keep in touch, I put a fortune into cable." Without cable television, he got one channel. With cable, which everyone in the north country has, he had access to the world.

The menu of possibilities presented by cable television influences the pastimes of the people in a community. The overall culture in which a school is located, and in which readers live certainly influences who they are as readers (Heath, 1983). A town faced with the decision to spend its money on cable or books may very well choose cable. The department chair in Conway was aware of students' ho-hum attitudes toward reading. He enticed his students by giving them some choices in what they read, but choice was not enough. He wanted his students to make personal connections to what they read. "That's evaluation: what connections they make." These connections challenged the students to think about what they valued (Simon, 1992), showed them the role reading can play in their lives, and kept them reading.

When his class read *Black Boy*, he asked them to write about the "basic insight the author is trying to make. I put them in groups of four. They exchanged papers." Various students had chosen different insights, and Frank stressed the necessity of that. He told them, "It comes out of your own context....There are different themes, depending on the reader." He listed their different themes on the board and said, "These come out of looking at the book from different points of view. All themes are fine. None are wrong." His belief is similar to a growing number of professionals in his field (Robertson, 1990), including Shana's English teacher.

When Terry Moher went to college, many aspects of instruction differed from what she does now. "I went to a Jesuit institution. All of my classes were lectures. I never expressed a thought of my own, only repeated back what they'd said." Now, she structures her classroom so that her students express thoughts of their own.

"When we read *To Kill a Mockingbird*, I asked them for one line or word that tells what the book is about. We listed them on the board, and I asked which one was right. They laughed, 'They all are!'...I didn't have to tell them whether their themes were valid. They knew their own themes were valid." Her students had to figure out what each book was about (Lewis, 1993), as opposed to listening to her tell them in a lecture what a book means.

A belief in the idiosyncrasies of readers was not held by large numbers of educators in our profession several years ago. When they were students, many present-day teachers were not expected to analyze what they read, and teachers did not learn in their teacher education programs to seek multiple interpretations. Now these teachers have to learn as they go. They take classes, attend workshops, and read to challenge themselves, to extend what they know about the teaching of reading.

The vice principal of Exeter High School, a former English teacher for 17 years, explained the use of literature in their English Department. "It's not so important what the students read, but how the teacher relates it to their world. There's a prescribed reading list with some flexibility." Then what sounded like a contradictory message came through. "The departments give common final exams. All teachers had better be teaching the same thing. Regardless of who's teaching a class, if the title of the class is the same as a class another teacher is teaching, they all teach the same thing. If the materials the various teachers use are totally different, then when students talk, some teachers will be seen as good and others as bad. That's one reason for the attempt to standardize the curriculum."

This double message reflected what I learned in Nicole's and Lindsay's earlier interviews. It was extremely difficult to find value in the different ways teachers, parents, school districts, and students responded to situations (Harman, 1991). In some instances in my interviews, worldviews matched those of tests, where difference, rather than being seen as evidence of individuals with a myriad of assets, is viewed as either better than or worse than. Difference is not valued, not sought. Evaluation is not a search for strengths; it is a process used to sort the chaff from the grain. This view, however, is changing, as some of my interviews showed.

This emergent thinking rests firmly on much research and common sense that underscore the complexity of lives and diversity of thought in readers (Willinsky, 1991). When teachers value this richness, they help students appreciate each other and gain confidence in themselves; these basic skills are not fostered in test-driven curricula.

Terry Moher told this story about a student who was inspired by her diversity-driven curriculum to become a reader. Terry has learned that choice is essential for her students to become readers. "This one student is reading *Black Boy*. I asked him, 'How's *Black Boy* coming?' 'Fine.' 'Have you ever finished a book before?' 'No, but I will this one.' Then I encouraged him to think of what he'll read next."

Other teachers often confirmed Terry's belief in book choice as a behavior of readers. When she gave workshops and taught in the UNH Summer Writing Program, she regularly asked teachers, "What are the characteristics of a reader?" In their answers, "Choice always comes up."

None of the readers I interviewed preferred to be told what to read. They all referred to books of their choice as important indicators in their stories about themselves as readers. I heard excitement about Stephen King, *Owen Meany*, *Garfield*, *Peter Pan*, The American Girl Series, and Carolyn Haywood, the author of the most significant book in Lindsay's life. Her most exciting experience as a reader was "When I finished my first chapter book. I knew, 'Now I can read chapter books.' It was the beginning of my reading chapter books. I read *B Is for Betsy*."

READERS INVEST THEIR EMOTIONS
IN THEIR READING

Everyone talked about the significance of the affective domain. My interviewees considered themselves readers when they started to like to read. To simply know the skills was not enough, and the skills often did not come without a desire. Teachers, schools, and families provided overall atmospheres in which reading was exciting, and in these contexts readers emerged and thrived. At the same time, negative settings contributed to uninvolvement, which often led to displeasure with reading. All my interviewees considered uninvolved students to be capable and attributed any lack of success to factors that caused a student not to be attached to reading.

When Mike's principal talked about what he valued for the readers in his school, he stated that he wanted the students to enjoy reading. His primary guiding question was, "Is there evidence of enthusiasm?" Readers do not simply comprehend books. "I do a lot of informal observation. In rooms I ask kids who are reading, 'What's it about?' I'll know very soon if they're really engaged or just waiting for the next activity to occur. You know quickly whether students are engaged purposefully.

"Student attitudes are important. It's happened here. Kids like to read more than they used to. Children choose their books. Learning isn't linear. We used to put some of them in an awkward situation with materials they couldn't read, and then they started to think poorly of themselves. Now teachers say, 'The children read a lot.' I hear parents say, 'You wouldn't believe how much my child reads at home.' The library's circulation has increased each year in the last 2 years."

This principal placed value on the reading of real books, as did the children, parents, and teachers in his school. He became even more convinced of his beliefs as he listened to himself talk about the positive changes he saw in the children in his school. In his excitement, he could not restrain himself. He had to mention tests, as some of my other interviewees did, even though I opened these interviews by saying, "We aren't going to talk about tests at all."

Tests bothered this principal a great deal. The fundamental values the tests rest on are at odds with the forces that help children become readers. "I have to say this. Until the college professors withdraw support for standardized tests, we won't make the impact we need to." I gulp, but I know I have withdrawn my support.

Lindsay's principal talked about the library as a gauge of students' interest. "They had a book swap last week to exchange paperbacks. I brought in 15. The exciting part for the new librarian was listening to children talk to each other about the books. 'This one was exciting. This one was awful.' They showed interest in books, enthusiasm. The library was crowded all week. I'm interested in how many books are being taken out of the library." The use of the library as a barometer of the reading in a school is an underused assessment tool.

In Nicole's school the librarian and the teachers recently received a grant to buy books for integrated units, as a way for the children to work together and learn from each other. The principal told me that one Grade 4 class had pen pals in Tucson as part of their unit. Some students in the class were doing research on New Hampshire to send information to Arizona. "Groups of children have different assignments" so that children found work of interest to them. "That's what we're all about, trying to get children excited."

Shana knew the importance of her excitement about what she read and talked about this in relation to history. She felt no emotional tie to the people in the text. "I have trouble reading history books. They're boring. I don't care about history. I have trouble remembering it....We read *Huck Finn* in English class. I learned so much about how people got along with slaves. And you can learn about how people are now. That book was banned in some places. I think that's ridiculous....In history they tell you, and you may hear it. But when you read a book (not a textbook), you know it."

Her mother added, "In social studies a few years ago, Shana was having an awful time. It was going over her head. We read it together. I don't think it was the reading. It was the book and the questions." It seems that Shana and her mother sensed the difference between an aesthetic and an efferent response (Rosenblatt, 1978). Shana realized the importance of stories to help her understand our nation; questions based on non-narrative information distanced her from people's lives.

Questions seldom elicit an emotional response from students. It is possible to answer them correctly, but not become involved; to remain aloof from a book is not to read it. When Michael talked about *God's Lost Children*, I could tell by the expression on his face and the information he shared that he had not only read it, but had experienced it. Michael's teacher confirmed this: "I confer with my students after each book they read. Even if I haven't read the book I can tell if they read it. I can tell by the details they use and the emotion in their voice." Emotion and involvement were themes that arose throughout these interviews.

Michael's teacher continued, "What's significant to me is how they relate to the characters in the book. Their emotional response is significant, particularly at this age level....Kids this age get lots of bad publicity," and it is important that the community realizes that they can be "so motivated to read." Test scores never tell the community this information. Scores tell only whether Michael answered the questions correctly, questions we know he does not value. Reading tests cannot tell the story of this junior high student who is now motivated to read.

Chris Fleming, Nate's English teacher when he was in eighth grade, said, "The most important thing is that...I want them to enjoy reading." Nate's enjoyment showed when he talked in great detail (more than one full page of single-spaced notes) about "The Most Dangerous Game," a short story his class read this year. "I liked it a lot. It was very interesting. It was one of the most interesting short stories I'd read. I really liked it." As he talked about it, his pace accelerated: "The General smokes his cigar, smiles, and looks halfway up the tree. He blows smoke up at Whitney. I'm freaking out at this point when I'm reading. I wonder what he's going to do next....I loved that story."

His father confirmed Nate's interest. He asked Nate about his reading: "When he's involved in a short story for class he enjoys, he'll relate, freely articulate what he's read."

Nate's involvement in his reading and other schoolwork came from an emotional state more than from a rational level. He did not work for the sake of doing well, as many students do. His father explained, "He's capable if he's interested, if he's motivated by the teacher. In Grade 7 he did very well in French. In Grade 8 he didn't like the teacher and got a D. This year he's in Spanish even though if he hadn't switched languages he would be finished in 2 years. He's getting all As. He thinks Spanish and his teacher are great. He loves it!"

Nate's grades told part of his story, but we needed this additional information about Nate's attitude toward his classes before the grades made sense. When we record only scores, we tell students the larger picture does not count. As preparation for life and citizenship, I wonder what we teach students when the letters A, B, C, D, or F receive more attention than the story of who the student is.

Shana's story of herself as a reader started years ago. "I started to read by myself at 4. I read Dr. Seuss and Golden books. My favorite was about a little puppy....At the one elementary school I attended they didn't have us read much...but at the other one I went to they always had us read. I read all the Judy Blume books, and I read *Bridge to Terrabithia*. I've always liked to read. I liked *The Chronicles of Narnia. The Lion, the Witch, and the Wardrobe* was my favorite."

As the principal of Nicole's school said, "Reading in the school is working when there's an aura. It's as difficult to define as trying to define a smell. In trying to define it, we alter it in some way. Unless the readers of your chapter, Jane, have felt it, they won't know what you're talking about....The fervor for reading is something you feel."

A good book begets emotion; an emotional investment is a characteristic of readers, of learners. People inherently want to learn. They want to find value and meaning in their lives, in what they do (Himley & Carini, 1991). Evaluation is a search for value in our work, in ourselves, in others. To flatten the power of reading, not to value the emotions it arouses, to assess a reader with a number, violates the core of a reader's soul.

8

Toward Reform: Lessons From Miscue Analysis

Standardized tests have not been the only vehicles used to assess reading. Teachers in classrooms have long developed their own sets of practices. As argued in chapters 5 and 6, these practices have been influenced by standardized tests principally because of the credence given to tests by those who overextended their uses so that performance on tests had significant implications. If standardized tests inscribe reading narrowly, with a definition of reading that does not involve much reading of connected discourse, and if the tasks on the tests do not hold up to fundamental design assumptions, then we must look to other measures to garner insight into more profitable directions for assessment. One such instrument is miscue analysis.

Miscue analysis is useful for a variety of reasons. First, miscue has a 30-year history of use to draw on,[1] unlike some other assessment reforms. Miscue analysis has been the subject of numerous studies and has been used in many contexts. Each of these experiences offers new insights, which have sometimes led to revision of the procedure or have added new interpretive lenses from which to view reading. Miscue analysis is thus a form of evidence about reading that can build on precedents.

Second, miscue analysis uses the idea of directness in assessment. A valid criticism of standardized multiple-choice testing is that it is an indirect form of assessment. The assumption that the samples of reading gathered in such assessments generalize to other areas of reading is fundamental in most tests of reading. Miscue analysis is a more grounded procedure, in which inferences about the reading of a text are made in relation to the text.

Third, miscue analysis developed out of the movement toward a more complex understanding of cognitive processes, and this understanding has fueled the critique of testing from within psychology. Consequently, some of the underpinnings of the critique are represented in its design. For

---

[1]For insight into the scope and depth of writing on miscue analysis, see Brown, Goodman, & Marek (1996).

instance, the design resists simplified or eclectic descriptions of the reader but favors those built out of a theoretical conception of reading.

Finally, the validity and reliability of miscue analysis have been extensively documented (see S. Murphy, in press). This documentation can be achieved only through a history of use. Even though the documentation may raise some questions about aspects of the procedure of miscue analysis, it can also provide insights for those who wish to formulate new evidentiary arguments in the drive toward assessment reform. Before turning to the ways in which miscue analysis can inform reform, a brief background to miscue analysis is provided.

A BRIEF BACKGROUND ON MISCUE ANALYSIS

Miscue analysis is an oral reading observational tool. Oral reading observation and its accompanying error analysis have long been used, formally and informally, as a form of instructional practice and assessment (Allington, 1984). At its most basic, an oral reading assessment requires that a student read a text aloud while the examiner makes annotations of the differences between the text as read and the text as written.[2] Early reading theorists, caught up in the drive toward establishing a science of education, not only put their energies into developing "quick and cheap" standardized tests but also attempted to incorporate some of the principles behind standardized tests into oral reading analysis. Procedures for gathering oral reading samples moved toward standardization; passages to be read were ranked in order of difficulty and were assigned grade levels. Gray's *Standardized Oral Reading Paragraphs*, published in 1915, was the first measure to use graded passages (Allington, 1984). Gray's test also included error analysis guidelines and norms. Payne (1930) went on to develop a classification system for word recognition errors derived from children's reading of the Gray Oral Reading Paragraphs. These early efforts were soon followed by others. Weber (1968) reviewed many of the different oral reading analysis systems that came into being in the first two thirds of the 20th century. Typically, in these oral reading analysis systems, examinees were to read the passages and then to answer questions asked by an examiner. These "comprehension questions" focused on elements such as the identification of characters, plot, story

---

[2]One popular test form developed over the past half century is referred to as the informal reading inventory.

details, and theme. In the review of individualized measures presented in chapter 4, the Gilmore represents an example of this kind of oral reading analysis scheme.

Oral reading analysis tools have appealed to educators because they are a more direct assessment of reading than standardized tests. They are much like the work that is being done in classrooms, and the evidence they provide about reading is similar to the evidence that teachers have to rely on in their day-to-day assessments. The popularity of oral reading analysis tools is such that instruments like the Gilmore continue to be used even in the early 1990s (Steele & Meredith, 1991) when their norms are over 20 years old. Yet, according to Allington (1984) little research was ever conducted on these instruments. In fact, Allington described these measures as psychometric and theoretical failures. Allington characterized these instruments as having a fair amount of relative consistency in classifying errors as omissions (of sounds or words), additions (of sounds or words), substitutions, mispronunciations, repetitions, self-corrections, word-aided hesitations, and punctuation omissions;[3] a view of errors as something to be eliminated even in the face of evidence that error patterns differ across grade levels; a belief in word-perfect reading as the only acceptable reading performance; a lack of supportive validity argumentation for the constructs of independent, instructional, and frustration levels proposed by Betts in 1946; and an absence of any adequate criteria indicating that placement in one text for instructional purposes is better than placement in some others. These critiques of the quasi-standardized oral reading analysis schemes have provided early hints about the hybridization of assessment schemes from different backgrounds.

Nevertheless, it was through a study of oral reading errors that, in the mid-1960s, Goodman (1982/1965) proposed that oral reading errors were really miscues—that is, they were not errors as such.[4] This view of oral reading was different in that it moved beyond simple description and cataloguing of oral reading behavior and sketched an interpretive framework. Drawing on the burgeoning research in child language development that had been fueled by the theories of Chomsky (K. S. Goodman, 1982/1967),

---

[3]It should be noted that in some of these schemes, the categories began to be used for interpretation rather than observation. For instance, mispronunciation errors could include what amounts to counting dialect against the reader. Similarly, hesitations were counted as errors in some systems. The observation that there was a hesitation became clouded with the interpretation that to hesitate was an inappropriate response to a text. This idea relates to Allington's (1984) observation about the tendency for these tests to assume that error-free reading was the only acceptable reading performance.

[4]At about the same time that Goodman was developing his theory, Marie Clay (1991) developed a somewhat similar conceptualization in New Zealand. In Clay's system, the observational and interpretive annotation systems are not separated as they are in miscue analysis.

Goodman proposed that readers used a variety of cuing systems (graphophonic, syntactic, and semantic) and strategies (initiating, predicting, confirming, terminating) when reading words in context. The term miscue did not merely mean that a reader had departed from the text but that departure could be accounted for in terms of the interface of the strategies and cuing systems in relation to the printed text.[5] This view represented a considerable departure from oral reading analysis schemes of the past and provided the kernel from which current reform initiatives can be informed.

THE DISTINCTION BETWEEN DESCRIPTION AND INTERPRETATION

With the desire for direct assessment of reading, more and more elements of assessment will likely be based on classroom observation or the collection of assessment artifacts (see chap. 9). As an observation-based instrument, miscue analysis offers a working example of the use of such an instrument for assessment.

One of the distinguishing characteristics of miscue analysis in comparison to other methods of reading assessment was the manner in which it separated the descriptive system for miscues from the interpretive system.[6] In miscue analysis, an annotation system provides a written description of the reader's oral reading. With this annotation system, someone trained in miscue analysis procedures can generate a rough approximation of the reading.[7] Although some additional categories were used, the descriptive system is much like oral reading error analysis systems of the past in terms of the categories assigned to descriptions of reading behavior—omissions, substitutions, insertions, repetitions, corrections (unsuccessful, successful, and abandoning of a successful reading), dialect, misarticulations, split syllables, intonation shifts, repeated miscues, and complex miscues. In

---

[5]Miscue then does not denote an error. Instead, it signifies that the textual information presented was used differently than might have been anticipated because of the way in which the reader used particular strategies and textual cues.

[6]I recognize that in a way it is impossible to separate description from interpretation. By using a language system that categorizes in particular ways, an interpretive system is automatically invoked. Additionally, the seeming neutrality of descriptive systems is itself an interpretive stance. Despite these drawbacks, I think that the idea of a descriptive system as separate from an interpretive system is useful in thinking about miscue analysis because one describes observable reading behaviors with a fairly definitive set of categories and the other allows for inferences to be made on the basis of the description.

[7]One feature that is not well described is intonation. See S. Murphy (in press) for a discussion of intonation in miscue analysis.

many other systems of oral reading analysis, the annotation system was then turned into a means of counting the number of individual words read incorrectly. In some cases in these other systems, results were reported by descriptive category (e.g., 3 omissions, 2 insertions). In effect, in these systems, the descriptive system was turned into an interpretive system because the manner of reporting highlighted that reading was no more than word identification. The task of the teacher, presumably, would be to get children not to omit or insert words and to identify all words correctly.

In miscue analysis, the descriptive system became the basis for considering the strategies and cuing systems that the reader used while reading. In other words, the raw data were then coded in an effort to determine their meaning. Miscues involving the reader's normal speech patterns (e.g., dialect or misarticulation miscues) were not coded. Additional procedures governed which miscues were coded (see K. S. Goodman & Burke, 1982/1973; Y. M. Goodman, Watson, & Burke, 1987). On the basis of an analysis of the use of language cues (graphophonic, syntactic, and semantic) and strategies (predicting, confirming), patterns of reading were identified. The significance of the separation of the descriptive and interpretive systems has not always been recognized by those conducting research into miscue analysis (see S. Murphy, in press, for a discussion). This oversight emphasizes all the more the reason for a consideration of this distinction in moving toward assessment reform.

The goal in attempting to separate the descriptive system from the interpretive system is not so much to make the basis of the evaluation objective. It is doubtful that any evaluation can be objective because value is at its core and valuing is fundamentally a subjective act. Instead, the objective of the description–interpretation distinction is to make the basis of evaluation transparent. Transparency demands that interpretations be defensible and tied to data. The system of description need not be like that of miscue analysis (in fact some assessment reforms use miscue analysis or a variation of it as a component), but, as Darling-Hammond, Ancess, and Falk (1995) noted in one of their school studies, evaluators take a new perspective on evaluation and interpretation when they must tie their judgments to data.

THE NEED FOR EVOLUTION
AND GRADUAL DEVELOPMENT

Miscue analysis is based on the study of readers engaged in the act of reading (K. S. Goodman, 1994). Miscue analysis did not emerge fully formed in the mind of Ken Goodman; it took a number of years to develop, and the theory that is informed by it has continued to evolve (e.g., K. S. Goodman 1985/1984, 1994; K. S. Goodman & Burke, 1968, 1973; K. S. Goodman & Goodman, 1978). As the emphasis has shifted from assessment in which the items used have a sketchy background at best and bear but a cursory relation to the curriculum in any one setting to assessment that is tightly linked to the activities of classrooms, space must be made for the new assessment to grow, shift, and refine itself. These new assessments are theories in the making, theories of literacy for individual students.

In examining miscue analysis, for example, its earliest versions contained the basic category systems still used in versions of miscue analysis today (e.g., Y. M. Goodman et al., 1987). The descriptive system remained relatively invariant across the 30 years of its use.[8] The system that changed was the interpretive (coding) system. The changes in this system were informed by successive encounters with readers, a refining of the system, and by increasing demands for creating coding systems that would be workable in the classroom. As a consequence, one can find the Goodman taxonomy (Goodman & Burke, 1973, 1982/1973) with 18 possible coding categories for miscues and up to 9 distinctions in each coding category; the Y. M. Goodman and Burke (1972) early version for classroom teachers contained 9 possible coding categories for each miscue with up to 3 declinations in each coding category; Procedure IV in the most recent version of miscue analysis (Y. M. Goodman et al., 1987) contains one question for each sentence read and only two distinctions in this category.

Expectancies that observationally based or interpretive systems should emerge fully formed into the world of assessment are simplistic. Miscue analysis indicates that it takes time to refine systems of interpretation so that they can account for different uses of the observational system and so that the system itself is reflexive. It cycles back onto itself to improve and move forward. In the most negative sense, this view of assessment could be taken to mean that we are trying out assessments on students. In one sense we are, in the same way that for years we tried out standardized assessments on children, but in those cases, the technologies of numbers, inferences that seemed to be derived mysteriously, and confidentiality of test procedures

---

[8]A few changes were made. For instance, the 1972 version annotated the text with an A in a circle to denote repetition of the text, and a line was drawn under the repeated portion of the text (Y. M. Goodman & Burke, 1972), while the 1987 version used an R in a circle. The difference is that the A in the earlier version stood for anticipating whereas the R in the later version stood for repetition. The second marking is a further step toward ensuring that the marking system is descriptive rather than interpretive.

left us willing to suppress our curiosities, worries, and tensions. If we can maintain the distinction between description and observation so that our assessments are transparent, any worries about the manner in which assessments are being conducted should be allayed.

THE PROS AND CONS OF HYBRIDIZATION

In its early published form for teachers (see Y. M. Goodman & Burke, 1972), miscue analysis represented a hybrid approach to assessment. The initial kit, for example, contained a booklet with hierarchically ranked stories that could be used for assessment. In other words, it built on the familiarity of the old oral reading approaches with their collections of graded passages even though the stories in this early form of miscue analysis for teachers were lengthier than those typically found in other oral reading assessments. This early version of miscue analysis also introduced procedures for examining proportions of miscue patterns to talk about reading proficiency. Although not quite the same as other oral reading analysis procedures, these procedures were, among other things, a deliberate attempt to use quantification, the currency of general assessment, so that teachers would be able to talk about numbers in their discussions with other reading professionals (Y. M. Goodman, personal communication). In essence, the quantification of patterns allowed teachers to "talk the talk" about what was deemed important in school assessment circles. Thus the miscue analysis of 1972, like some of the current reform initiatives, was a bit of a hybrid: It took on some of the characteristics of the procedures and processes to which it was a counterpoint. The hybridization of miscue analysis also reflected the simple nature of the development of a new scheme—building on the old to some extent, but forging ahead with the new.

What was the net result of this hybridization? First, miscue analysis was not dismissed as an assessment project, although it did bear some criticism from those associated with other assessment paradigms (e.g., Groff, 1980). The sound theoretical and research base combined with the hybridization probably eased miscue analysis into the mainstream so that it became a descriptor in the Educational Resources Information Center (ERIC) database. The term *miscue analysis* grew so widespread that it was often used without citation of its originator. Hybridization also seemed to serve as a transitional device. In the revisions to miscue analysis for teachers produced in 1987 by Y. M. Goodman, Watson, and Burke, the fact that the patterns relating to quantification were dropped was not discussed. Numbers still played a part, but the part they played is much more interpretive than procedural. In other words, there are not simple rules to follow. Instead, interpreters of miscues must look at inter-relationships and particularities within the miscue data in relation to the percentages calculated for each coding category. Interestingly, the changes did not meet with criticism. Instead, it appeared that the shifting assessment climate and the hybridization of the earlier version had gradually prepared miscue users for these changes.

Hybridization appears to offer the benefits of a tutorial device for those who are still learning about alternative forms of assessment. On the other hand, it does place in partial jeopardy the theoretical purity of the assessment form. If, however, theoretical purity results in the dismissal of the form, then the whole point of the construction of the alternative assessment form is lost.

ASSESSMENT AS A SOCIAL CONSTRUCT

Miscue analysis as an assessment system made transparent both the manner of collecting data and the means of interpretation. Like many of the new assessment reform initiatives, it was not a great secret that one had to have particular credentials to read about or purchase. Instead, as miscue analysis developed, its proponents published what they discovered, and miscue analysis moved from the private domain of assessment developers into the public domain of other teachers and researchers.

The effect of the availability of miscue analysis was that other researchers and teachers tried it out, examined its use in varied contexts, and played with different configurations of the coding categories and interpretive system (see, for example, Bean, 1979; Cunningham, 1984; Pappas, Kiefer, & Levstik, 1990; Siegel, 1979; Tortelli, 1976). The availability of miscue analysis demonstrated what standardized assessment had hidden, that assessment is a social construct—it is used by people who obtain their own insights, share those insights, revise, and try again.

Assessment is modified as different uses are found for it. Because miscue analysis was derived in research contexts, miscue analysis needed to change to answer questions for the classroom teacher. Several of the versions of miscue analysis noted earlier set out to accomplish such a task. Indeed, both the Y. M. Goodman and Burke (1972) and the Y. M. Goodman et al. (1987)

miscue analysis procedures were attempts to make miscue analysis more "teacher friendly" while retaining the insights that could be gained from miscue analysis procedures.

These adaptations made to miscue analysis demonstrated that assessment is socially constructed. There is not a finite assessment or a perfect and infallible assessment. To think so is to be deluded. Instead, assessment is merely people working collectively and individually to try to describe what is valued.

THE IMPORTANCE
OF SITUATIONAL SPECIFICITY

In studies of the validity and reliability of miscue analysis (see S. Murphy, in press), miscue analysis has repeatedly highlighted the situational specificity of reading knowledge. That is, the performances of readers are intertwined with the genre of the text being read, the reader's knowledge of the content in the text, the reader's familiarity with the specific text (i.e., the number of times the text has been read previously by the reader), the number of pictures in the text and their relation to the written text, the length of the text, and the linguistic features used in the text. The knowledge that reading contains a situationally specific element suggests the limitations of measures that produce a definitive report about reading. But this fact also indicates the scope and depth of insight that can be gained from using measures that present a textured view of reading, a view that focuses on the strategies that a reader might use in different textual situations.

Many of the assessment reforms in reading are like miscue analysis in that they too are situationally specific. They examine the reader's strategies and knowledge in different contexts under different conditions. If inferences are made about general aspects of reading performance, they are made based on the reader's performance in varied contexts. The inferences clearly are inferences rather than definitive statements, but they are inferences tied to the varied data collected.

RECOGNIZING LIMITATIONS

The final lesson that miscue analysis can offer current reform initiatives is that all assessments have their limitations. For instance, miscue analysis is an oral reading assessment procedure. Although it correlates well with silent reading procedures (see S. Murphy, in press), it still remains an oral reading procedure and is limited by the peculiarities that oral reading is wont to create.

The limitations of miscue analysis as a reading assessment procedure were not lost on its originator. When Ken Goodman wrote about miscue analysis in 1973, he talked about miscues as "windows on the reading process" (K. S. Goodman, 1982/1973, p. 93). He and Yetta Goodman (1978) later went on to acknowledge that the full reading process is not revealed through observable behavior. For instance, in their discussion of correction, they noted that "all correction is not overt. Readers may correct silently, satisfying themselves with no overt correction" (K. S. Goodman & Goodman, 1978, p. 4.31). Perhaps the most fundamental lesson of miscue analysis is that all assessments have limitations and all assessments are but windows on the complexities of literacy learning. We always need to augment our assessments by peering in through the other windows that varied assessments allow.

Part V

Reform Initiatives

In this section, I consider current reform initiatives in terms of the tasks they use, the assumptions underlying these tasks, and the relation between these tasks and traditional psychometric measurements. I consider the potential perils that continue to plague assessment as it is used to play out high-stakes games in the name of education when matters like finance and power are at stake.

Finally, I consider what matters. At the heart of the assessment of reading is a vision of schooling. We need to think of what education means for us to truly come to terms with assessment at all levels. We need to consider how we build on what we know and what kinds of assessments are needed to truly build an educated citizenry who are prepared to speak when it is unpopular to speak, to read and analyze propaganda and fact, and to mold the social institutions of the future.

9

Reforms in Assessment:
Perils and Possibilities

Since the mid- to late-1980s, a groundswell of support has emerged for alternatives to traditional, standardized norm-referenced multiple-choice testing. Given energy, perhaps, by the Lake Wobegon fiasco, by repeated indictments from both the curriculum and educational psychology branches of educational study, and by teachers' questioning of the wasted time spent on multiple-choice tests, new forms of educational assessment have found room to grow and, in some quarters, flourish. The efforts in analyzing these reforms add to the discussion of evidence in reading because the reforms provide a different answer to the question of "What constitutes evidence of reading?"

Critics of these newly emerging challenges to what reading (indeed schooling) is all about have tended to speak from the vantage point of security, from the seeming solid ground of the culture of a multiple-choice, standardized, and norm-referenced past. They often have poked and prodded at challenges to old ways by asking cloaked versions of the question, "Why aren't these measures perfect?" while failing to acknowledge that nothing can be perfect, that developing a new culture of assessment takes time, and that their own ideas about testing have been challenged, to some extent, and are no longer sufficient. Yet, those developing these new measures can learn something from their predecessors by honing and distinguishing their arguments about what constitutes evidence of reading.

THE SURGE OF REFORM IN ASSESSMENT

Evidence for the surge of reform in assessment can be found in many places. In the past 3½ years alone, the Educational Resources Information Center (ERIC) database listed 1,000 articles[1] on authentic assessment, perfor-

---

[1]This search spans the period of 1992 to June 1996. The breakdown is 175 performance-based assessment, 533 portfolio assessment, and 407 authentic assessment. The combined total is 1,005. If the terms *portfolio* and *assessment*, *authentic* and *assessment*, and *performance* and *assessment* are used, a total of 1,332 citations exist. This search was conducted using the Win SPIRS 2.0 database.

mance-based assessment, and portfolios.[2] A perusal of the catalogues of
most major educational publications reveals a proliferation of recent books
about assessment reform.[3] Numerous initiatives have been planned or are
already underway at the state level in several states.[4] In one way or another,
all these efforts are attempts to answer the question, "What constitutes
evidence of reading?"

Characteristics of Authentic, Performance-Based, and Portfolio Assessment

In some senses, it is easier to describe reform initiatives in terms of what
they are not than of what they are. They are usually not multiple choice in
format, although sometimes statewide initiatives retain a multiple-choice
component.[5] Broadly speaking, the three terms most associated with reform
initiatives in assessment are *authentic, performance based,* and *portfolio.* These

---

[2]Examples include Darling-Hammond et al. (1995); Gough (1993); Koretz, Stecher, Klein, & McCaffrey (1994); Moss et al. (1992); Stiggins (1987); Valencia, Hiebert, & Afflerbach (1994).

[3]Examples of such publications include the following: Anthony, Johnson, Mickelson, & Preece (1991); Barrs, Ellis, Hester, & Thomas (1988); Belanoff & Dickson (1991); Bennett & Ward (1993); Black, Daiker, Sommers, & Stygall (1994); Byrd, Goodman & Goodman (1992); Darling-Hammond et al. (1995); Education Department of South Australia (1991); Goodman, Goodman, & Hood (1989); Griffin, Smith, & Burrill (1995); Holland, Bloome, & Solsken (1994); Jervis (1996); Johnston (1992); R. Murphy & Torrance (1988); Roderick (1991); Taylor (1993); Tierney, Carter, & Desai (1991); Valencia, Hiebert, & Afflerbach (1994); Wiggins (1993).

[4]Examples of documents referring to the need for reform in assessment or documenting the states involved in assessment reform include Bond, Freidman, & Vander Ploeg (1993), Consortium for Policy Research in Education (1993), Educational Testing Service (1993), House Committee on Education and Labor (1993), Kolanowski (1993), Linn (1991), Moody (1991), Rebarber (1991), Traiman (1993), and Zinser (1994).

[5]It is difficult to say why some reform initiatives retain a multiple-choice component. In part, I suspect it is because those associated with multiple-choice formats continue to advocate them. In addition, I suspect that it is the fear of going forward without a fallback position. And finally, I suspect that multiple-choice approaches to assessment are so embedded into the culture of schooling and issues of schooling's accountability to the public that it takes some time to excavate them from school culture. A further irony to reform initiatives is that, despite criticism about the evidentiary and consequential arguments of multiple-choice measures, many new initiatives seem to be put in a position of arguing for the validity of these new measures by correlating them to performance on the older measures—and so there is a danger of reforms being crumbled by the stranglehold on the system of large-scale multiple-choice standardized testing.

Bond et al. (1993) provided an overview of initiatives in educational assessment. They noted that although only 29 states had mandated students' assessment programs in 1980, the figure had grown to 46 by 1992. Seventeen states reported using performance assessments, and six used portfolios, while four (Arizona, California, Kentucky, and New Mexico) reported using both. Even so, they reported that, with a few exceptions, these initiatives are extensions of existing programs rather than replacements, and most states have indicated that they are continuing to use criterion-referenced or norm-referenced tests.

terms are neither mutually exclusive nor hierarchically ordered. They have been discussed and defined in varying ways by many different writers (e.g., Brandt, 1991; Gough, 1993; Pearson, 1994). The following general characterizations can be made about the context for the emergence of these terms and the intent that undergirds them.

Authentic, performance-based, and portfolio assessment were as counterpoints to features of traditional forms of assessment. The term authentic assessment has arisen as a contrast to standardized assessment forms that appeared antiseptic and disconnected to any reality but that of a particular culture of assessment with its roots in the days of early experimental psychology. As noted by Shannon and Johnston (see chaps. 5 and 6), these earlier assessments intruded on the reality of the classroom and bore little resemblance to the realities of the social world outside schools. The use of the term *authentic* in relation to assessment reform attempts to capture an assessment form that is located in the realities of either school activities or extraschool (sometimes referred to as real-world) activities.[6]

Performance assessment emphasizes a process assessment that occurs in situ, during a performance. To understand the concept behind performance assessment it is useful to think about a performance-based discipline such as dance or theater. In these disciplines, a judgment of ability is not made by exercises or written tests from which one would have to infer dance or theatrical ability; the judgment is based on observation of an actual dance or theatrical production. In practice in schools, science, for instance, is assessed not by paper and pencil tasks but through observation of a student's

---

[6]In many assessments termed as authentic, it appears that there is a certain amount of ambivalence about exactly what reality the authenticity is meant to embrace. Authenticity as imagined in classrooms also involves a particular visioning of classrooms that goes beyond traditional content-coverage activity into inquiry-driven engagements. But authenticity is also conceived of as bearing some kind of mirrored relation to real-world literacy engagements. Both these conceptualizations have their problems.

If authenticity remains in relation to schools, then the next question is what kinds of schools are envisioned. Typically, the schools envisioned in discussions about authenticity in reform refer to progressive schools, schools that privilege inquiry, reflection, collaboration, and self-regulation. These schools are organized around a liberal arts focus rather than a functionalist focus.

If authenticity remains in relation to real-world engagements, it becomes an open question as to how far schools should mirror society. Society is, after all, diverse. For instance, reading and writing engagements of participants in society can range from minimal to extensive. What relation do occupational literacy and business interests play in determining the engagements of students in classrooms? Is this education one that focuses on producing an active citizenry? Or are the kinds of activities really personal— completing forms, reading for pleasure, reading for information, and so on? Does implementing writing process programs in our classrooms mirror what writers who write for a living do?

It may be that we need an integrated school- and societal-based view of authenticity—one that allows learners to explore the limits of their literacy, whether or not that literacy mirrors society, while importing some daily living concerns of the literate person in society.

engagement with a scientific problem in the manner a scientist would deal with the problem. Paper and pencil may be a part of the task but only insofar as they would be part of a scientist's daily activity. In reading, performance assessment could involve everything from observing participation in a book study group, to analysis of reports of material read, to observation of oral reading events. The overlap between performance and authentic assessment can occur when the tasks and behaviors documented deal with real-world activities as they are occurring in their natural environment or in simulations of this environment.

Portfolio assessment emphasizes the form rather than the process of assessment, even though most writers assume a particular process informs this type of assessment. The artist's portfolio is at the root of this concept of assessment. In the artist's portfolio are self-selected pieces that represent an aspect or aspects of the artist's work. Selection often occurs in relation to the purpose or audience for the display of the portfolio. Two assumptions undergird the artist's portfolio: that there is a more extensive collection of work underlying the portfolio, and that the artist has the ability to select appropriate pieces in relation to a specific purpose. As the concept of portfolios is emerging in the educational literature, there has been considerable variation in both these assumptions. Some portfolio assessments have teachers choosing the pieces to be included (e.g., Koretz, 1992), whereas others have encouraged students to be active participants in the selection of materials (e.g., Snider, Lima, & DeVito, 1994). Some uses of portfolios have specified the nature of the pieces to be included (e.g., Saylor & Overton, 1993), while others are more open to diversity in the collection (e.g., Taylor, 1990b), and others contain a mix of both (e.g., Valencia & Place, 1994). Some uses of portfolios, whether for local or state assessment, include holistic numerical or categorical scales, while others may or may not rely on student–parent–teacher conferencing and discussion (e.g., Darling-Hammond, Ancess, & Falk, 1995; Jervis, 1996).

Although the terms *authentic*, *performance-based*, and *portfolio assessment*, sometimes appear interchangeably in the educational literature, an authentic assessment need not be a performance assessment, which in turn need not be a portfolio assessment. For instance, an unemployment insurance form that has been completed could be an example of one type of literacy that is not examined in the process of its production and need not be part of a larger portfolio of work but yet is vital and authentic to someone applying for unemployment benefits. This example highlights the possibility of the distinctiveness of the concepts; but, other examples indicate that in some implementations these assessments might not even share the core feature of narrowing the gap between the nature of what is assessed and the inferences drawn about reading ability. A portfolio that contains mostly worksheets or a student performance on a spelling test is an example of performances that occur nowhere but in school. These possibilities suggest that assessment reform is not just about collecting data about literacy in a different way. Assessment reform, for some, is also about the reformation of schooling. This reformation adds a new dimension to any consideration of "What constitutes evidence of reading?" because it implicates the acts of reading in classrooms as part of the answer to the question.

Features of Tasks Used in Reform Initiatives in Reading Assessment

The tasks used in reform initiatives in reading are one kind of evidence of reading ability. In general, except for some of the large-scale[7] reading initiatives that continue to include multiple-choice items, tasks used in reform initiatives tend to be ones that occur in the daily routine of particular classes, the inferred prototypical activities of daily living, or some simulation of either or both of these. Examples of tasks that occur in the daily routine of the classroom include reading texts, responding to texts, discussions, and journal keeping. These tasks have as their underpinning the assumption that it is important to society that graduates of school have a broad education in literature, arts, mathematics, and sciences, regardless of future employment destinations. These tasks of the liberal arts classroom are not especially set up for an assessment. Instead, the assessment must draw from the life of the classroom. For instance, students in literature discussion groups may form the basis for considering reader response in one class; in another class, written literature response logs may be the way that students and teachers work through their response to literature.

Tasks that are categorized as typical activities of daily living may or may not be intrusive into the daily life of the classroom. For instance, if students live in an urban setting, then it might be part of the routine of regular class outings that they read the bus schedule if they are taking a field trip on public

---

[7]By large-scale initiatives, I refer to assessments that are designed to be administered to large groups such as a sample of the students across the state or the nation. By small-scale initiatives, I refer to samples of students in small jurisdictions such as the school district level. The assumption embedded in this distinction is that small-scale initiatives stand a better chance of being designed to consider local contextual issues. For example, portfolio assessments that operate at the state level very likely cannot account for local contextual issues (such as the teaching of a particular skill) as well as can those developed at a school or even a district level.

transit. In some instances, curricular demands combined with the local context may make some prototypical activities of daily living impossible to enact for genuine purposes. In such cases, simulations might occur, and these would form the basis of the assessment. The tasks involve oral reading performances; self-documentation of reading; written, photographed, or dramatically enacted responses to reading; and observational notes of reading made by the reader or someone else. Specific exemplars of the documentation[8] of tasks are presented in Table 9.1.

These types of documentation focus on the cues (graphophonic, syntactic, semantic) and strategies (sampling, predicting, inferring, confirming) readers use in the process of reading rather than on measuring discrete skills and inferring that the skills relate to reading. Additionally, these types of documentation expand on the idea of comprehension so that it involves reconstructing, responding to, or interpreting a text rather than merely answering questions about a text. The variety of genres read is treated as something to record keep (except in some of the large-scale assessments in which genre becomes a method for deciding on text prompts around which students answer questions [e.g., Weiss, 1994]). Attitude toward reading in general or toward the material read plays some part in some assessments as does documentation of metacognitive knowledge about reading.

Neither the tasks nor the data collected as a result of the tasks are what make up any assessment. Fundamentally, an assessment is an interpretation. The interpretive motifs that have been implemented for reform assessment initiatives are varied and sometimes appear internally contradictory; but they are the early efforts toward effecting new models of assessment. Unlike their standardized multiple-choice counterparts, these approaches have usually actively involved teachers in analyzing the results of any assessment;[9] but there is considerable variation in the ways teacher knowledge is utilized.

---

[8]The very fact that such documentation is being done, when it might not be done in the "natural" situations, is one circumstance that demands consideration. The situations themselves may be somehow changed as a result of all of this documentation. Such a change might alter the behavior under observation. Additionally, the purpose of the documentation must also be considered. The culture of schools has demanded documentation of performance of academic tasks but it is, in some senses, the artifice of schooling that some reform initiatives are attempting to escape. The ambivalence of some reform initiatives in this regard is understandable (e.g., Darling-Hammond et al., 1995), but the lack of recognition in others demands attention.

[9]This is not to say that teachers cannot be involved in the analysis or interpretation of large-scale multiple-choice standardized tests. Once test administration occurs, the next task is to scan answer sheets into a machine, a task usually conducted in a centralized location. The output of a computer analysis typically presents raw score and standardized score derivative information, and the teacher's task is to interpret these scores to parents. In assessment reform initiatives, teachers are actively involved in examining answers to questions and determining what they mean in terms of literacy behaviors. The way in which the teacher's knowledge is drawn on is qualitatively different.

TABLE 9.1

Examples of Reading Assessment Documentation

Focal Aspect	Documentation	Examples of Use
Cue use and reading strategies	Miscue analysis (with audio tape)	Bembridge, 1994; Goodman, Watson, & Burke, 1987
	Running record	Au, 1994
	Oral cloze	Griffin, Smith, & Burrill, 1995; Johnston, 1992
Response to reading, interpretation, and understanding	Written responses to questions and prompts	Garcia & Verville, 1994; Johnston, 1992; Weiss, 1994
	Essays	Darling-Hammond et al., 1995
	Response journals	Anthony, Johnson, Mickelson, & Preece, 1991; Griffin et al., 1995; Johnston, 1992; Valencia & Place, 1994
	Book reports	Anthony et al., 1991; Valencia & Place, 1994
	Drawings and photos	Darling-Hammond et al., 1995
	Observational notes	Anthony et al., 1991; Au, 1994; Hancock, Turbill, & Cambourne, 1994; Hansen, 1994; Johnston, 1992
	Self-assessments	Anthony et al., 1991
	Oral and written retellings	Bembridge, 1994; Y. M. Goodman et al., 1987; Griffin et al., 1995; Valencia & Place
	Project folders	Griffin et al., 1995
Breadth of reading	Booklists and logbooks	Anthony et al., 1991; Au, 1994; Darling-Hammond et al., 1995; Griffin et al., 1995; Snider, Lima, & DeVito, 1994; Valencia & Place, 1994
	Nonschool reading artifacts	Hansen, 1994
Awareness of reading process	Reflections on process	Darling-Hammond et al., 1995; Snider et al., 1994; Valencia & Place, 1994
	Retrospective miscue analysis	Y. M. Goodman & Marek, 1996
	Notes on student or parent interviews	Anthony et al., 1991; Darling-Hammond et al., 1995; Griffin et al., 1995
Attitudes toward reading	Observational notes	Anthony et al., 1991; Au, 1994; Darling-Hammond et al., 1995; Griffin et al., 1995; Hancock et al., 1994; Hansen, 1994; Johnston, 1992
	Notes on student or parent interviews	see previous references
	Reflective/response journals	see previous references
	Logbooks	see previous references

143

As Table 9.2 indicates, the act of interpretation in these new models has tended to be characterized by specific features. The interpretive lens in educational assessment currently appears to be shifting from a psychological to an anthropological stance. As a result, the product of the interpretative act, the role of theory in this act, and the people engaged in the first level of interpretation can differ on the basis of the stance.

In interpretive approaches that take an anthropological stance toward generating an answer to the question, "What constitutes evidence of reading?", the data have typically been gathered from the context of classroom activity. Usually, the teacher is the interpreter of the data, although sometimes small cohorts of teachers team together to make sense of students' work (e.g., Darling-Hammond et al., 1995; Hansen, 1994; Jervis, 1996). Inevitably, like any interpreters, teachers draw on their own background knowledge and experience in interpreting the data before them. In other words, the teachers do not use a list of a priori categories to describe student work; they draw on the work to generate the categories. When small collectives of teachers are involved, interpretations are presented, and either negotiation occurs until consensus is reached, or the divergences are accounted for in the summary of students' work. The product of this approach is either a descriptive overview or a conference in which the data as a whole are considered. Interpretive approaches influenced by an anthropological stance tend to be school- or district-based approaches, while large-scale assessment initiatives remain oriented toward the psychological approach.

In interpretive approaches that take a psychological stance, the data have typically been gathered by injecting into the classroom a set of tasks that were designed specifically for the assessment. Most large-scale reform

TABLE 9.2
Interpretive Stance in Assessment Reform Initiatives

Factors in Interpretation	Anthropological Stance	Hybrid Stance	Psychological Stance
Product of interpretation	Descriptive report	Descriptive and categorical or numerical report	Categorical or numerical report
Role of external theory	Grounded theory[a] approach	Grounded theory and imported theory	Imported theory
Generator(s) of interpretation	Individual or small group	Individual or small group and unknown expert(s)	Unknown expert(s)

[a]The term *grounded theory* was coined by the sociologists Glaser and Strauss (1967) to refer to "the discovery of theory from data" (p. 1). In its usage here, I am trying to signal that ultimately interpreters develop a theory of a child's ability to read in relation to the data they are provided. The theory is only as good as the data.

initiatives in reading have continued to take this approach;[10] but these differ from past approaches in that students engage in prereading experiences, the texts are drawn from children's trade books, and response modes are open ended (e.g., Garcia & Verville, 1994; Kapinus, Collier, & Kruglanski, 1994; Weiss, 1994) and sometimes contain a group collaborative component (e.g., Weiss, 1994). In these approaches, even though teachers are engaged in scoring the assessments, the scoring is typically done in accordance with a prepared rubric. In other words, either numerical or categorical labels indicating students' competencies in relation to the task(s) at hand are assigned to performances. Often these labels have been developed out of a pilot study that also may have involved teachers in ranking and generating scoring criteria and selecting sample pieces as prototypical benchmarks for each category of competence used in the assessment. Although there was a point at which a grounded theory approach to data analysis was used in the creation of the benchmarks, for the "real" assessment, teachers used the theoretical framework implied in the scoring rubrics and benchmark pieces. The product of the assessment sessions was usually a categorical label, a numerical label, or both.

The hybrid stance typically involves situations in which educational workers have blended aspects of the anthropological and psychological stances. For instance, Griffin et al. (1995) and Valencia and Place (1994) gathered multifaceted classroom data, used a rating scale or rubrics built on the work of other classroom teachers, and used both descriptive notes and numerical or categorical labels as the product of their work.

REFORM INITIATIVES AND VALIDITY

Reform efforts can be framed in terms of Messick's (1988) view that validity should include consideration of the evidence for and the consequences of test interpretation and use. Messick's framework is a concept that can be applied even when the assessment tool lacks traditional psychological attributes.

Evidence for Interpretation in New Assessment Initiatives

Reform initiatives have struggled with, and taken seriously, the creation and assembly of tasks that strengthen certain aspects of test interpretation. In

[10]This is not the case for writing. Reform initiatives in several states in the United States either designate the types of samples to be included or invite students and teachers to select samples for inclusion. Although this openness has produced some difficulties in using traditional psychometric approaches to validity and reliability (see, for example, Koretz, 1992, 1994; Koretz, McCaffery, Klein, Bell, & Stecher, 1992), it demonstrates that external testing can depart considerably from traditional formats.

particular, these new assessments have attempted to narrow the gap between generalizing from the test to the real-world situation by using real classroom tasks occurring in the regular routine of the classroom or simulations of real-world tasks. In essence, these initiatives have framed the answer to the question, "What constitutes evidence of reading?" by having people look to real-world activities of reading and use them as the models from which to generate assessment designs. The greater the degree of synchrony and semblance between the real-world activities of reading and reading assessment models, the less fragile is the claim that what is being assessed is the same thing.

On the basis of what one accepts as evidence and what traditions one uses to argue that the evidence is worthwhile, the fragility or strength of assessment reforms is open to interpretation. For instance, many large-scale reform initiatives have tended to stay close to psychological traditions, and the arguments that relate to them draw from these traditions. Alternatively, smaller scale initiatives, which often adapt methods from fields like anthropology, challenge some of the traditional psychological arguments.

The following concerns about assessment reforms are rooted in the evidentiary arguments of psychology especially in relation to the issue of generalizability,[11] that is, whether the inferences made about reading on the basis of these assessments can be generalized to a broader concept of reading.

Differential Exposure to Test Texts. Because many texts used in assessment reforms are sampled from the world of published children's texts rather than constructed for the purposes of the test, some children might have already read them. Others meet these texts for the first time on the test. This differential exposure to texts may unduly advantage some children over others.[12] The concern over undue advantage is such in some quarters that, in 1994, in California, the publication of the name of a text to be included in the state test resulted in that text's being removed from the test (Gladstone, 1994, March 10). Yet it is naive to think that knowledge of texts can be controlled, and Thorndyke's (1977) study demonstrated that exposure to the macrostructure of a text could be an advantage in retelling that text.

---

[11]It is an irony that many of these problematics exist with multiple-choice tests; yet somehow these flaws are presented as much more of a problem for new assessments to the extent that multiple-choice tests are often favored as a kind of litmus test for these newer alternatives.

[12]In such an instance, it would not be surprising that success is positively related to socioeconomic status as availability of books for reading is, in part, an economic condition. Additionally, it should be noted that even minimal exposure to texts has been demonstrated to affect their comprehensibility (see, for example, Thorndyke, 1977).

The episode in California and the work of Thorndyke have also high-lighted the fact that there are many students who have specific or general reading experiences that can advantage them on the test. Some have already read the exact texts without knowing that they were to be included on a test, and others have read texts with similar macrostructures. Can an assessment of reading that operates on the premise of strictly controlling variables ever be adequate for the assumptions governing it?

Fewer but Lengthier Texts.   With the inclusion of published children's trade books in assessments, text excerpts have become longer. As a result, fewer texts are used to sample competence (Pearson, 1994) simply because of the time that lengthy text samples take. Although matrix sampling[13] can be used to compensate for this problem, the pressure to produce scores for every student rather than for a sample of students may make matrix sampling unpopular (e.g., Weiss, 1994). Here again, the idea of a comprehensive sampling appears at the root of this concern. With the variety of genres that can be identified and the stylistic variations of authors, the likelihood of comprehensive sampling in large-scale assessment is low because of the magnitude of the tasks that would result.

Fewer Texts and Ceiling or Floor Effects.   With a reduced number of texts comes the likelihood of ceiling or floor effects in performance (Pearson, 1994). That is, with fewer texts to read, the range of difficulty of the texts used is automatically lessened. Consequently, students of very high or very low proficiencies may not find texts that tap them to their greatest potential.

Fewer Texts and the Restriction of Applicable Background Experiences. The reduction in the number of texts also increases the likelihood that certain background knowledge and cultures may be unduly privileged because of the restricted range. Researchers such as Johnston (1984a) and Langer (1984), among others, have documented the influence of back-ground knowledge on performance in reading.

---

[13]Matrix sampling should not be confused with multitrait–multimethod analysis in which "more than one attribute and more than one method are used in the validation process" (Kerlinger, 1986, p. 424). Matrix sampling is a process in which "each student takes only one version or one part of a total test in any given content area" (Weiss, 1994, p. 214). Matrix sampling allows for a greater variety of types of work to be sampled across the population but means that no individual student will have completed all of the tasks. This type of sampling is intended to provide an overview of the general competencies of children in the state being assessed rather than provide an overview of the work of an individual child.

Unknown Influences in Text Selection.   Practices used in text selection reveal ideological underpinnings and assumptions governing texts. In the California test in which a text was pulled, the governor, Pete Wilson, lobbied to have the decision reversed. Whether his efforts were politically motivated is an open question;[14] but they represent an explicit attempt to affect the material contained in tests and may raise the question of how texts are selected for inclusion on tests.

The Desire for Common Tasks.   Common tasks on which all students can be compared still remain a desire of some large-scale assessments that retain this feature (Peters, 1994). Underlying the common task is the idea that by controlling one source of variability, the task, there is greater likelihood that performance can be attributed to differences in abilities (rather than differences in tasks). Of course, even if the tasks are held in common, the administration of assessments can differ, and the relation between the cultures of the students and texts remains varied.

Response Mode As a Confounding Factor.   For many large-scale assessments, multiple-choice formats have been discarded in favor of written responses (e.g., Weiss, 1994). Writing may take the form of anything from jot notes to short essays. Despite the efforts of assessment developers to ensure that the quality of writing does not interfere with the assessment, the fact that the results of the assessment are open to being influenced by how well a student can write should not be overlooked (Pearson, 1994). The counterargument might be raised that writing is a typical form of classroom response to reading; but because it is often the only form of response on large-scale assessments, its influence on who gets selected into the category of reader because of writing skills means that the test is more of a literacy test than a reading test.

More Publicness for Tasks As a Means of Developing Insight Into Assessment.   The publicness of many of the new large-scale assessment tasks (Pearson, 1994) as they occur in classrooms across several days means that some of the insider knowledge that influenced assessments of the past is gone. Knowledge of the highly specialized task of test taking with its accompanying security around administration practices is being replaced by assessment situations that are more open to public scrutiny and that mimic

---

[14]The story in question was written by Alice Walker, who refused a gubernatorial arts award from the state of California.

real-life reading events rather than correlate with them. Even so, some measures are still open to the general critique of schools and school knowledge as class and culture based (see, for example, Gee, 1990; Mitchell & Weiler, 1991; Woods & Hammersley, 1993). The fundamental question of whose life is being imitated and how these patterns operate to exclude many from high participation in schooling has yet to be tackled in serious and focused ways in new assessments.

Evaluation As Applying an Interpretive Rating. The use of written responses, oral reading samples, and other forms of response in assessment reforms usually means that the act of assessing these artifacts is not like that of standardized multiple-choice tests; it does not require a yes or no response. Instead, panels of assessors are usually convened or teachers are "trained" to do the assessment. Although the assessment teams repeatedly comment on the benefits of the assessment as a professional development exercise (e.g., Weiss, 1994; Wixson, 1994) , a critical question is "What is being accomplished by the training?" In psychometric terms, the training ultimately requires that raters of files achieve a reasonable degree of inter-rater reliability—in other words, that they rate as similarly as possible any data gathered to demonstrate evidence of reading.

Some different perspectives can be brought to bear on this idea. Raters are being trained to "see" the files similarly in the same way that we learn to "see" our world around us through the lens of language, the names we give to things in our culture. In a sense, this move to consensus is a move toward enculturating the file assessors to a particular way of seeing and a particular way of naming. Although the rating schemes or rubrics that are being used to rate files may have been developed by teachers (e.g., Weiss, 1994), the teachers who rate the files are usually different from those who generated the rating scheme or rubrics. Thus the rating scheme is imposed or, one could argue, is like the language of the extant culture—you enter this language world and have to figure out how to use it. An alternative way of thinking about using multiple raters is to consider the information that may be lost by learning to "see" in a single way.[15] Raters might be asked to

---

[15]As an example of how language can determine what we see, one can consider how people's environment often demands that they create ways for naming things that help them relate to their environment. For instance, some people have multiple words for the different colors of green. Similarly, people who live where ice is hazardous may use a variety of phrases (e.g., slush, slab, or pack ice) to describe the ice as the kind of ice in the water can determine accessibility to water routes. Arriving at consensus or being trained in seeing in a particular way means that those doing the training are prepared to be satisfied that information may be lost because of the imposition of a uniform view. Of course, even

pool information and consider the implications of differences rather than strive to eliminate the differences. Moss (1994) suggested this latter approach when she described a hermeneutic approach to reliability.

These issues demonstrate a way of thinking about whether assessment tasks demonstrate the nature of reading in classrooms or in the real world, both in terms of breadth (variety of materials read) and depth (intensity of reading). They echo concerns that assessment of any kind should not become a sorting mechanism that is based on the culture or status that children bring into the classroom; instead, the desire is to have a system that either recognizes differences and somehow accounts for them or at least does not penalize students for who they are. Finally, these issues raise the question of how we know quality when we see it and whether different ways of ascribing quality to performances and artifacts yield more insight.

Yet, assessment reforms have also raised some questions that challenge the traditional psychometric approach to evidentiary arguments. For instance, small-scale assessments that are often characterized by a diversity of artifacts (e.g., audiotapes, photographs, journal entries, and drawings can sit next to miscue analysis coding sheets, observational notes, and literature response logs) require a different way of thinking about evidence. Issues like the trade-offs between the artificiality of a task and the identicality of the task to the domain being assessed must be framed in a way that goes beyond the traditional paralyzing stalemate. The particularity and directness of small-scale assessment of the reading of common tasks forces a different way of thinking about the marshaling of evidence, but these new directions also bring some familiar strengths and weaknesses.

Directness. The strength of the small-scale reform initiatives is their directness. Unlike some of the new large-scale initiatives and the traditional standardized tests, many small-scale assessments are not sets of tasks that require inferencing back to abilities in context. Instead, the abilities are assessed in context. With the advantage of directness in validity argumentation, though, come other issues that call for shifting from the psychometric tradition in validity argumentation.

Variability in Data as a Strength. Variability in assessment data introduces an area of concern in arguing from a traditional psychometric base. In

---

within the uniform view there may be variation. For instance, when the word *table* is said, in each person's mind a prototypical version of that word is evoked, but the images can differ from person to person (e.g., a four-legged pine table, a single pedestal oak table, etc.).

psychology, the use of such multiple methods to capture reading or any other construct is laudable in principle. In fact, it echoes the multitrait–multimethod matrix in which, in part, researchers must find different measures to measure the same construct (Crocker & Algina, 1986). The multitrait–multimethod approach assumes common measures—the same measures for all students. In most small-scale assessment reform initiatives, not only is there variability in terms of the items contained in any one portfolio, often there is variability in the items collected from portfolio to portfolio. Building on the assumption of variability (rather than controlling it) continues to run counter to many large-scale assessment practices. In psychometric terms, task variability introduces competing explanations for differential performances among students. An example of task variability might be a student's differential reading performance as assessed on the basis of a written response versus miscue analysis. Variations in tasks make it difficult to use traditional psychological validity arguments such as reliability statistics. Newer assessment intiatives do not discount the differences or treat them as disparities. Instead, they raise questions like: What insight is to be gained from examining these differential performances? What do these differential performances say about the reader that either one alone does not say?

Newer assessments demand even more of a shift because they ask for consideration of the individual performance in relation to contexts—the contexts of the classroom and its particular culture, the contexts of the school, and the contexts of the community. For instance, as indicated in chapter 7, some classroom contexts allow for the sociality of reading to make itself manifest. In examples provided by Darling-Hammond et al. (1995) and Jervis (1996), it would appear that diversity in student demonstrations of efficacy is typical. Sometimes very broad guidelines govern what the data should demonstrate, and it is expected that there are many different routes toward the guidelines. Darling-Hammond et al. (1995) referred to this situation as "standards without standardization" (p. 22). The particularity of the task is not the goal of educational attainment; instead, the goal is evidence of general skills and knowledge. The individuality in assessment data not only avoids the problem of ceiling and floor effects of large-scale assessments with controls on texts, but it also can be considered revealing of the particular strengths of students. This approach to data analysis and making inferences about the data strongly echoes qualitative research traditions.

Sampling Breadth and Depth.   In the small-scale reform initiatives, sometimes concern has been raised over the evenness of sampling—making sure that a similar number of samples of similar types are collected from each student. Although this approach has some echoes of traditional psychological approaches to assessment, it raises interesting points. First, depth of samples may be as revealing as or more revealing than breadth of samples. For instance, examining how a student closely works with one text over an extended period offers different information than does examining how a student superficially works with several different texts. How sampling breadth and depth are played out largely depend on an interpretive process. The process can either remain relatively constrained or it can take up questions of the complexities of reading and the contexts from which it emerges.

Second, the samples assessed may, in large part, reflect the kind of classroom that students find themselves in—especially when the data become the source of decisions about the student's academic future. The influence of the classroom cannot be expunged from an assessment but must be weighed in it. The material and pedagogical conditions available in classrooms constitute the "opportunity to learn"[16] factor. The opportunity to learn can be addressed only when the local context is well known. This factor must be accounted for in assessments so that students are not penalized for curricular variations.

Selection of Data for Analysis.   The potential pool of data gathered in the course of classroom life can be overwhelming. Consequently, not all data produced by students become the fodder for assessment. Instead, some selection process must be used to make the data manageable. This selection process has important validity implications. For example, much is currently made of ensuring that students participate in choosing samples for inclusion in an assessment process. This choice may be entirely self-directed or may occur in negotiation between teacher and student. Regardless of who makes the choice, the best choices are likely to be made when those doing the selection are fully aware of the criteria used to judge their selections and the implications of these selections. Darling-Hammond et al. (1995) presented

---

[16]The "opportunity to learn" issue is complex and may even be a nonissue depending on how learning is conceptualized. For instance, students may be presented with an opportunity to learn but may not take advantage of it. Students may also be able to perform a skill and yet not have the underlying competence. The work of Ferreiro and Teberosky (1982) offers insight in this regard. Their research, describing the emerging literacy knowledge of young children, explicitly demonstrated that children develop literacy knowledge that is never explicitly taught. Furthermore, these researchers suspected that direct teaching of some aspects of literacy may not just be futile but may be counterproductive to learning if a student is engaged in learning about something for which the direct teaching provides confounding information.

several detailed examples of workable processes in which both these elements come into play. Without knowledgeable choices informed by transparent evaluation criteria, the validity of the data set can be questioned. Perhaps even worse, when those choosing samples for evaluation are not aware of the purposes and stakes involved, they may become implicated in processes that may misportray who they are.

Process and Product. Part of the current rhetoric of portfolio assessment asks teachers to assess both the process and the product. Yet, in writing portfolios, at least, the assessment of process has been problematic. For example, White (1994) argued that the role of drafts in writing folders is difficult to evaluate; if such evaluation were to occur, the consequences of disclosures about the process could ultimately influence writing in a way that constrains writers.

For some areas of reading assessment, the issue of differentiating the assessment of the process and the product of reading is not as problematic as writing. For instance, oral reading miscues (K. S. Goodman, 1982/1973) are considered an "online" indicator of the strategies and cues a reader is using when reading aloud a text. Miscues are acknowledged to be a "window on the reading process" (K. S. Goodman, 1982/1973) and as such reveal only as much as performative oral reading allows. Furthermore, the process of marking miscues is public to the student and bypasses some problems inherent in process writing. Understanding the process of silent reading is more difficult, although there is sufficient evidence to argue for the generalizability of miscue research to silent reading (see S. Murphy, in press) and some evidence to attest to the comparability of reading strategies in a silent reading mode (see Cowie, 1985).

In reading, products are typically viewed as responses that occur after the reading of the text. Products interact with the mode of generating the product. For instance, a reader's ease in discussing a story with an adult may influence the reader's demonstrated competence in an oral retelling. Similarly, if a written response or a recall of text is required, then writing facility interacts with the demonstration of competence in interpretation. If writing is the product mode, then questions such as the stage of the writing (draft or final; process or product) intersect with those of reading.

Products are also framed by the question of "What does it mean to have read a text?" Background knowledge about text structure and content predisposes the reader toward certain readings of the text (R. C. Anderson 1985/1984; Bartlett, 1932; Thorndyke, 1977); products are inherently framed to the extent that a range of possible interpretations of text is not only possible but likely (Rosenblatt, 1994). In addition, because children begin to learn textual interpretive skills very early (Heath, 1983 ; Michaels, 1981, 1983, 1985), the role of how an individual has learned to read a text from within the framework of a particular interpretive community (Fish, 1980) must also be considered. Learning how to recognize the relative contributions of text and reader to a reading is a matter that is beginning to be untangled by reading researchers. Even so, how such contributions play out in an evaluation of reading must be given some consideration by assessors or interpreters.

The process and product dimensions in assessment are artifacts of time and tangibility. The process dimension is typically considered as actions or productions that occur temporally before the generation of what is named an outcome or a final product. The outcome or final product is often bounded by distinct opening and closing markers and can often take the form of a paper-and-pencil product. Yet, the linearity underlying the process and product dimensions is deceptive and masks the recursiveness of intellectual activity. Even though the oral production of words requires a linear progression through the text, thought may shift backward and forward and may reconcile textual, social, and personal elements both in oral reading and in any postreading activity. As a consequence, assessors of portfolios might consider how readers draw from previous texts and experiences in the compilation of readings and postreading activities. In other words, assessors should themselves adopt a recursive stance when judging evidence of reading. They must move between pieces of data to create an interpretation of a student's ability to read. Peter Elbow (1994), in discussing writing portfolios, argued that "when we read a portfolio we get a much stronger sense of contact with the person behind the texts: an author with a life history, a diversity of facets, a combination of strengths and weaknesses, someone who has good days and bad days" (p. 53). This notion suggests that interpreters of data collected using multiple methods and contexts must know the conditions under which data were created so that their interpretations may be both informed and reasoned. Otherwise the validity of their interpretations is suspect.

The Data Interpretation Process.   At the heart of new reform initiatives that are small in scale is the interpretive process. Some processes are guided by a set of common goals, others build consensus, others engage in some kind of aggregative process. Not all the processes are about achieving inter-rater reliability.[17] Instead, the means through which the process is accomplished vary and reflect more of an anthropological approach to ideas of validity and reliability.

The participants in the process are the first consideration. Through the participants the nature of expertise is defined, and the evaluation is partially embodied. Most interpretive processes involve more than one person (though a teacher may choose to engage in his or her own assessment) and focus on building a community of interpreters. Many successful processes involve parents. In this way, as suggested in chapter 7, aspects of background knowledge that might be overlooked by interpretivists can be brought to bear on the problem. In addition, students (not necessarily the student being assessed) are often involved in the process, and this procedure is another step in making transparent the evaluation criteria.

Second, the data interpretation process is usually an open one that makes room for the act of contestation. The seemingly uncontestable forms of interpretation characteristic of traditional standardized assessment gives way to dialogue that crystallizes the essence of validity. As Deborah Meier explained it, "It's an act of judgment. It reminds kids that we're making decisions here. You and me, we're making judgments....You've got to persuade us and we've got to persuade you of our case if we give you an assessment different than you think....The notion that everybody's got to make persuasive cases, they've got to bring in their evidence" (Darling-Hammond et al., 1995, p. 59). This approach to assessment echoes that of Moss's (1994) hermeneutic approach (see chap. 2).

This interpretive approach is more reminiscent of the everyday concept of validation than are the approaches that are rooted in the tradition of psychology. It stresses the fact that assessment is about values and judgments, and it makes these aspects explicit.

Consequences of New Assessments

All talk of assessments is moot unless they are used for some purpose. Assessments can be used for anything from self-awareness to employment. Assessment reform initiatives have covered this range. Because of their newness, studies of the consequences of interpretations of new assessments are scant, but there are some suggestive signs in the existing literature.

---

[17]In fact, it should be noted that large-scale assessment projects that use inter-rater reliability and varied data sets have difficulty achieving acceptable statistical levels (see, for example, Koretz, 1994; Koretz et al., 1992).

High-Stakes Assessment. For large-scale assessments in particular, a
key issue in standardized multiple-choice assessment was the use of these
assessments for high-stakes purposes: The results of the assessment determined issues like student placement, funding, support for districts and
schools, and teacher salaries. The cases of Vermont and Kentucky, states
that developed large-scale assessments in writing, are examples of different
implementations of assessment—one high stakes and one not.

The writing assessments used in Vermont and Kentucky bear a strong
similarity. For instance, in the Kentucky assessment,[18] the writing portfolios
contain a table of contents; a personal narrative; a poem, play or script, or
piece of fiction; a piece of writing the purpose of which is to present or
support an opinion, tell about a problem and its solution, or inform; a
non-English language arts sample; a best piece; a letter to the reviewer
(Saylor & Overton, 1993). In the Vermont assessment, the portfolio contains a table of contents; a best piece; a letter explaining the composition
and selection of the best piece; a poem, short story or personal narration; a
personal response to a book, event, current issue, mathematical problem,
or scientific phenomenon; a prose piece for a non-English language arts area.
Both states have rubrics that govern the assessment of the portfolios, but
the implications of the assessments are significantly different.

Kentucky's assessment reform came about with a significant reform of the
entire educational system as the consequence of a successful litigation in
which the educational system was found to be discriminatory.[19] A period of
intense development followed the decision and culminated in transitional
and reform assessment plans. The transitional assessment plan involved a
test like the National Assessment of Educational Progress (NAEP) test "for
purposes of providing the state with national comparisons" (Kentucky State
Department of Education, 1992, p. 74). A catalogue of certificate revoca-
tion, dismissals, suspensions, along with cases pending is one part of the
outcome of the assessment, but there are additional sanctions and rewards

---

[18]The Kentucky assessment, like most reform initiatives, is a work in progress. The particular items
used have changed somewhat in 1997. For instance, in the spring 1997 assessment, the portfolio
contained six entries—five different pieces and a letter. The pieces were selected in collaboration with
a teacher and should be exemplars of best work. In addition, an on-demand writing task in which students
respond to one of two prompts is part of the assessment. The same scoring guide is used for both the
portfolio and the on-demand assessment. (Personal communication from Sue Rigney, Dvisional Director
for Portfolio Initiatives, Kentucky State Department of Education, April, 1997.)

The general point I want to make in this section is that what is noteworthy is not so much the
particularity of the artifacts but the consequences of their use in two somewhat similar contexts.

[19]See J. L. Smith, Rhodes, & Jensen (1992) for the sequence of events from the time the complaint
was issued in November 1985 to the enactment of law on July 13, 1990.

when both the transitional and reform plans are implemented (Guskey, 1994). The transitional assessment is the beginning step in the development of the Accountability Index (AI).[20] The AI is calculated for the biennium and takes into account, with a five sixths weighting, information from the transitional tests as well as performance-based tests and portfolio scores. The remaining one-sixth is made up of noncognitive factors like attendance rates, retention rates, dropouts, transitions, and the reduction of barriers to learning. Improvement goals are set for each school by calculating the gap between their current AI score and an AI score of 100 at the end of a 20-year period. The required rate of progress is calculated by dividing the differential by 10. Rewards are given to schools that exceed their biennial goal by 1% and sanctions are to be imposed in increasing severity depending on the degree to which goals are not met.

Needless to say, the nature of the stakes in the Kentucky assessment has been criticized. Despite its gestures toward authenticity, its uses appear even more problematic than those outlined for traditional standardized tests. Among the issues raised are the time it takes for teachers to develop strategies to deal with the assessment as previously they worked on multiple-choice strategies; the costs and additional time it takes to track the school-based descriptive information; the fact that students are not held accountable (the assessment uses a matrix approach so that no one student takes all tasks) while teachers and schools are held accountable in the extreme; the fact that schools start at different points on the AI and consequently those who do well now are already at an advantage because they have to make only small improvements to meet their targets; and the need for staff development so that teachers deal with the assessment effectively (Oldham, 1993).

In contrast is the Vermont initiative. Vermont's assessment program began in a different context with differently couched goals: "To provide rich data on student performance; to encourage better teaching and the adaptation of higher standards; to co-exist with Vermont's strong tradition of local control and innovation; and to encourage greater equity of educational opportunity" (Koretz, 1992, p. 7). Educators also had considerable input into the assessment they needed. In fact, attempts to implement a traditional standardized assessment test in 1989 were dropped because of the criticism of educators (Bond, Freidman, & Vander Ploeg, 1993).

---

[20]This description of the Accountability Index is taken from Oldham (1993, pp. 5–10). See also Guskey (1994).

The process imagined by the Vermont State Department of Education was "a long and decentralized process in which committees of teachers, with the help of outside consultants and substantial trial and error, would gradually build the assessment program. Thus...the 'pilot' effort was not a true pilot in the traditional sense of a field test of an already designed program. Rather the pilot was a developmental effort" (Koretz, 1992, p. 7). Although there have been some indications that the state would hold schools accountable for results, the accountability seems qualitatively different from that of Kentucky. For instance, the state indicated it had no intention of using portfolios for the determination of high school exit requirements or class placements (Bond et al., 1993). In short, the Vermont process is much more focused on the collaborative effort of creating assessments that can capture what goes on in schools and classrooms and can be used by teachers for the benefit of students rather than for meeting test requirements. The Vermont assessment initiative recognizes the implications of high-stakes assessment and has said no to them. As Koretz, Stecher, Klein, McCaffrey, and Deibert (1992) argued:

> Programs that hold people accountable for scores on assessments are not self-evaluating. That is, increases in scores on the assessments for which people are held accountable are not sufficient to indicate that the programs are meeting their goals. This fact is now widely recognized in the case of programs using traditional, multiple choice tests, but is no less true of performance-assessment programs. (p. 19)

Clearly, not all jurisdictions accept this argument and the potential for distorting the results of assessment reforms is real.

Assessment as a Tool of Educational Reform

One of the new uses of reformed assessment is derived from the critique of the uses of traditional, standardized assessment, which was accused of being a significant influence on the narrowing of the curriculum and of pedagogical strategies. Consequently, some behind the new reform initiatives have suggested that educational assessment can be used as a tool of pedagogical and curricular reform, while others have been critical of this use of assessment (e.g., Shepard, 1991). What underlies this situation is partly the assumption of high stakes, but there may also be the professional desire of teachers to keep up with innovations.

Once again, the Vermont and Kentucky initiatives provide some insight into whether assessment can be successful in driving reform. In both Vermont and Kentucky, preliminary findings have suggested that reform in assessment can affect reform in instruction. In a study of four rural districts in Kentucky comparing accountable and nonaccountable schools (State Policy Program, 1994), assessment reform appeared to influence instructional reform. Students were being asked to do complex activities, and a new emphasis on writing characterized classroom instruction. Those teachers with the most training and background on writing and portfolio use were the most enthusiastic, but issues such as the time-consuming nature of keeping portfolios proved to be a major complaint.

In Vermont, Lipson, Mekkelsen, Mosenthal, and Daniels (1996)[21] undertook a study of the impact of reform on assessment. Their study did not rely solely on perceptions of teachers and administrators participating in the assessment. Pre- and postassessment questionnaires about teaching beliefs were administered with follow-up interviews of teachers. Their findings provided some evidence for the impact of assessment on reform across a relatively contained timespan, but they noted that Vermont's long history of involvement and professional development in the area of writing paved the way for the assessment reforms. For instance, most teachers already used writing folders as part of their classroom practices. Lipson and her colleagues made the argument that there is much to be said for the professional development of teachers in preparing for reform and reaping any benefits that might accrue.

Affective Effects

Permeating the reports of the critique on standardized assessment are undercurrents of feelings of powerlessness and anger and a sense of distance from the tests. For example, a report by Paris, Lawton, Turner, and Roth (1991) revealed that some students' sense of disengagement is such that they randomly fill in the bubbles of their answer sheets. One consequence of the uses of some small scale-reform initiatives appears to be an enhanced commitment to the project of education. Darling-Hammond et al.'s (1995) study of the reform initiatives in five different schools echoed with the comments of teachers, students, and parents alike on how being involved

---

[21]The description presented is from notes taken at a session presented at the International Reading Association Conference (April 28–May 3, 1996) in New Orleans, LA.

in assessment is an enlightening activity that ultimately makes them more committed to education. The comments from interviewees at the Bronx New School, investigated by Darling-Hammond et al. (1995), are illustrative:

> I learned that parent involvement could be very rewarding—not for the right…to lobby for good evaluation reports about my children, but so I might have the opportunity to help shape the quality of their education, and participate in workshops to learn about a philosophy of education that was different than the one I was raised in. (Einbender, cited in Darling-Hammond et al., 1995, p. 237)

> This is a place where teachers have the opportunity for the kind of support and reflection that they are trying to give to children.…What it takes to do this is to always be observing, always reflecting, always evolving. (Unnamed teacher, cited in Darling-Hammond et al., 1995, p. 244)

VALIDITY AND REFORM INITIATIVES IN SUMMARY

According to Messick (1988), key issues in validation are an assessment that discriminates among those being assessed, that provides results similar to those of other measures of the skill, that takes into consideration the values inherent in it and the values assigned to the test in particular circumstances, that provides evidence for the relevance of what is being assessed, that provides evidence for the usefulness of its results, and that considers the consequences of its uses. These concerns were not well answered by either individualized or group multiple-choice standardized tests of reading.

Reform initiatives have challenged and perpetuated many of the validity problems of large-scale, multiple-choice standardized tests. Direct assessment is a counterpoint to indirect assessment, which broadly samples using a single format and relies considerably on generalizability of the sample to other contexts. Authenticity enhances validity by narrowing the generalization gap between what is assessed and the construct being assessed. Because reform initiatives focus on real classroom literacy events or some facsimile of real-world literacy events, validating these new initiatives by comparing them with other assessments becomes difficult. If standardized tests are inadequate as a way to enhance student performance, as even the head of the Educational Testing service has acknowledged (Grady, 1992), then correlating scores on these measures with reform measures appears illogical.[22] What is the relation of the ratings of literacy in schools to literacy accomplishments in the nonschool world? Rating scales build in a different way of discriminating among those being assessed. In this case, it is not item discrimination indexes that indicate differences among those being assessed but judgments of teachers and others involved in assessments.

Reform initiatives may better answer the question of the values underlying the competencies being assessed if those participating in the assessment represent the interests of the cultures and backgrounds of students. The large question facing those involved in revisioning reading assessment is how to provide an assessment system that does not perpetuate the naturalization[23] of the values of the dominant groups in society and that recognizes the varied knowledge that readers bring to classrooms (see, for example, Fitzpatrick Reardon, Scott, & Verre, 1994). This issue remains difficult. Consider, for instance, a culture that values oral tradition[24] or a culture in which the narrative structure does not match that of middle-class North America[25]—how does an assessment account for these differences and at the same time move students toward practices that differ from their own and are valued by school? Should the school reconsider its objectives in relation to its community context? Much attention in assessment reform has focused on authentic tasks, but there has been less attention on how these tasks interface with the diversities that exist in classrooms. Whose authenticity is being considered? How does the assumption of authenticity work against some groups to the extent that questions about the meaning of authenticity are unbearable and, as a result, are ignored? These are the questions that must face the next set of struggles in assessment reforms.

Because these assessment reforms are located in classrooms, they tend to be intimately tied to teaching. When aspects depart from the work of teachers, such as achieving inter-rater reliability, complaints about the relevance of the task begin (e.g., Stecher & Hamilton, 1994). As noted previously, the directness of the assessment is an argument for its usefulness,

---

[22]I admit that there are plenty of cases where this is done and continues to be done because of the power that standardized tests hold in some assessment circles. I myself have reported studies of test scores that correlate with miscue analysis scores as part of an argument for the validity of miscue analysis (see S. Murphy, in press). However, I did so with expressed doubt over exactly what the correlations signify.

[23]In this usage, naturalization refers to the ways in which dominant ideologies (assumptions, values, and beliefs) "become rationalized as 'common-sense' assumptions about the way things are and the way things should be. A process of naturalization takes place to the extent that people are often no longer aware of the hierarchies and systems which shape their social interaction" (Simpson, 1993, p. 6).

[24]One example of this might be the Appalachian culture described in Purcell-Gates (1995).

[25]The work of Sarah Michaels (1981, 1983, 1985) is one example.

but like any assessment, the ends to which assessments are used are often the purview of others. Reforms like those in Kentucky suggest that the implications of test results are being assigned much more weight than even some of the standardized measures of the past. Somehow, when politicians become involved in assessment, assessment becomes less about assessment and more about power and control.[26] There is no easy answer to these kinds of uses.

In short, reform measures leave some validity concerns unanswered and have answered others, sometimes in ways that the psychometric community may not have anticipated. These steps toward reform are significant because of the relative lethargy that has existed in the assessment industry for much of this century.

---

[26]It would indeed be interesting to set an accountability index for politicians relating their promises to actuality and enacting more severe penalties the further away their promises are from what actually happens. This idea is ludicrous because politicians operate in a social system in which there are many factors impinging on their performance other than their living up to a promise. We need to help our politicians see that schools are in similar circumstances.

10

Toward a Revisioning of Reading Assessment: What Matters?

Two characteristics of assessment reforms shape the emerging answer to what matters in reading assessment. The first is the gathering of data in naturally occurring contexts, and the second is the use of an interpretive process focused on seeing the patterns that exist in the data. Both of these suggest that a qualitative approach to the answer of "What counts as evidence?" is being forged. The evidence is still fragile, but unlike standardized multiple-choice group tests and individualized measures, the practices of the assessment seem to be more in harmony with theorization about assessment and reading.

Assessment reforms have transformed reading assessment from norm-referenced, multiple-choice standardized tests toward a multitask, multicontextual assessment that occurs in natural contexts. Multitask, multicontextual assessment assumes that reading is complex, and, as a consequence, this type of reading assessment attempts to consider reading in all its complexity. Such assessment requires the collection of samples of reading across time, and the temporal factor alone creates new contexts. In addition to the collection of samples across time is the collection of samples across different situations. Situations can include the reading of different genres, reading a text for different purposes (e.g., specific "on-demand" tasks, lengthy investigatory tasks, reading for enjoyment), reading a text on multiple occasions, reading a text to different audiences, responding to a text in multiple modes of representation. Each of these dimensions differentially affects reading.[1]

Because of a focus on authenticity, in a multitask, multicontextual approach, questions of transfer of skills and abilities are bypassed. Instead, new descriptive criteria focus on such things as situated reading strategies (i.e., recognizing, sampling, predicting, inferring, correcting, and confirming

---

[1]See, for example, Golden & Pappas (1990); Guzzetti (1984); Herman (1985); Hood (1982); and Leslie (1980).

163

while reading a particular text under particular circumstances), cue use (i.e., graphophonemic, lexicogrammatic, and semantic-pragmatic cues),[2] and modes of representation of textual interpretation.[3] Key facets considered also include engagement with and response to the text. Both engagement with and response to the text introduce cognitive and affective influences into the assessment process. The demands of the response (e.g., analytical, emotive, synthesizing, reconstructing) combined with the form of the response (e.g., oral, written, artistic, dramatic) are additional influences that must be considered.[4]

The multiple lines of data that exist in multitask, multicontextual assessment become the object of interpretation by individual interpreters or groups of interpreters. The goal of interpretive acts is not to achieve a definitive interpretation but one that is reasonable in light of the data and is situated in a knowledge of both the individual being assessed and the contexts of assessment. There is a recognition of the openness of interpretation to contestation. Examples of similar practices of adjudication and evaluation occur on a daily basis in a variety of institutions. For instance, Moss (1994) pointed out that university hiring committees, like many engaged in hiring practices, review files that resemble portfolios of individuals' work. The committee members interpret the content of such files and debate each other as to the reasonableness of their interpretation of the data. The desire is not to standardize the information received across all applicants although some rudimentary expectations might be articulated. Differences in files are expected. The role of committee members is to debate each other's interpretation of the data; throughout this process of debate, interpretations may shift as the nuances revealed through the discussion become another aid to judging the "portfolio." In hiring committees, the outcome may be the result of consensus or of compromise, but an ethic of fairness is invoked to guide the decision. Once decisions are made, the committee must provide the evidentiary basis for its recommendation to senior administrators at the university.

In essence, then, variability in a file or portfolio is not something to be discounted; rather, it is "an empirical puzzle to be solved by searching for a more comprehensive or elaborated interpretation that explains the inconsistency or articulates the need for additional evidence"(Moss, 1994, p. 8).

---

[2]For research on strategy and cue use, see S. Murphy (in press).

[3]For research on text interpretation, see, for example, Ruddell & Unrau (1994).

[4]For research documenting these influences, see, for example, Golden & Pappas (1990); K. S. Goodman & Burke (1968, 1973); Hansen (chapter 7, this volume); and Menosky (1971).

Consequently, patterns such as differences in the repeated reading of a text would not be a source of reliability problems but would become something to be explained in an overall pattern of a reader's cue and strategy use. Moss et al. (1992) argued that "the validity of the conclusions are warranted in the process of data analysis and the transparency of the evidentiary trail, which allows the reader [i.e., the interpreter of the assessment data] to trace the teacher's arguments" (p. 19).

This revisionist view of assessment and the role of interpretation in assessment places validity at the heart of the assessment process. It compels the interpretive community in such assessments to decide whether the data collected and summarized provide the evidentiary and argumentative basis for the reasonableness of the interpretations drawn from the data. Yet, this ethic is no different from what current tests and measurement theorists articulate as a necessary condition of validity argumentation (see, for example, American Psychological Association, 1985; Joint Committee on Testing Practices, 1988). The shift in the field of reading assessment does not require so much an alteration of the principles of validity as it requires an alteration of the answer to the question "What counts as evidence?"

As suggested in chapter 2, all acts of validation are about more than the provision of evidence. They are about values, the values that a community holds, the values that a community says it is important to have even when the physical evidence points in other directions. This sense of validation leads to what underlies all assessments of reading in school. With an emphasis on qualitative assessment, this sense of validation asks us even more now than before to raise questions like: What do we want of schooling? What are satisfactory experiences for children? What role do we believe schools have in our society? What matters?

Currently there is no end to books debating what matters in education.[5] They are written by business people, politicians, academics; conservatives, liberals, social democrats, eclectics; newspaper journalists, lobbyists, unionists. Each eyes the other suspiciously, but they all are concerned about what matters from their own unique perspectives. What matters is the foundation on which schooling and its ultimate assessment are built.

Schools are, on the one hand, institutional tributes to the conserving forces in society, but they are also places of hope. Society locates its hope

---

[5]Examples include books by people such as the head of IBM, Louis Gerstner, (Gerstner, Semerad, Doyle, & Johnston, 1994), books by academics who served as political advisors at one time (e.g., Ravitch & Vinovksis, 1995); books drawing in politicians and others to write of key educational issues (e.g., Jennings, 1993, 1995a, b), and books by professional academics (e.g., Arnstine, 1995; Levine, Lowe, Peterson, & Tenorio, 1995; Maxcy, 1995; D. C. Paris, 1995).

for the future in its children. As Roger Simon (1992) said, "Hope is the acknowledgement of more openness in a situation than the situation easily reveals"(p. 3). Hope, then, gives us the opportunity to make something of the societal invention of schooling in spite of the self-doubts, superstitions, beliefs, and fears, despite the walls, real or imagined, that exist among the many participants who engage in the life of schools. "Hope," Simon wrote, "is directed toward the future" (p. 79). But hope is not enough. The vision that underlies our schooling practices is the instantiation of this hope, and assessment is the distillation of what this hope is all about.

The conservative historian and critic Diane Ravitch (1995) argued that standardized tests and standardized textbooks were among the key influences in creating an implicit standard in U.S. education. Speaking in support of the current standards movement spawned in part by America 2000 and Goals 2000, Ravitch (1995) takes a content-view of education and argues for standards that identify "what knowledge is of most worth and what knowledge is most valuable to children who will live and work in the twenty-first century" (p. 187). Yet, Ravitch acknowledged the paradox in setting standards in the title of her work—"the search for order and the rejection of conformity" (p. 167).

The philosopher Donald Arnstine (1995) took a different tack. He argued that schools are not really about knowledge at all. Instead, he suggested that *schooling* is about socialization, about learning how to conform to the group, while the result of *education* is independent judgment (p. 13). Arnstine compellingly identified the absence of research on long-term memory of the knowledge that schools are supposed to impart in the knowledge-driven paradigm. He argued that dispositions and skills are the core of education and used reading to exemplify his point:

> But we don't simply "read" in the sense of deciphering or decoding words on a page. We always confront written materials with an aim in mind, and we read in terms of fulfilling that aim. Confronted by a poem or a newspaper editorial, our aims determine whether we'll even start reading, and whether we'll continue to read once we've begun. We read the poem and the editorial in different ways. The poem, for meaning and intrinsic satisfaction; the editorial, critically and judgmentally. Reading isn't the exercise of a skill, nor even the exercise of several skills. It's a complex human activity involving skills and dispositions, and it is governed by aims, intentions, attitudes and understandings. If reading were taught simply as a skill, you might enable a child to decipher words on a page. But if that's all the child could do, you wouldn't [have] called him a "reader" unless you qualified what you meant. (Arnstine, 1995, p. 60)

Arnstine (1995) suggested that we need to rethink standards. After all, he claimed, an education system that is driven by standards does not go far because we try to meet standards while ideals are what we strive for. His discussions located the faddishness of standards for schools in the pragmatics of everyday life. For instance, if we fail to meet the standards in our jobs, we can look elsewhere. If, however, students fail to meet standards, they are sentenced to repeating grades. Few areas of society have such limitations.

If poorly designed and inappropriately used standardized tests are being replaced by new assessments, we need to keep in mind both Ravitch's (1995) idea of order without conformity as well as Arnstine's (1995) ideas of dispositions and ideals. Ultimately, we all recognize that we do not value a culture of identicality, but we also realize that the common good must not give way to total individualism. Our assessments need to address this delicate balance as well. Not only do we need to have standards without standardization, as Darling-Hammond et al. (1995) suggested, we need to have a vision of what it means to be educated. This vision must consider individual and collective diversity not as disparity but as the grounds for considering a different kind of education and a different kind of assessment—an assessment that begins from the premise of the strengths that the diversities in each classroom can bring to the education and, ultimately, the assessment of all children in the classroom.

This view places tremendous responsibility in the hands of teachers. Revisionist forms are not as controlling of classrooms, teachers, or curriculum. They ask teachers to consider "What matters?" In answering this question, teachers, who are now placed in the posture of continuously gathering information about the children they are teaching, must think of their dispositions to education—processes, skills, and knowledge. They must also consider their own positionality with respect to race, language, culture, gender, and class. They must work to develop ways to read the positionality of the children they teach and honor the diversity inherent in their classes.

In some ways, this posture or stance toward evaluation is more complicated and dangerous than any standardized reading test because, depending on how it is done, children may have no moments of solitude, no moments when they feel free from surveillance. But it is not the gathering of information that has changed, as teachers have always gathered such information about the students they teach. What has changed is the value placed on the information and the room given to interpretation. So, even more than ever before, we must continuously remind ourselves of whom evaluation is for. In the practice of education, evaluation is for students. Unfortunately, as

Madaus (1994) pointed out, achievement tests, as they evolved in the United States, were less for teachers and students and more for politicians and bureaucrats. Once assessment is conceptualized as being for the student, then its inevitable focus is on documenting and enhancing the improvement of learning. If evaluation is for someone else, then students are subjected to surveillance. The instrumentality of assessment shifts away from the student and onto the objectives of others. In multitask, multicontextual forms of assessment, it is possible to leave nothing unobserved, nothing uncollected. Problems arise when students are being actively or subtly deceived as to the value of their performances and productions. In such climates, if students perform or engage in selecting pieces for inclusion in folders without a clear idea of the stakes involved, then teachers and administrators are engaging in acts of subterfuge that likely further entrench those who know the privileged discourses of schools and disenfranchise those who do not.

Ultimately, revisioning assessment means a revisioning of schools. For assessment to shift, the curriculum must shift, teachers must change their practices, literacy in special education must be constructed out of the theoretical insights of literacy researchers, the local school community must become an integral part of schooling, and the distribution of resources must be more equitable. This revisioning process is not one that can be mandated. Rather, as Darling-Hammond (1994) suggested, there should be "top-down support for bottom-up reform"(p. 18). In this way the focus is kept on teaching and learning. Darling-Hammond argued that because of the implementation of authentic assessment, "students should actually learn more as a result of assessment, rather than being more precisely classified, and schools should be able to inquire into and improve their practices more intelligently, rather than being more rigidly ranked" (p. 18). In such a vision, assessment resists bureaucratic and political uses while maintaining its ethic of responsibility to its fundamental users—the learners. Our hope should be our new starting point.

TOWARD THE FUTURE

The future of reading assessment looks more promising than its past simply because of the acknowledgment that traditional multiple-choice standardized reading tests are insufficient. This movement creates many possibilities. Old ways of constituting evidence for reading still resist and rub up against the new ways. Reading itself continues to be contested. The resistance and contestations are not troubling. In fact, it is just the opposite. The lethargy in conceptualizing new visions of reading assessment in the past century seems amazing in a period that has seen the birth of the information age, the emergence of doubts about the positive effects of industrialization on the condition of the planet, the perversity of the Holocaust and "ethnic cleansing" in Europe, civil wars in Africa, the hope of glasnost and perestroika, the rise and fall of antibiotics, the devastation of AIDS, the birth of test-tube babies along with numerous other medical advances, the fall of apartheid in South Africa, and the ebb and flow of told and untold developments and counterdevelopments in human civilization. In this panoply of the key events of the century, it is certain that reading played significant roles. At some level, print has been used as a tool to document and record both the mundane and the horrific; it has been used to broker and transmit progressive and regressive knowledge; it has been used to educate and to propagandize. To offer evidence of reading, to name someone as a reader, represents significant power.

The key principles in the shifting future of the kinds of evidence that are necessary for reading assessment lie in recognizing the role of the "interpretive community" (S. Fish, 1980), both the interpretive community that bounds any reader and the interpretive community that names someone as a reader. It is ultimately from the interpretive community that arguments about kinds of evidence take shape. From the interpretive community comes an understanding of what matters in reading. And it is from the interpretive community new interpretations arise and are contested. If future revisionings of reading assessment recognize this dynamic, then entire worlds of possibility arise for considering what counts as reading.

Appendix

Attributes Of Individualized and Group Tests Analyzed

For each of the tests reviewed, the number of items possible per grade was tallied. In some cases, a tally was not possible. Examples include cases in which error scores on reading passages constitute items. In these cases, individual performance is indicative of item performance to some extent even though, arguably, the passage being read might be considered the item.

BRIGANCE DIAGNOSTIC COMPREHENSIVE INVENTORY OF BASIC SKILLS

The number of items per grade is not determinable, but the following is a list of the number of items per subtest:

Word Recognition Grade Placement Test	120
Oral Reading	* * *
Reading Comprehension (Vocabulary)	120
Reading Comprehension (Comprehension)	65
Auditory Discrimination	26
Identifies Initial Consonants in Spoken Words	21
Pronounces Initial Consonants	21
Substitutes Initial Consonant Sounds	21
Substitutes Short Vowel Sounds	5
Substitutes Long Vowel Sounds	5
Identifies Final Consonants in Spoken Words	18
Substitutes Final Consonant Sounds	18
Pronounces Written Initial Blends and Digraphs	30
Substitutes Initial Blend and Digraph Sounds	31
Reads Words With Common Endings	58
Reads Words With Vowel Digraphs and Diphthongs	18
Reads Words With Phonetic Irregularities	16
Reads Suffixes	36
Reads Prefixes	36

Identifies Number of Syllables in Spoken Words	3
Divides Words Into Syllables	9
Basic Sight Vocabulary	400
Direction Words	75
Contractions	40
Abbreviations	80
Warning and Safety Signs	40
Informational Signs	58
Warning Labels	16
Food Labels	19
Number Words	42

For oral reading there are two sets of 14 passages on which errors are counted; the possible total items (not including the oral reading) are 1,447.

BRIGANCE DIAGNOSTIC INVENTORY OF BASIC SKILLS

The number of items per grade is not determinable, but the following is a list of the number of items per subtest:

Word Recognition Grade Level Test	60
Basic Sight Vocabulary	250
Direction Words	37
Abbreviations	57
Contractions	35
Common Signs	40
Oral Reading	***
Oral Reading Comprehension	30
Oral Reading Rate	1
Auditory Discrimination	26
Initial Consonant Sounds Auditorily	21
Initial Consonant Sounds Visually	20
Substitution of Initial Consonant Sounds	84
Ending Sounds Auditorily	24
Vowels	6
Short Vowel Sounds	5
Long Vowel Sounds	10
Initial Clusters Auditorily	33
Initial Clusters Visually	33
Substitution of Initial Cluster Sounds	33
Digraphs and Diphthongs	20
Phonetic Irregularities	15
Common Ending of Rhyming Words	75

Suffixes	18
Prefixes	14
Meaning of Prefixes	14
Number of Syllables Auditorily	18
Syllabication Concepts	6
Context Clues	***
Classification	15
Analogies	15
Antonyms	18
Homonyms	24

There are 1,076 items plus oral reading error items.

CALIFORNIA ACHIEVEMENT TESTS CAT5

The number of items per grade is not clearly derivable as individual tests can sometimes be multilevel tests. For each level, the number of items is indicated here:

Reading Subtest	Level 11 Gr 1.6–2.2	Level 13 Gr. 2.6–4.2	Level 15 Gr. 4.6–6.2
Word analysis	28	30	0
Vocabulary	32	34	40
Comprehension	34	40	50
Total	94	104	90

DURRELL ANALYSIS OF READING DIFFICULTY

The number of items per grade cannot be determined. The following is a listing of the number of items per subtest:

Oral Reading	***
Oral Reading Comprehension	60
Silent Reading	***
Listening Comprehension	44
Word Recognition	100
Learning Vocabulary	75
Sounds in Isolation	68
Spelling	40
Phonic Spelling	15
Visual Memory of Words	35

Identifying Sounds in Words	29
Syntax Matching	6
Identifying Letter Names in Spoken Words	22
Identifying Phonemes in Spoken Words	25
Naming Letters (Lower Case)	26
Writing Letters	26
Naming Letters (Upper Case)	26
Writing From Copy	26
Identifying Letters Named	26

For Oral Reading and Listening Comprehension, the scoring is based on the number of student miscues. Consequently, an item count is not possible for these. Excluding these two tests, the total number of items is 649.

GATES–MACGINITIE READING TESTS (3RD EDITION)

Subtest	Level R Gr. 1.0–1.9	Level 1 Gr. 1.4–1.9	Level 3 Gr. 3	Level 5/6 Gr. 5–6
Initial consonants and consonant clusters	15	—	—	—
Final consonants and consonant clusters	15	—	—	—
Vowels	15	—	—	—
Use of sentence context	15	—	—	—
Vocabulary	—	45	45	45
Comprehension	—	46	48	48

For administration purposes, the Level R test is divided into three parts, but the scores and score transformations are presented in the format of four subtests.

GILMORE ORAL READING TEST

The number of items per grade level is not derivable because it is impossible to anticipate errors on the oral reading passage. For comprehension, there are 50 questions (5 questions on each of 10 passages). In addition, it is possible to calculate speed ratings possible for each passage.

IOWA TESTS OF BASIC SKILLS

Subtest	Level 7 Grade 1	Level 9 Grade 3	Level 11 Grade 5
Word analysis	47	—	—
Vocabulary	30	30	39
Pictures	23	—	—
Sentences	14	—	—
Stories	19	—	—
Reading comprehension	—	44	54
TOTAL	143	74	93

METROPOLITAN ACHIEVEMENT TESTS

The number of items per grade level is not derivable as the individual tests are multigrade tests. For each level, the number of items is indicated here:

Subtest	Primary 1	Primary 2	Elementary
Vocabulary	(22)	(22)	(22)
Subject/predicate	6	6	6
Adjective, adverb, preposition	8	8	8
Direct & indirect objects	8	8	8
Word recognition	(28)	(28)	(29)
Phoneme/grapheme:	10	6	6
Consonants	10	13	14
phoneme/grapheme: Vowels/word part/clues	8	9	9
Reading comprehension	(53)	(55)	(60)
Rebus			
Sentences	4	0	0
Stories	4	0	0
Literal	24	23	17
Inferent	11	20	28
Critical	10	12	15
Analysis			
Total	(103)	(105)	(111)

PEABODY INDIVIDUAL ACHIEVEMENT TEST—REVISED

It is not possible to derive the number of items on a per grade basis, but a general description of the number of items is presented here. Only the first three subtests were considered in the present analysis.

General Information	100
Reading Recognition	100
Reading Comprehension	82 (18 required on RR to administer)
Mathematics	100
Spelling	100
Written Expression I	(evaluation of writing sample)
Written Expression II	24 (evaluation of writing sample)
Total	482 plus the writing checklist items = 524

Although individual items per grade are not strictly derivable, for each of the subtests of 100 items, the following planned distribution was outlined:

K = 15 items	7 = 6
1 = 11	8 = 6
2 = 9	9 = 5
3 = 8	10 = 5
4 = 8	11 = 5
5 = 8	12 = 4
6 = 6	12 + = 4

The argument is made that the distribution focuses more on the lower grade levels because this is where it is anticipated that the test is most likely used.

STANFORD DIAGNOSTIC READING TEST

For each level, the number of items varies as indicated below:

Subtest	Red Gr. 1–3	Green Gr. 3–5	Brown Gr. 5–8
Decoding	70	108	108
Vocabulary	36	40	40
Comprehension	78	48	60
Rate	0	0	33
Total	184	196	241

TEST OF READING COMPREHENSION

The number of items per grade level is not derivable. The following is a listing of the number of items per subtest:
The total number of items in the test is 185.

General Vocabulary	25
Syntactic Similarities	20
Paragraph Reading	30
Mathematics Vocabulary	25
Social Studies Vocabulary	25
Science Vocabulary	25
Reading the Directions of Schoolwork	25
Sentence Sequencing	10

WIDE RANGE ACHIEVEMENT TEST—REVISED

There are 100 possible items for Level 1 Reading and 89 possible items for Level II. It is not possible to derive the number of items on a grade level basis.

WOODCOCK READING MASTERY TESTS—REVISED

It is not possible to derive the number of items on a grade level basis. The number of items per subtest is presented here:

Visual-Auditory Learning (Form G only)	134 items
Letter Identification (Form G only)	51 items
Supplementary Letter Checklist (Form G only)	27 items
Word Identification	106 items
Word Attack	45 items
Word Comprehension	146 items
Antonyms	
Synonyms	(65)
Analogies	(79)
General Reading Vocabulary	(30)
Science–Mathematics Vocabulary	(40) (39 for Form H)
Social Studies Vocabulary	(38) (39 Form H)
Humanities Vocabulary	(38)
Passage Comprehension	68 items

From these cluster scores may be derived:

Readiness Cluster = Visual-Auditory Learning + Letter Identification; Basic Skills Cluster = Word Identification + Word Attack; Reading Comprehension Cluster = Word Comprehension + Passage Comprehension; Total Reading — Full Scale = Word Identification + Word Attack + Word Comprehension + Passage Comprehension; Total Reading — Short Scale = Word Identification + Passage Comprehension.

References

Adams, M. (1990). *Beginning to read: Thinking and learning about print.* Cambridge, MA: MIT Press.

Afflerbach, P. (1990). Statewide reading assessment: A survey of the states. In P. Afflerbach (Ed.), *Issues in statewide reading assessment* (pp. 101–161). Washington, DC: ERIC Clearinghouse on Tests, Measurement, & Evaluation.

Allington, R. (1983). The reading instruction provided readers of differing ability. *Elementary School Journal, 83,* 548–559.

Allington, R. L. (1984). Oral reading. In P. D. Pearson, R. Barr, M. L. Kamil, & P. Mosenthal (Eds.), *Handbook of reading research* (pp. 829–864). New York: Longman.

Allington, R., & McGill-Franzen, A. (1989). Different programs, indifferent instruction. In D. Lipsky & A. Gartner (Eds.), *Beyond separate education: Quality education for all* (pp. 75–97). Baltimore, MD: Brookes Publishing.

Allington, R., & McGill-Franzen, A. (1992). Does high stakes testing improve school effectiveness? *Spectrum: Journal of School Research and Information, 10*(2), 3–12.

American Psychological Association, American Educational Research Association, & National Council on Measurement in Education. (1985). *Standards for educational and psychological testing.* Washington, DC: American Psychological Association.

Anastasi, A. (1982). *Psychological testing* (5th ed.). New York: Macmillan.

Anderson, A. B., & Stokes, S. J. (1984). Social and institutional influences on the development and practice of literacy. In H. Goelman, A. A. Oberg, & F. Smith (Eds.), *Awakening to literacy* (pp. 24–37). Portsmouth, NH: Heinemann.

Anderson, R. C. (1985/1984). Role of the reader's schema in comprehension, learning, and memory. In H. Singer & R. B. Ruddell (Eds.), *Theoretical models and processes of reading* (3rd ed., pp. 372–384). Newark, DE: International Reading Association.

Anderson, R. C., Hiebert, E., Scott, J., & Wilkinson, I. (1985). *Becoming a nation of readers.* Washington, DC: National Institute of Education.

Angoff, W. H. (1988). Validity: An evolving concept. In H. Wainer & H. I. Braun (Eds.), *Test validity* (pp. 19–32). Hillsdale, NJ: Lawrence Erlbaum Associates.

Anthony, R. J., Johnson, T. D., Mickelson, N. I., & Preece, A. (1991). *Evaluating literacy: A perspective for change.* Toronto, Ontario: Irwin.

Arnstine, D. (1995). *Democracy and the arts of schooling.* Albany, NY: SUNY Press.

Au, K. H. (1994). Portfolio assessment: Experiences at the Kamehameh Elementary Education Program. In S. W. Valencia, E. H. Hiebert, & P. P. Afflerbach (Eds.), *Authentic reading assessment: Practices and possibilities* (pp. 103–126). Newark, DE: International Reading Association.

Austin, M., & Morrison, C. (1963). *The first r.* New York: Wiley.

Avery, C. (1993). *With a light touch: Learning about reading, writing and teaching with first graders.* Portsmouth, NH: Heinemann.

Ayres, L. (1915). Making education definite. *NSSE Bulletin, 11*(13), 72–87.

Bandura A., & Schunk, D. (1981). Cultivating competence, self-efficacy, and intrinsic interest through proximal self-monitoring. *Journal of Personality and Social Psychology, 41*(3), 586–598.

Barrs, M., Ellis, S., Hester, H., & Thomas, A. (1988). *The primary language record: Handbook for teachers*. Portsmouth, NH: Heinemann.

Bartlett, F. C. (1932). *Remembering*. Cambridge, England: Cambridge University Press.

Barton, A., & Wilder, D. (1964). Research and practice in the teaching of reading. In M. Miles (Ed.), *Innovations in education*. New York: Teachers College Press.

Baumann, J. F. (Ed.). (1991). [Special issue.] *The Reading Teacher, 44*, 370–395.

Bean, T. W. (1979). The miscue mini-form: Refining the informal reading inventory. *Reading World, 18*(2), 400–405.

Belanoff, P., & Dickson, M. (1991). *Portfolios: Process and product*. Portsmouth, NH: Boynton/Cook.

Belenky, M., Clinchy, B. M., Goldberger, N. R., & Tarule, J. M. (1986). *Women's ways of knowing: The development of self, voice and mind*. New York: Basic Books.

Bellah, R., Madsen, R., Sullivan, W., Swidler, A., & Tipton, S. (1985). *Habits of the heart: Individualism and commitment in American life*. New York: Harper & Row.

Bembridge, T. (1994). A multilayered assessment package. In S. W. Valencia, E. H. Hiebert, & P. P. Afflerbach (Eds.), *Authentic reading assessment: Practices and possibilities* (pp. 167–184). Newark, DE: International Reading Association.

Bennett, R. E. (1993). On the meanings of constructed response. In R. E. Bennett & W. C. Ward (Eds.), *Construction versus choice in cognitive measurement: Issues in constructed response, performance testing, and portfolio assessment* (pp. 1–27). Hillsdale, NJ: Lawrence Erlbaum Associates.

Bennett, R. E. & Ward, W. C. (Eds.). (1993). *Construction versus choice in cognitive measurement: Issues in constructed response, performance testing, and portfolio assessment*. Hillsdale, NJ: Lawrence Erlbaum Associates.

Berliner, D., & Biddle, B. (1995). *The manufactured crisis: Myths, frauds, and the attack on America's public schools*. Reading, MA: Addison-Wesley.

Black, L., Daiker, D. A., Sommers, J., & Stygall, G. (Eds.). (1994). *New directions in portfolio assessment: Reflective practice, critical theory and large-scale scoring*. Portsmouth, NH: Heinemann–Boynton-Cook.

Bliss, D. (1918). Standard tests and a basal method of teaching reading. *Elementary School Journal, 18*, 795–801.

Bond, L., Freidman, L., & Vander Ploeg, A. (1993). *Surveying the landscape of state educational assessment programs: Ed talk*. Washington, DC: Council for Educational Development and Research. (ERIC Document Reproduction Service No. ED 367 664.)

Bormuth, J. R. (1970). *On the theory of achievement test items*. Chicago: University of Chicago Press.

Brandt, R. (Ed.). (1991). Using performance assessment. *Educational Leadership, 49*(8).

Brigance, A. H. (1977). *Brigance diagnostic comprehensive inventory of basic skills*. North Billerica, MA: Curriculum Associates.

Brigance, A. H. (1983). *Brigance diagnostic inventory of basic skills*. North Billerica, MA: Curriculum Associates.

Brodkey, L. (1991). Tropics of literacy. In C. Mitchell & K. Weiller (Eds.), *Rewriting literacy: Culture and the discourse of the other* (pp. 161–168). Toronto, Ontario: OISE.

Brown, D. L. (1995, November 23). Reading scores up but still below par. *Washington Post*, 1, 2, 3.

Brown, J., Goodman, K. S., & Marek, A. M. (Eds.). (1996). *Studies in miscue analysis: An annotated bibliography*. Newark, DE: International Reading Association.

Brown, V. L., Hammill, D. D., & Wiederholt, J. L. (1978). *TORC—The test of reading comprehension: A method for assessing the understanding of written language*. Austin, TX: Pro-Ed.

Buros, O. K. (1972). *The seventh mental measurements yearbook.* Highland Park, NJ: Gryphon Press.

Buros, O. K. (1977). Fifty years in testing: Some reminiscences, criticisms, and suggestions. *Educational Researcher,* 6(7), 9–15.

Buros, O. K. (1992). *The ninth mental measurements yearbook.* Highland Park, NJ: Gryphon Press.

Buros, O. K. (1993). *The tenth mental measurements yearbook.* Highland Park, NH: Gryphon Press.

Byrd, L., Goodman, K. S., & Goodman, Y. M. (Eds.). (1992). *The whole language catalog: Supplement on assessment.* Santa Rosa, CA: American School.

Cannell, J. J. (1988). Nationally normed elementary achievement testing in America's schools: How all 50 states are above the national average. *Educational Measurement: Issues and Practice,* 7(Summer), 5–9.

CAT5: California Achievement Tests, Fifth Edition. (1992). Monterey, CA: CTB/Macmillan McGraw-Hill.

Cattell, J. (1886). The time it takes to see and name objects. *Mind,* 11, 63–65.

Chandler, J. (1996, March 26). Half of Cal State freshmen needed English, Math help. *Los Angeles Times,* A1, A20.

Chittenden, E. A. (1987). Styles, reading strategies and test performance: A follow-up study of beginning readers. In R. O. Freedle & R. P. Duran (Eds.), *Cognitive and linguistic analyses of test performance: Volume XXII—Advances in discourse processes* (pp. 369–390). Norwood, NJ: Ablex.

Church, S., & Newman, J. M. (1985). Danny: A case history of an instructionally induced reading problem. In J. Newman (Ed.). *Whole language: Theory and use* (pp. 169–179). Portsmouth, NH: Heinemann.

Clay, M. (1991). *Becoming literate: The construction of inner control.* Portsmouth, NH: Heinemann.

Colvin, R. L. (1995, September 13). State report urges return to basics in teaching reading. *Los Angeles Times,* A1, A24.

Connelly, J. B. (1985). Published tests—Which ones do special education teachers perceive as useful? *Journal of Special Education,* 19(2), 149–155.

Consortium for Policy Research in Education. (1993). *Developing content standards: Creating a process for change.* CPRE Brief. New Brunswick, NJ. (ERIC Document Reproduction Service No. ED 362 981.)

Corbett, H., & Wilson, B. (1989). *Raising the stakes in statewide mandatory minimum competency testing.* Philadelphia: Research for Better Schools.

Covington, M., & Beery, R. (1976). *Self-worth and school learning.* New York: Holt, Rinehart & Winston.

Cowie, R. (1985). Reading errors as clues to the nature of reading. In A. L. Ellis (Eds.), *Progress in the psychology of language* (pp. 73–107). Hillsdale, NJ: Lawrence Erlbaum Associates.

Cremin, L. (1988). *American education: The metropolitan experience 1876–1980.* New York: Harper & Row.

Crocker, L., & Algina, J. (1986). *Introduction to classical and modern test theory.* New York: Holt, Rinehart & Winston.

Cronbach, L. J. (1988). Five perspectives on validity argument. In H. Wainer & H. I. Braun (Eds.), *Test validity* (pp. 3–17). Hillsdale, NJ: Lawrence Erlbaum Associates.

Cronbach, L. J. (1989). Construct validation after thirty years. In R. Linn (Ed.), *Intelligence: Measurement, theory and public policy* (pp. 147–171). Urbana: University of Illinois Press.

Cubberley, E. P. (1917). Editor's introduction. In W. Monroe, *Educational tests and measurements* (pp. i–xv). Boston: Houghton Mifflin.

Cunningham, J. W. (1984). A simplified miscue analysis for classroom and clinic. *Reading Horizons, 24* (2), 83–89.

Darling-Hammond, L. (1994). Performance-based assessment and educational equity. *Harvard Educational Review, 64* (1), 5–30.

Darling-Hammond, L., Ancess, J., & Falk, B. (1995). *Authentic assessment in action: Studies of schools and students at work.* New York: Teachers College Press.

Deci, E., Spiegel, N., Ryan, R., Koestner, R., & Kauffman, M. (1982). The effects of peformance standards on controlling teachers. *Journal of Educational Psychology, 74,* 852–859.

DeSaint-Exupéry, A. (1971). *The little prince.* New York: Harcourt Brace.

Diener, C., & Dweck, C. (1978). An analysis of learned helplessness: Continuous changes in performance, strategy, and achievement cognitions following failure. *Journal of Personality and Social Psychology, 36,* 451–462.

Dorr-Bremme, D., & Herman, J. (1986). *Assessing student achievement: A profile of classroom practices (CSE Monograph No. 11).* Los Angeles: Center for the Study of Evaluation, University of California at Los Angeles.

Dorr-Bremme, D., Burry, J., Catterall, J., Cabello, B., & Daniels, L. (1983). *The costs of testing in American public schools (CSE Technical Report No. 198).* Los Angeles, CA: Center for the Study of Evaluation, University of California at Los Angeles.

Drahozal, E. C., & Frisbie, D. A. (1988). Riverside comments on the friends for education report. *Educational Measurement: Issues and Practice, Summer,* 12–16.

Durrell, D. (1939). Individual differences and their implications with respect to instruction in reading. In W. S. Gray (Ed.), *The teaching of reading: A second report. Thirty-sixth yearbook of the National Society for the Study of Education* (pp. 325–358). Chicago: University of Chicago Press.

Durrell, D. D., & Catterson, J. H. (1980). *Durrell analysis of reading difficulty: Manual of directions.* Cleveland, OH: Psychological Corporation.

Edelsky, C. (1996). *With literacy and justice for all: Rethinking the social in language and education.* Washington, DC: Taylor & Francis.

Education Department of South Australia. (1991). *Literacy assessment in practice: Language arts.* Urbana, IL: National Council of Teachers of English.

Educational Testing Service. (1993). *Performance assessment sampler: A workbook.* Princeton, NJ: Policy Information Center. (ERIC Document Reproduction Service No. ED 361 371.)

Elbow, P. (1994). Will the virtues of portfolios blind us to their potential dangers? In L. Black, D. A. Daiker, J. Sommers, & G. Stygall (Eds.), *New directions in portfolio assessment: Reflective practice, critical theory, and large-scale scoring* (pp. 40–55). Portsmouth, NH: Heinemann–Boynton/Cook.

Elliott, E., & Dweck, C. (1988). Goals: An approach to motivation and achievement. *Journal of Personality and Social Psychology, 54,* 5–12.

Farr, R. (1992). Putting it all together: Solving the reading assessment puzzle. *Reading Teacher, 46,* 26–37.

Ferreiro, E., & Teberosky, A. (1982). *Literacy before schooling* (K. Goodman Castro, Trans.). Portsmouth, NH: Heinemann.

Fillmore, C. J. (1982). Ideal readers and real readers. In D. Tannen (Ed.), *Analyzing discourse: Text and talk. Georgetown University Round Table on Languages and Linguistics 1981.* Washington, DC: Georgetown University Press.

Fish, J. (1988). *Responses to mandated standardized testing.* Unpublished doctoral dissertation, University of California at Los Angeles.

Fish, S. (1980). *Is there a text in this class? The authority of interpretive communities.* Cambridge, MA: Harvard University Press.

Fitzpatrick Reardon, S., Scott, K., & Verre, J. (Eds.). (1994). Symposium on equity in educational assessment. *Harvard Educational Review, 64* (1), 1–95.

Freeman, Y. (1986). *The contemporary Spanish basal in the United States.* Unpublished doctoral dissertation. University of Arizona, Tucson.

Friedman, I. (1991). High- and low-burnout schools: School culture aspects of teacher burnout. *Journal of Educational Research, 84*(6), 325–333.

Fyans, L. J. (1979). Test anxiety, test comfort, and student achievement test performance. Paper presented at Educational Testing Service, Princeton, NJ.

Garcia, M. W., & Verville, K. (1994). Re-designing teaching and learning: The Arizona student assessment program. In S. W. Valencia, E. H. Hiebert, & P. P. Afflerbach (Eds.), *Authentic reading assessment: Practices and possibilities* (pp. 228–246). Newark, DE: International Reading Association.

Gardner, H. (1985). *The mind's new science.* New York: Basic Books.

Gardner, H. (1993). *Frames of mind: The theory of multiple intelligences* (2nd ed.). New York: Basic Books.

Garrison, R. (1990). Graduation before graduation: Social involvement and English. *English Journal, 79* (6), 60–63.

Gates, A. (1927). *The improvement of reading.* New York: Macmillan.

Gates, A. (1937). The measurement and evaluation of achievement in reading. In W. S. Gray (Ed.) *The teaching of reading: A second report. Thirty-sixth yearbook of the National Society for the Study of Education* (pp. 391–418). Chicago: University of Chicago.

Gee, J. (1990). *Social linguistics and literacies: Ideology in discourses.* New York: Falmer Press.

Gerstner, L. V. (1995, December 30). Don't retreat on school standards. *The New York Times,* 27.

Gerstner, L. V., Semerad, R. D., Doyle, D. P., & Johnston, W. B. (1994). *Reinventing education: Entrepreneurship in America's public schools.* New York: Dutton.

Gilmore, J. V., & Gilmore, E. C. (1968). *Gilmore Oral Reading Test: Manual of directions.* New York: Harcourt Brace.

Gladstone, M. (1994, March 10). Wilson opposes deletions in reading test. *Los Angeles Times,* A3, A31.

Glaser, B. G., & Strauss, A. L. (1967). *The discovery of grounded theory: Strategies for qualitative research.* New York: Aldine de Gruyter.

Glaser, R. (1986). The integration of instruction and testing. In E. E. Freeman (Conference Proceedings Ed.), *The redesign of testing for the 21st century: Proceedings of the 1985 Educational Testing Service Invitational Conference* (pp. 45–58). Princeton, NJ: Educational Testing Service.

Glover, M. K. (1993). *Two years: A teacher's memoir.* Portsmouth, NH: Heinemann.

Golden, J. M., & Pappas, C. C. (1990). A sociolinguistic perspective on retelling procedures in research on children's cognitive processing of written text. *Linguistics and Education, 2,* 21–41.

Goodman, K. S. (1982). A linguistic study of cues and miscues in reading. In F. V. Gollasch (Ed.), *Language and literacy—The selected writings of Kenneth S. Goodman. Volume 1: Process, theory and research* (pp. 115–120). Boston: Routledge & Kegan Paul. (Original work published 1965)

Goodman, K. S. (1982). Reading: A psycholinguistic guessing game. In F. V. Gollasch (Ed.), *Language and literacy—The selected writings of Kenneth S. Goodman. Volume 1: Process, theory and research* (pp. 33–43). Boston: Routledge & Kegan Paul. (Original work published 1967)

Goodman, K. S. (1982). Miscues: Windows on the reading process. In F. V. Gollasch (Ed.), *Language and literacy: The selected writings of Kenneth S. Goodman. Volume 1: Process, theory and research* (pp. 93–101). London: Routledge & Kegan Paul. (Original work published 1973)

Goodman, K. S. (1985/1984). Unity in reading. In H. Singer & R. B. Ruddell (Eds.), *Theoretical models and processes of reading* (pp. 813–840). Newark, DE: International Reading Association. (Original work published 1984)

Goodman, K. S. (1994). Reading, writing, and written texts: A transactional sociopsycho-linguistic view. In R. B. Ruddell, M. R. Ruddell, & H. Singer (Eds.), *Theoretical models and processes of reading* (pp. 1093–1130). Newark, DE: International Reading Association.

Goodman, K. S., & Burke, C. L. (1968). *Study of children's behavior while reading orally: Report of Project No. 5425.* Washington, DC: U.S. Dept. of Health, Education & Welfare.

Goodman, K. S., & Burke, C. L. (1973). *Theoretically based studies of patterns of miscues in oral reading performance: Final report of Project 920.9-0375, Grant No. OEG-0-9370375-4269.* Washington, DC: U.S. Dept. of Health, Education & Welfare.

Goodman, K. S., & Burke, C. L. (1982). The Goodman taxonomy of reading miscues. In F. V. Gollasch (Ed.), *Language and Literacy: The selected writings of Kenneth S. Goodman. Volume 1: Process, theory and research* (pp. 215–302). Boston: Routledge & Kegan Paul. (Original work published 1973)

Goodman, K. S., & Goodman, Y. M. (1978). *Reading of American children whose language is a stable rural dialect of English or a language other than English.* (National Institute of Education contract NIE-C-00-3-0087).Washington, DC: U.S. Department of Health, Education, & Welfare.

Goodman, K. S., Goodman, Y. M., & Hood, W. J. (Eds.). (1989). *The whole language evaluation book.* Portsmouth, NH: Heinemann.

Goodman, K. S., Shannon, P., Freeman, Y., & Murphy, S. (1988). *Report card on basal readers.* New York: Richard C. Owen.

Goodman, Y. M., & Burke, C. (1972). *Reading miscue inventory manual: Procedure for diagnosis and evaluation.* New York: Holt, Rinehart & Winston.

Goodman, Y. M., & Marek, A. (1996). *Retrospective miscue analysis.* New York: Richard C. Owen.

Goodman, Y. M., Watson, D., & Burke, C. (1987). *Reading miscue analysis: Alternative strategies.* New York: Richard C. Owen.

Gough, P. B. (Ed.). (1993). Special section on authentic assessment. *Phi Delta Kappan, 74*(6), 444–478.

Grady, E. (1992). *The portfolio approach to assessment: Fastback series 341.* Bloomington, IN: Phi Delta Kappan Educational Foundation. (ERIC Document Reproduction Services No. ED 356 273.)

Graves, D. (1990). *Discover your own literacy.* Portsmouth, NH: Heinemann.

Gray, C. (1917). *Types of reading ability as exhibited through tests and laboratory experiments. Supplemental education monographs, 5*(1). Chicago: University of Chicago Press.

Gray, C. (1922). *Deficiencies in reading ability: Their diagnosis and treatment.* Boston, MA: Heath.

Gray, W. S. (1915). Selected bibliography upon practice tests of reading ability. In H. Wilson, (Ed.) *Minimal essentials in elementary school subjects. Fourteenth yearbook of National Society for the Study of Education, Part I* (pp. 59–61). Bloomington, IL: Public School.

Gray, W. S. (1916). Methods of testing reading I. *Elementary School Journal, 16,* 231–246.

Gray, W. S. (1917). *Studies of elementary school reading through standardized tests.* Chicago: University of Chicago Press.

Gray, W. S. (1918). The use of tests in improving instruction. *Elementary School Journal, 19,* 121–141.

Gray, W. S. (1919). Principles of methods in teaching reading, as derived from scientific investigation. In E. Horn (Ed.) *Report of the Committee on Economy of Time in Learning:*

Eighteenth yearbook of the National Society for the Study of Education, Part II. Bloomington, IL: Public School.

Greenwood, T. (1992). Look Ma, no grades: A new teacher, parents and portfolios. *Portfolio News, 3* (3), 9–10.

Griffin, P., Smith, P. G., & Burrill, L. E. (1995). *The American literacy profile scales: A framework for authentic assessment.* Portsmouth, NH: Heinemann.

Groff, P. (1980). A critique of an oral reading miscue analysis. *Reading World, 19*(3), 254–264.

Guskey, T. R. (Ed.). (1994). *High stakes performance assessment: Perspectives on Kentucky's educational reform.* (ERIC Document Reproduction Services No. ED 379 288.)

Guzzetti, B. J. (1984). The reading process in content fields: A psycholinguistic investigation. *American Educational Research Journal, 21*(3), 659–668.

Hacking, I. (1990). *The taming of chance.* Cambridge, England: Cambridge University Press.

Hall, B. W. (1985). Survey of the technical characteristics of published educational achievement tests. *Educational measurement: Issues and practice, Spring*, 6–14.

Hancock, J., Turbill, J., & Cambourne, B. (1994). Assessment and evaluation of literacy learning. In S. W. Valencia, E. H. Hiebert, & P. P. Afflerbach (Eds.), *Authentic reading assessment: Practices and possibilities* (pp. 46–62). Newark, DE: International Reading Association.

Hansen, J. (1994). Literacy portfolios: Windows on potential. In S. W. Valencia, E. H. Hiebert, & P. P. Afflerbach (Eds.), *Authentic reading assessment: Practices and possibilities* (pp. 26–40). Newark, DE: International Reading Association.

Hanson, F. A. (1993). *Testing testing: Social consequences of the examined life.* Berkeley: University of California Press.

Harman, S. (1991). National tests, national standards, national curriculum. *Language Arts, 68*(1), 49–50.

Harp, B. (1995, May). *Regional survey of assessment practices.* Paper presented at the Annual Convention of the International Reading Association, Annaheim, CA.

Harry, B. (1992). An ethnographic study of cross-cultural communication with Puerto Rican–American families in the special education system. *American Educational Research Journal, 29*(3) 471–494.

Harste, J. C., Short, K. G., & Burke, C. (1995). *Creating classrooms for authors and inquirers.* Portsmouth, NH: Heinemann.

Hartley, J., & Treuman, M. (1986). The effects of typographic layout of cloze-type tests on reading comprehension. *Journal of Research in Reading, 9*(2), 116–124.

Heath, S. B. (1983). *Ways with words: Language, life, and work in communities and classrooms.* Cambridge, England: Cambridge University Press.

Herman, J. & Golan, S. (1991). *Effects of standardized testing on teachers and learning—another look: CSE Technical Report #334.* Los Angeles: Center for the Study of Evaluation, University of California at Los Angeles.

Herman, P. A. (1985). The effect of repeated readings on reading rate, speech pauses, and word recognition accuracy. *Reading Research Quarterly, 20*(5), 553–565.

Hiebert, E. (1983). An examination of ability grouping for reading instruction. *Reading Research Quarterly, 18*, 231–255.

Hieronymous, A. N., Hoover, H. D., Frisbie, D. A., & Dunbar, S. B. (1990). *Iowa Tests of Basic Skills: Manual for school administrators supplement, levels 5–14.* Chicago: Riverside.

Hieronymous, A. N., Hoover, H. D., Oberly, K. R., Cantor, N. K., Frisbie, D. A. (1990). *Iowa Tests of Basic Skills teacher's guide.* Chicago: Riverside.

Hill, K. T., & Sarason, S. B. (1966). The relation of test anxiety and defensiveness to test and to test and school performance over the elementary school years. *Monographs of the Society for Research in Child Development, 31* (Serial No. 104) .

Himley, M., & Carini, P. (1991). The study of works: A phenomenological approach to understanding children as thinkers and learners. In M. Himley (Ed.), *Shared territory: Understanding children's writing as works*. New York: Oxford University Press.

Hirsch, E. D. (1987). *Cultural literacy: What every American needs to know*. Boston, MA: Houghton Mifflin.

Hoffman, J. V. (1991). Research directions: Illiteracy in the 21st century: Who can prevent it? *Language Arts, 68*(1), 60–66.

Holland, K., Bloome, D., Solsken, J. (Eds.). (1994). *Alternative perspectives in assessing children's language and literacy*. Norwood, NJ: Ablex.

Holmes, E. G. (1911). *What is and what might be: A study of education in general and elementary in particular*. London: Constable & Co.

Hood, J. (1982). The relationship of selected text variables to miscue scores of second graders. *Journal of Reading Behavior, 14*(2), 141–158.

House, E. (1978). Evaluation as scientific management in United States school reform. *Comparative Educational Review, 22*, 388–401.

House Committee on Education and Labor. (1993). *Hearing on H. R. 6: Assessment: Hearing before the Subcommittee on Elementary, Secondary, and Vocational Education of the Committee on Education and Labor*. House of Representatives, One hundred third Congress of the United States, Washington, DC. (ERIC Document Reproduction Service No. Ed 362 551.)

Huey, E. B. (1968). *The psychology and pedagogy of reading with a review of the history of reading and writing and of methods, texts, and hygiene in reading*. Cambridge, MA: MIT Press. (Original work published 1908)

IRA/NCTE Joint Task Force on Assessment. (1994). *Standards for the assessment of reading and writing*. Newark, DE: International Reading Association.

Jastak, J. F., & Jastak, S. (1978). *The Wide Range Achievement Test: Manual of instructions*. Wilmington, DE: Jastak Associates.

Jastak, S., & Wilkinson, G. S. (1984). *WRAT-R: Wide Range Achievement Test administration manual*. Wilmington, DE: Jastak Associates.

Jenks, C., & Roberts, J. (1990, November). Reading, writing, and reviewing: Teacher, librarian, and young readers collaborate. *Language Arts, 67*(7), 742–745.

Jennings, J. F. (Ed.). (1993). *National issues in education: The past is prologue*. Bloomington, IN: Phi Delta Kappa.

Jennings, J. F. (Ed.). (1995a). *National issues in education: Elementary and secondary education act*. Bloomington, IN: Phi Delta Kappa.

Jennings, J. F. (Ed.). (1995b). *National issues in education: Goals 2000 and school-to-work*. Bloomington, IN: Phi Delta Kappa.

Jerdon, R. (1921). *Nationality and school progress*. Bloomington, IN: Public School.

Jervis, K. (1996). *Eyes on the child: Three portfolio stories*. New York: Teachers College Press.

Johnston, P. H. (1983). *Reading comprehension assessment: A cognitive basis*. Newark, DE: International Reading Association.

Johnston, P. H. (1984a). Prior knowledge and reading comprehension test bias. *Reading Research Quarterly, 19*(2), 219–239.

Johnston, P. H. (1984b). Assessment in reading. In P. D. Pearson, R. Barr, M. L. Kamil, & P. Mosenthal (Eds.), *Handbook of reading research* (pp. 147–182). New York: Longman.

Johnston, P. H. (1992). *Constructive evaluation of literate activity*. New York: Longman.

Johnston, P. H. (1993). Assessment as social practice. In D. Leu & C. Kinzer (Eds.), *Examining central issues in literacy research, theory, and practice*. Chicago: National Reading Conference.

Johnston, P. H. (1997). *Knowing literacy: Constructive literacy assessment*. New York: Stenhouse.

Johnston, P. H., Afflerbach, P., & Weiss, P. (1993). Teachers' evaluation of the teaching and learning of literacy and literature. *Educational Assessment, 1*(2), 91–117.

Johnston, P. H., Guice, S., Baker, K., Malone, J., & Michaelson, N. (1995). Assessment of teaching and learning in "literature based" classrooms. *Teaching and Teacher Education, 11* (4), 359–371.

Joint Committee on Testing Practices. (1988). *Code of fair testing practices in education.* Washington, DC: American Psychological Association.

Judd, C. (1914). Reading tests. *Elementary School Journal, 14,* 365–373.

Judd, C. (1915). Reading tests—Report of Committee on Tests and Standards of Efficiency in Schools and School Systems. *National Educational Association: Addresses and Proceedings, 53,* 560–565.

Kaestle, C. F., Damon-Moore, H., Stedman, L. C., Tinsley, K., & Trollinger, W. V. (1991). *Literacy in the United States: Readers and reading since 1880.* London: Yale University Press.

Kapinus, B., Collier, G. V., & Kruglanski, H. (1994). The Maryland school performance assessment program: A new view of assessment. In S.W. Valencia, E. H. Hiebert, & P. P. Afflerbach (Eds.), *Authentic reading assessment: Practices and possibilities* (pp. 255–276). Newark, DE: International Reading Association.

Karlsen, B., &. Gardner, E. F. (1986). *Stanford diagnostic reading test 3rd edition: Manual for interpreting.* Cleveland, OH: Psychological Corporation.

Kentucky State Department of Education. (1992). *Office of Education Accountability annual report.* Frankfort, KY. (ERIC Document Reproduction Services No. ED 361 839.)

Kerlinger, F. N. (1986). *Foundations of behavioral research* (3rd ed.) New York: Holt, Rinehart & Winston.

Kliebard, H. (1986). *The struggle for the American curriculum, 1893–1958.* Boston, MA: Routledge & Kegan Paul.

Koenigs, S., Fiedler, M., & DeCharms, R. (1977). Teacher beliefs, classroom interaction and personal causation. *Journal of Applied Social Psychology, 7,* 95–114.

Koerner, J. D. (1968). *Reform in education: England and the United States.* New York: Delacorte Press.

Kolanowski, K. (1993). *Use of portfolios in assessment of literature learning: Report series 3.7.* Albany, NY: National Research Center on Literature Teaching and Learning.

Kolers, P. (1968). Introduction for reissue. In E. B. Huey (Ed.), *The psychology and pedagogy of reading* (pp.xiii–xxxix). Boston, MA: MIT Press.

Koretz, D. (1992). *The Vermont portfolio assessment program: Interim report on implementation and impact, 1991—92 school year. Project 3.2: Collaborative development of statewide systems. Report of year 1, Vermont study.* Los Angeles: National Center for Research on Evaluation, Standards and Student Testing. (ERIC Document Reproduction Services No. ED 351 345.)

Koretz, D. (1994). *The evolution of a portfolio program: The impact of the Vermont portfolio program in its second year (1992–93).* Los Angeles: National Center for Research on Evaluation, Standards and Student Testing. (ERIC Document Reproduction Services No. ED 379 301.)

Koretz, D., McCaffery, D., Klein, S., Bell, R., Stecher, B. (1992). *The reliability of scores from the 1992 Vermont portfolio assessment program—Interim report.* Los Angeles: National Center for Research on Evaluation, Standards and Student Testing. (ERIC Document Reproduction Services No. ED 355 284.)

Koretz, A., Stecher, B., Klein, S., & McCaffrey, D. (1994). The Vermont portfolio assessment program: Findings and implications. *Educational Measurement: Issues and Practice, 13*(3), 5–16.

Koretz, D., Stecher, B., Klein, S., McCaffrey, D., & Diebert, E. (1992). *Can portfolios assess student performance and influence instruction? The 1991–92 Vermont experience.* Los Angeles: National Center for Research on Evaluation, Standards and Student Testing. (ERIC Document Reproduction Services No. ED 365 699.)

Langer, J. (1984). Examining background knowledge and text comprehension. *Reading Research Quarterly, 19*(4), 468–481.

Leslie, L. (1980). The use of graphic and contextual information by average and below-average readers. *Journal of Reading Behavior, 12*(2), 139–149.

Levine, D., Lowe, R., Peterson, B., & Tenorio, R. (Eds.). (1995). *Rethinking schools: An agenda for change.* New York: New Press.

Lewis, C. (1993). "Give people a chance": Acknowledging social differences in reading. *Language Arts, 70*(6), 454–461.

Linn, R. L. (1986). Educational testing and assessment: Research needs and policy issues. *American Psychologist, 41* (10), 1153–1160.

Linn, R. L. (1991). *Cross-state comparability of judgments of student writing: Results from the New Standards Project, CSE Technical Report 335.* Los Angeles: CRESST. (ERIC Document Reproduction Service No. ED 343 933.)

Linn, R. L., Graue, M. E., & Sanders, N. M. (1990). Comparing state and district test results to national norms: The validity of claims that "everyone is above average." *Educational Measurement: Issues and Practice, 9* (Fall), 5–14.

Lipson, M., Mekkelson, J., Mosenthal, J., & Daniels, P. (1996, April 28–May 3). *Change: Teachers as agents, teachers as targets in a statewide assessment program.* Paper presented at the International Reading Association Annual Convention, New Orleans.

Locke, J. (1705/1976). *Some thoughts in education.* New York: Vintage.

Luke, A. (1988). *Literacy, textbooks and ideology.* Philadelphia: Falmer.

MacGinitie, W. H., & MacGinitie, R. K. (1989a). *Gates–MacGinitie reading tests* (3rd ed.). Chicago: Riverside.

MacGinitie, W. H., & MacGinitie, R. K. (1989b). *Gates–MacGinitie reading tests: Technical report* (3rd ed.). Chicago: Riverside.

MacIver, D., Stipek, D., Daniels, D. (1991) . Explaining within-semester changes in student effort in junior and senior high school courses. *Journal of Educational Psychology, 83,* 201–211.

Madaus, G. F. (1994). A technological and historical consideration of equity issues associated with proposals to change the nation's testing policy. *Harvard Educational Review, 64*(1), 76–95.

Madaus, G. F., & Airasian, P. W. (1977). Issues in evaluating student outcomes in competency-based graduation programs. *Journal of Research and Development in Education, 10*(3), 79–91.

Madaus, G. F., & McDonagh, J. T. (1979). Minimum competency testing: Unexamined assumptions and unexplored negative outcomes. In R. T. Lennon (Ed.), *New directions for testing and measurement: No. 3, Impactive changes on measurement* (pp. 1–14). San Francisco: Jossey-Bass.

Mann, D. (1986). Can we help dropouts: Thinking about the undoable. *Teachers College Record, 87,* 307–323.

Markwardt, F. C. (1989). *Peabody Individual Achievement Test Revised (PIAT—R) manual.* Circle Pines, MN: American Guidance Services.

Marvin, C. (1988). Attributes of authority: Literacy tests and the logic of strategic conduct. *Communication, 11,* 63-82.

Maxcy, S. J. (1995). *Democracy, chaos, and the new school order.* Thousand Oaks, CA: Corwin.

McCall, W. & Crabbs, L. M. (1925). *Standard test lessons in reading. Five volumes.* New York: Teachers College Press.

McCormick, T. W. (1988). *Theories of reading in dialogue: An interdisciplinary study.* New York: University Press of America.

McDermott, R. P. (1993). The acquisition of a child by a learning disability. In S. Chaiklin & J. Lave (Eds), *Understanding practice: Perspectives on activity and context* (pp. 269–305). Cambridge University Press.

McGill-Franzen, A., & Allington, R. L. (1991). The gridlock of low achievement: Perspectives on policy and practice. *Remedial and Special Education, 12*, 20–30.

McGill-Franzen, A., & Allington, R. L. (1993). Flunk'em or get them classified: The contamination of primary grade accountability data. *Educational Researcher, 22*(1), 19–22.

McLaughlin, M. (1975). *Evaluation and reform.* Cambridge, MA: Ballinger.

Mehan, H. (1984). Institutional decision-making. In B. Rogoff & J. Lave (Eds.), *Everyday cognition: Its development in social context* (pp. 41–66). Cambridge, MA: Harvard University Press.

Menosky, D. (1971). *A psycholinguistic description of oral reading miscues generated during the reading of varying portions of text by selected readers from grades two, four, six and eight.* Unpublished doctoral dissertation; Wayne State University, Detroit, MI.

Messick, S. (1988). The once and future issues of validity: Assessing the meaning and consequences of measurement. In H. Wainer & H. I. Braun (Eds.), *Test validity* (pp. 33–45). Hillsdale, NJ: Lawrence Erlbaum Associates.

Messick, S. (1989). Validity. In R. Linn (Ed.), *Educational measurement* (3rd. ed., pp.13–103). New York: Macmillan.

Michaels, S. (1981). "Sharing time": Children's narrative styles and differential access to literacy. *Language in Society, 10*, 423–442.

Michaels, S. (1983). Influences on children's narratives. *Quarterly Newsletter of the Laboratory of Comparative Human Cognition, 5*(2), 30–34.

Michaels, S. (1985). Hearing the connections in children's oral and written discourse. *Journal of Education, 167*(1), 36–56.

Milner, B. (1991, April 30). Ritchie issues challenge: Competitiveness rests with all. *Globe and Mail,* B6.

Milofsky, C. (1989). *Testers and testing: The sociology of school psychology.* New Brunswick, NJ: Rutgers University Press.

Milroy, J., & Milroy, L. (1991). *Authority in language: Investigating language prescription and standardisation* (2nd ed.). London: Routledge.

Minium, E. W. (1978). *Statistical reasoning in psychology and education* (2nd ed.). New York: Wiley.

Mislevy, R. J. (1993). Foundations of a new test theory. In N. Frederiksen, R. J. Mislevy, & I. I. Bejar (Eds.), *Test theory for a new generation of tests* (pp. 19–39). Hillsdale, NJ: Lawrence Erlbaum Associates.

Mitchell, C., & Weiler, K. (Eds.). (1991). *Rewriting literacy: Culture and the discourse of the other.* Toronto, Ont.: OISE Press.

Monroe, W. (1917). *Monroe's standardized silent reading tests.* Bloomington, IN: Public School.

Moody, D. (1991). *Strategies for statewide assessment: Policy briefs, Number 17.* San Francisco: Far West Lab for Educational Research and Development. (ERIC Document Reproduction Service No. ED 342 798.)

Moore, K. (1993). Ask them. In T. Newkirk (Ed.), *Workshop 4: The teacher as researcher* (pp. 78–87). Portsmouth, NH: Heinemann.

Mosenthal, P. (1990/1991). Understanding documents (series). *Journal of Reading, 34.*

Moss, P. A. (1992). Shifting conceptions of validity in educational measurement: Implications for performance assessment. *Review of Educational Research, 62*, 229–258.

Moss, P. A. (1994). Can there be validity without reliability? *Educational Researcher, 23*(2), 5–12.

Moss, P. A. (1996). Enlarging the dialogue in educational measurement: Voices from interpretive traditions. *Educational Researcher, 25* (1), 20–28.

Moss, P. A., Beck, J. S., Ebbs, C., Matson, B., Muchmore, J., Steele, D., & Taylor, C. (1992). Portfolios, accountability, and an interpretive approach to validity. *Educational Measurement: Issues and Practice, 11*(3), 12–21.

Murphy, P., & Brown, M. (1970). Conceptual systems and teaching styles. *American Educational Research Journal, 7*, 529–540.

Murphy, R., & Torrance, H. (1988). *The changing face of educational assessment.* London: Open University Press.

Murphy, S. (1994). Neither gone nor forgotten: Testing in the contemporary basal reading program. In P. Shannon & K. Goodman (Eds.), *Basal readers: A second look* (pp. 103–113). New York: Richard C. Owen.

Murphy, S. (1997). Literacy assessment and the politics of identities. *Reading and Writing Quarterly, 13*, 261–278.

Murphy, S. (In press). The validity and reliability of miscue analysis. In C. Edelsky & A. Marek (Eds.), *Reflections and connections: Essays on the influence of Kenneth S. Goodman.* New York: Hampden Press.

Neill, D., & Medina, N. (1989). Standardized testing: Harmful to educational health. *Phi Delta Kappan, 70*, 688–702.

Newkirk, T., with McLure, P. (1992). *Listening in: Children talk about books and other things.* Portsmouth, NH: Heinemann.

Nicholls, J. (1989). *The competitive ethos and democratic education.* Cambridge, MA: Harvard University Press.

Nicholls, J. G., McKenzie, M., & Shufro, J. (1994) Schoolwork, homework, life's work: The experience of students with and of students without learning disabilities. *Journal of Learning Disabilities, 27*(9), 562–569.

O'Connor, M. C. (1989). Aspects of differential performance by minorities on standardized tests: Linguistic and sociocultural factors. In B. R. Gifford (Ed.), *Test policy and test performance: Education, language, and culture* (pp. 129–181). Boston: Kluwer.

Ohlhausen, M., & Jepsen, M. (1992). Lessons from Goldilocks: "Somebody's been choosing my books but I can make my own choices now!" *The New Advocate, 5*(1), 31–46.

Oldham, B. R. (1993). *High stakes assessment: A local district perspective.* Paper presented at the Annual Convention of the American Educational Research Association, Atlanta, GA. (ERIC Document Reproduction Services No. ED 358 123.)

O'Neal, S. (1991). Leadership in the language arts: Student assessment, present and future. *Language Arts, 68*, 67–73.

Pappas, C. C., Kiefer, B. Z., & Levstik, L. S. (1990). *An integrated language perspective in the elementary school: Theory into action.* New York: Longman.

Paris, D. C. (1995). *Ideology and educational reform: Themes and theories in public education.* San Francisco: Westview.

Paris, S., Calfee, R. C., Filby, N., Hiebert, E., Pearson, P. D., Valencia, S. W., & Wolf, K. P. (1992). A framework for authentic literacy assessment. *Reading Teacher, 46*, 88–99.

Paris, S. G., Lawton, J. C., Turner, J. C., & Roth, J. L. (1991). A developmental perspective on standardized achievement testing. *Educational Researcher, 20*, 12–30.

Payne, C. S. (1930). The classification of errors in oral reading. *Elementary School Journal, 31* (2), 142–146.

Pearson, P. D. (1994). Commentary on California's new English language arts assessment. In S. W. Valencia, E. H. Hiebert, & P. P. Afflerbach (Eds.), *Authentic reading assessment: Practices and possibilities* (pp. 218–227). Newark, DE: International Reading Association.

Pearson, P. D., & Fielding, L. (1991). *Comprehension instruction.* New York: Longman.

Pearson, P. D., & Valencia, S. W. (1987). Assessment, accountability, and professional prerogative. In J. E. Readence (Ed.), *Research in literacy: Merging perspectives. Thirty-sixth yearbook of the National Reading Conference* (pp. 3–16). Chicago: National Reading Conference.

Peters, C. W. (1994). Commentary on redesigning teaching and learning: The Arizona student assessment program. In S. W. Valencia, E. H. Hiebert, & P. P. Afflerbach (Eds.), *Authentic reading assessment: Practices and possibilities* (pp. 247–254). Newark, DE: International Reading Association.

Pikulski, J. (1990). The role of tests in a literacy assessment program. *Reading Teacher, 43,* 686–688.

Prescott, G. A., Balow, I. H., Hogan, T. P., & Farr, R. C. (1986). *Metropolitan Achievement Tests MAT6: Survey battery. Teacher's manual for interpreting.* Cleveland, OH: Psychological Corporation.

Prescott, G. A., Balow, I. H., Hogan, T. P., & Farr, R. C. (1988). *Metropolitan Achievement Tests MAT6: Survey battery. Technical manual.* Cleveland, OH: Psychological Corporation.

Pressley, M. (1994). Commentary on the ERIC whole language debate. In C. Smith (Ed.), *Whole language: The debate.* Bloomington, IN: ERIC.

Pugh, A. K., & Ulijn, J. M. (1985). Realistic reading tasks in research in reading. *I.T.L. Review of Applied Linguistics, 69,* 29–41.

Purcell-Gates, V. (1995). *Other people's words: The cycle of low literacy.* Cambridge, MA: Harvard University Press.

Ravitch, D. (1995). The search for order and the rejection of conformity: Standards in American education. In D. Ravitch & M. A. Vinovskis (Eds.), *What history teaches us about school reform: Learning from the past* (pp. 167–190). Baltimore: Johns Hopkins University Press.

Ravitch, D., & Vinovskis, M. A. (Ed.). (1995). *What history teaches us about school reform: Learning from the past.* Baltimore: Johns Hopkins University Press.

Rebarber, T. (1991). *Accountability in education: Better education through informed legislation series.* Washington, DC: National Conference of State Legislatures. (ERIC Document Reproduction Service No. ED 338 713.)

Renshaw, P., & Gardner, R. (1987, May). *Parental goals and strategies in teaching contexts: An exploration of "activity theory" with mothers and fathers of preschool children.* Paper presented at the annual meeting of the Society for Research in Child Development, Baltimore, MD.

Rief, L. (1991). *Seeking Diversity.* Portsmouth, NH: Heinemann.

Robertson, S. (1990). Text rendering: Beginning literary response. *English Journal, 79*(1), 80–84

Roderick, J. A. (1991). *Context-responsive approaches to assessing children's language,* Urbana, IL: National Conference on Research in English.

Romaines, G. (1884). *Mental evolution in animals.* New York: Appleton.

Romberg, T. A., & Zarinnia, E. A. (1989). *The influence of mandated testing on mathematics instruction: Grade 8 teachers' perceptions.* Madison, WI: National Center for Research in Mathematical Science Education, University of Wisconsin.

Rosenblatt, L. M. (1978). *The reader, the text, the poem: The transactional theory of the literary work.* Carbondale: Southern Illinois University Press.

Rosenblatt, L. M. (1994). The transactional theory of reading and writing. In R. B. Ruddell, M. R. Ruddell, & H. Singer (Eds.), *Theoretical models and processes of reading* (pp. 1057–1092). Newark, DE: International Reading Association.

Routman, R. (1996). *Literacy at the crossroads: Critical talk about reading, writing, and other teaching dilemmas.* Portsmouth, NH: Heinemann.

Ruddell, R. B., Ruddell, M. R., & Singer, H. (Eds.). (1994). *Theoretical models and processes of reading* (4th ed.). Newark, DE: International Reading Association.

Ruddell, R. B., & Unrau, N. J. (1994). Reading as a meaning-construction process: The reader, the text, and the teacher. In R. B. Ruddell, M. R. Ruddell, & H. Singer (Eds.),

Theoretical models and processes of reading (pp. 996–1056). Newark, DE: International Reading Association.

Saylor, K., & Overton, J. (1993, March). *Kentucky writing and math portfolios.* Paper presented at the National Conference on Creating the Quality School. (ERIC Document Reproduction Service No. ED 361 382.)

Schmitt, C. (1914). School subjects as material for tests of mental ability. *Elementary School Journal, 15,* 150–161.

Schon, D. (1983). *The reflective practitioner: How professionals think in action.* New York: Basic Books.

Schunk, D. (1984). Self-efficacy perspective on achievement behavior. *Educational Psychology, 19,* 48–58.

Scientific progress, reading lag. (1994, August 20). *Washington Post,* A18.

Scruggs, T.E., White, K. R., & Bennion, K. (1985). Teaching test-taking skills to elementary-grade students: A meta-analysis. *Elementary School Journal, 87,* 69–82.

Segel, E. (1990). Side-by-side storybook reading for every child: An impossible dream? *New Advocate, 3*(2), 131–137.

Shannon, P. (1986). Teachers' and administrators' thoughts on changes in reading instruction within a merit pay program based on test scores. *Reading Research Quarterly, 21,* 20–35.

Shannon, P. (1989). *Broken promises: Reading instruction in twentieth-century America.* Granby, MA: Bergin & Garvey.

Shannon, P. (1990). *The struggle to continue: Progressive reading instruction in the United States.* Portsmouth, NH: Heinemann.

Shannon, P. (1992). Choosing our own way: Subjectivity in the literacy classroom. In P. Shannon (Ed.), *Becoming political: Readings and writings in the politics of literacy education* (pp. 42–49). Portsmouth, NH: Heinemann.

Shepard, L. A. (1989). Why we need better assessments. *Educational Leadership, 46*(7), 4–9.

Shepard, L. A. (1990). Inflated test score gains: Is the problem old norms or teaching the test? *Educational Measurement: Issues and Practice*(Fall), 15–22.

Shepard, L. A. (1991). Psychometricians' beliefs about learning. *Educational Researcher, 20*(6), 2–16.

Shepard, L., & Smith, M. L. (1986). Synthesis of research on school readiness and kindergarten retention. *Educational Leadership, 44*(3), 78–86.

Short, K. & Kauffman, G. (1993). Hearing students' voices: The role of reflection in learning. *Portfolio News, 4*(2), 12–15.

Siegel, F. (1979). Adapted miscue analysis. *Reading World, 19*(1), 36–43.

Silvey, A. (1989). The basalization of trade books (editorial). *The Horn Book,* September/October, 549–550.

Simon, R. I. (1992). *Teaching against the grain: Texts for a pedagogy of possibility.* Toronto: Ontario Institute for Studies in Education.

Simpson, P. (1993). *Language, ideology and point of view.* London: Routledge.

Smith, J. L., Rhodes, J. W., & Jensen, T. (1992). *Restructuring the urban school: A collaborative approach to developing a nongraded curriculum.* Paper presented at the Annual Convention of the American Educational Research Association, San Francisco, CA. (ERIC Document Reproduction Services No. ED 347 231.)

Smith, K. (1995, May). *Survey of changes in standardized testing.* Paper presented at the Annual Convention of the International Reading Association, Annaheim, CA.

Smith, M. L.(1991). Put to the test: The effects of external testing on teachers. *Educational Researcher, 20*(5), 8–11.

Smith, M. L., Edelsky, C., Draper, K., Rottenberg, C., & Cherland, M. (1991). *The role of testing in elementary schools. CSE Technical Report No. 321.* Los Angeles: Center for the Study of Evaluation.

Smith, M. L., & Shepard, L. A. (1988). Kindergarten readiness and retention: A qualitative study of teachers' beliefs and actions. *American Educational Research Journal, 25*, 307–333.

Smith, N. B. (1936). *American reading instruction.* Boston: Silver Burdett.

Snider, M. A., Lima, S. S., & DeVito, P. J. (1994). Rhode Island's literacy portfolio assessment project. In S. W. Valencia, E. H. Hiebert, & P. P. Afflerbach (Eds.), *Authentic reading assessment: Practices and possibilities* (pp. 71–88). Newark, DE: International Reading Association.

Snow, R. E. (1991). Construct validity and constructed-response sets. In R. E. Bennett & W. C. Ward (Eds.), *Construction versus choice in cognitive measurement: Issues in constructed response, performance testing, and portfolio assessment* (pp. 45–60). Hillsdale, NJ: Lawrence Erlbaum Associates.

Stake, R. E. (1991), The teacher, standardized testing, and prospects of revolution. *Phi Delta Kappan* (November), 243–251.

Stanovich, K. E. (1986). Matthew effects in reading: Some consequences of individual differences in the acquisition of literacy. *Reading Research Quarterly, 21*, 360–407.

Stanovich, K. (1994). Romance and reality. *Reading Teacher, 47*, 280–291.

State Policy Program (1994, December). Instruction and assessment in accountable and nonaccountable grades. Charleston, WV: Appalachia Educational Lab. (ERIC Document Reproduction Service No. ED 378 007)

Stecher, B. M., & Hamilton, E. G. (1994). *Portfolio assessment in Vermont, 1992–93. The teachers' perspective on implementation and impact.* Washington, DC: Office of Educational Research and Improvement. (ERIC Document Reproduction Services No. ED 372 112.)

Steele, J. L., & Meredith, K. (1991). Standardized measures of reading achievement for placement of students in Chapter 1 and learning disability programs: A nationwide survey of assessment practices. *Reading Research and Instruction, 30*(2), 17–31.

Stiggins, R. J. (1987). NCME instructional module on design and development of performance assessments. *Educational Measurement Issues and Practice, 6*(3), 33–42.

Stipek, D., Recchia, S., & McClintic, S. (1992). Self-evaluation in young children. *Monographs of the Society for Research in Child Development No. 226, 57.* Chicago: University of Chicago Press.

Stodolsky, S. (1988) . *The subject matters: Classroom activity in math and social studies.* Chicago: University of Chicago Press.

Taylor, D. (1990a). *Learning denied.* Portsmouth, NH: Heinemann.

Taylor, D. (1990b). Teaching without testing. *English Education, 22*(1), 4–74.

Taylor, D. (1993). *From the child's point of view.* Portsmouth, NH: Heinemann.

Taylor, D., & Dorsey-Gaines, C. (1988). *Growing up literate: Learning from inner-city families.* Portsmouth, NH: Heinemann.

Teale, W. H. (Ed.). (1991). [Special Issue]. *Language Arts, 68.*

Thorndike, E. L. (1906). *The principles of teaching based on psychology.* New York: A.G. Seeler.

Thorndike, E. L. (1914). The measurement of ability in reading. *Teachers College Record, 15*, 1–67.

Thorndike, E. L. (1917). Reading as reasoning: A study of mistakes in paragraph reading. *Journal of Educational Psychology, 8*, 323–332.

Thorndike, E. L. (1918). Fundamental theories of judging men. *Teachers College Record, 19*, 278–288.

Thorndike, E. L. (1919). *An introduction to the theory of mental and social measurement* (2nd ed.). New York: Teachers College Press. (Original work published 1904)

Thorndike, R. L. (1982). *Applied psychometrics.* Boston: Houghton Mifflin.

Thorndyke, P. W. (1977). Cognitive structures in comprehension and memory of narrative discourse. *Cognitive Psychology, 9*, 77–110.

Tierney, R. J. (1990). Verbocentrism, dualism, and oversimplification: The need for new vistas for reading comprehension research and practice. In R. Beach & S. Hynds (Eds.), *Developing discourse practices in adolescence and adulthood* (pp. 246–260). Norwood, NJ: Ablex.

Tierney, R. J., Carter, M. A., & Desai, L. E. (1991). *Portfolio assessment in the reading–writing classroom.* Norwood, MA: Christopher-Gordon.

Tortelli, J. P. (1976). Simplified psycholinguistic diagnosis. *Reading Teacher, 29*(7), 637–639.

Toy, V. S. (1995, June 13). In reversal, test scores rise at New York City's schools. *New York Times,* pp. A1, B3.

Traiman, S. L. (1993). *The debate on opportunity-to-learn standards.* Washington, DC: National Governors' Association. (ERIC Document Reproduction Service No. 371 487.)

Valencia, S. W., Hiebert, E. H., & Afflerbach, P. P. (Eds.). (1994). *Authentic reading assessment: Practices and possibilities.* Newark, DE: International Reading Association.

Valencia, S. W., & Pearson, P. D. (1986). *New models for reading assessment: Reading education No. 71.* Champaign: Center for the Study of Reading, University of Illinois at Urbana-Champaign.

Valencia, S. W., & Pearson, P. D. (1987). Reading assessment: Time for a change. *Reading Teacher, 40,* 726–732.

Valencia, S. W., & Place, N. A. (1994). Literacy portfolios for teaching, learning, and accountability: The Bellevue literacy assessment project. In S. W. Valencia, E. H. Hiebert, & P. P. Afflerbach (Eds.), *Authentic reading assessment: Practices and possibilities* (pp. 134–156). Newark, DE: International Reading Association.

Venezky, R. (1984). The history of reading research. In P. D. Pearson, R. Barr, M. Kamil, P. Mosenthal (Eds.), *Handbook of reading research, Vol. 1* (pp. 3–38). New York: Longman.

Vogel, M. & Zancanella, D. (1991). The story world of adolescents in and out of the classroom. *English Journal, 80*(6), 54–60.

Waller, R. (1991). Typography and discourse. In P. D. Pearson, R. Barr, M. Kamil, & P. Mosenthal (Eds.), *Handbook of reading research* (pp. 341–380). New York: Longman.

Weber, R. (1968). The study of oral reading errors: A survey of the literature. *Reading Research Quarterly, 4*(1), 96–119.

Weiss, B. (1994). California's new English language arts assessment. In S. W. Valencia, E. H. Hiebert, & P. P. Afflerbach (Eds.), *Authentic reading assessment: Practices and possibilities* (pp. 197–217). Newark, DE: International Reading Association.

White, E. M. (1994). Portfolios as an assessment concept. In L. Black, D. A. Daiker, J. Sommers, & G. Stygall (Eds.), *New directions in portfolio assessment: Reflective practice, critical theory, and large-scale scoring* (pp. 25–39). Portsmouth, NH: Heinemann-Boynton/Cook.

Wiggins, G. (1989). A true test: Toward a more authentic and equitable assessment. *Phi Delta Kappan, 70*(9), 703–13.

Wiggins, G. (1993). *Assessing student performance: Exploring the purpose and limits of testing.* San Francisco: Jossey Bass.

Wilkinson, G. (1987). *WRAT—R: Wide Range Achievement Test—Monograph 1.* Wilmington, DE: Jastak Associates.

Willinsky, J. (1991). *The triumph of literature/The fate of literacy: English in the secondary school curriculum.* New York: Teachers College, Columbia University.

Winterson, J. (1995). *Art objects: Essays on ecstasy and effrontery.* Toronto: Knopf.

Wixson, K. K. (1994). Commentary on the Maryland school performance assessment program: A new view of assessment. In S. W. Valencia, E. H. Hiebert, & P. P. Afflerbach (Eds.), *Authentic reading assessment: Practices and possibilities* (pp. 277–283). Newark, DE: International Reading Association.

Wolf, S. A., & Heath, S. B. (1992). *The braid of literature: Children's worlds of reading.* Cambridge, MA: Harvard University Press.

Woo, E. (1996, March 28). Governors agree to set higher goals for nation's schools. *Los Angeles Times,* A23.

Wood, K., & Muth, D. (1991). The case for improved instruction in the middle grades. *Journal of Reading, 35*(2), 84–90.

Woodcock, R. W. (1987). *Woodcock Reading Mastery Tests—Revised: Examiner's manual.* Circle Pines, MN: American Guidance Service.

Woods, P., & Hammersley, M. (Eds.). (1993). *Gender and ethnicity in schools: Ethnographic accounts.* London: Routledge.

Zinser, J. (1994). *Reinventing education: Issue paper. No. 1. Investing in people project.* Cambridge, MA: Jobs for the Future. (ERIC Document Reproduction Service No. ED 370 241.)

Author Index

Subject Index